TOP
STOCKS

SPECIAL EDITION

☑ ETHICAL
☑ SUSTAINABLE
☑ RESPONSIBLE

ERICA HALL

TOP STOCKS

SPECIAL EDITION

☑ **ETHICAL**

☑ **SUSTAINABLE**

☑ **RESPONSIBLE**

WILEY

First published in 2024 by John Wiley & Sons Australia, Ltd
Level 4, 600 Bourke St, Melbourne, Victoria 3000, Australia

Typeset in Garamond Premier Pro 10pt/14pt

© John Wiley & Sons Australia, Ltd 2024

The moral rights of the author have been asserted

ISBN: 978-1-394-24346-4

A catalogue record for this book is available from the National Library of Australia

Cover design by Wiley
Cover and part opener image by © diyanadimitrova/Adobe Stock

Disclaimer

Printed in Singapore
M128181_280224

CONTENTS

PREFACE

We live in interesting times. In a globalised world, offshore trends filter through to local markets. A company's value is linked to its ability to operate sustainably over the longer term. The game has changed. From the pursuit of short-term profits for shareholders, the approach has shifted to generating value for multiple stakeholders while making sustainable profits that take into account environmental, social and governance (ESG) factors. In a nutshell, profits still matter but *how* those profits are generated matters just as much.

BlackRock chairman Larry Fink coined the phrase 'stakeholder capitalism' to describe this phenomenon. He laid out the groundwork for this concept in his 2018 letter to CEOs, asserting that to be prosperous in the long term a company needs to benefit *all* stakeholders. And for the successful long-term investor, a company's ESG attributes are increasingly important: ESG capability has become a proxy for quality.

Grappling with ESG issues can be daunting. Determining which factors matter most can rest on an individual values decision. Climate change, however, has emerged as a mega-theme. Increasingly, investors and regulators are pushing companies to report on climate-related activities, including data related to transition and physical risks as well as their plans to manage those risks. To that end, many large-cap Australian listed companies have made net zero carbon emissions commitments, despite there being no regulatory requirement (yet) to do so. According to KPMG, approximately three-quarters of listed companies are reporting to the Task Force on Climate-related Financial Disclosures (TCFD), which has been the gold standard for the depth and breadth of reporting. TCFD reporting will be incorporated by the International Sustainability Standards Board from 2024, requiring baseline sustainability disclosures to help inform investors.

After years of limited activity in the ESG space in Australia, regulatory changes — particularly in relation to climate risks — and opportunities are proliferating. Australia is expected to introduce mandatory climate reporting through a staged approach in 2024. With changing requirements and expectations as we transition to a low-carbon economy, investors are being encouraged to consider the management of ESG risks and opportunities to help identify companies likely to be successful in the long term.

Different sectors face inherently different ESG risks, and some companies will find the transition to decarbonisation easier than others. A company's management of ESG risks is an important component of its likely transition success. The data shows us that the two best business sectors from an ESG perspective, taking into account both the risks inherent in the sectors and the management of those risks, are Industrials and Australian real estate investment trusts (REITs). Companies facing the highest risk are those operating within the materials sector (specifically diversified metals mining) and the energy sector (especially those involved with coal and oil and gas exploration and production). Typically, sustainability investors have avoided companies operating in the energy and materials sectors because of a lack of alignment, as these companies have rated poorly from an ESG perspective. That said, there is plenty of room for improvement across the board. Only 10 listed companies in Australia have achieved the top-ranking Morningstar Sustainalytics five-globe ESG risk assessment, which signals they face negligible ESG risks. Interestingly, though, there are far more companies to choose from if only climate risk is considered: 68 companies are rated as having 'negligible risk' for overall carbon risk.

Given that many sustainable investors tend to have systemic sector underweights and overweights to align with their values, recent market conditions have been tough for them to navigate. The energy sector, which is either not held or is underweighted by sustainable investors, had a significant performance boost in 2022. This was due largely to the Russia–Ukraine conflict. As Russia is a significant supplier of global crude oil and natural gas the conflict caused an energy supply shock, which buoyed the energy sector's returns. Fossil fuel companies' stock prices catapulted as a result of the imbalance between supply and demand and, after years of benign returns, energy became the standout sector on a returns basis in the 2022 calendar year. Those not holding this sector missed out on this short-term performance uptick in 2022, although it was short-lived, as energy subsequently became one of the worst performing sectors in the ASX for 2023.

To combat rising inflation caused by an expansive monetary policy used to stimulate economies during the disruption caused by the COVID pandemic, central banks around the world, including the Reserve Bank of Australia (RBA), started to raise interest rates. The RBA hiked rates 13 times between May 2022 and December 2023. This strategy created jitters in the stock market and impacted investor confidence.

This, in turn, has contributed to recent pockets of scepticism in relation to sustainable investing, particularly in the US where some states have gone so far as to seek to restrict ESG considerations through anti-ESG bills. This action is out of step with a global commitment to transition to net zero carbon in order to slow climate change, which includes imposing more reporting on ESG risks and opportunities alongside financial metrics. Even in purely investment terms, to ignore the collaborative global decarbonisation commitment is ill-advised, because the trend is clear: 193 nations signed the Paris Agreement commitment to net zero carbon emissions by 2050. As they say in the markets, 'the trend is your friend'; you disregard it at your peril.

Mandatory reporting of climate-related risks is already in place in many countries around the world. Such regulation is being developed in Australia, but we are late to the party and local companies face the real risk of losing out to competitors who have already committed on ESG issues. Predictions are that they may find it increasingly difficult to attract capital. They may potentially find themselves holding 'stranded assets' that have no financial value because of lack of demand or because of a change in regulations or laws.

Recognising the changing landscape and global commitment to ESG, prudent investors will carefully assess the risks and opportunities ahead. They will pay attention to how companies are transitioning their operations as the market evolves into a more regulated ESG environment, which is leading to better ESG reporting and standards.

There are clear signals that embracing ESG factors is likely to secure long-term financial prospects for companies. KPMG's 2022 Sustainability Reporting Survey found that 90 per cent of the ASX top 100 companies by market capitalisation recognise climate as a financial risk; 89 per cent report on carbon targets. Despite pockets of dissent, most governments, companies and investors are committed to ESG and particularly to managing climate risks, although not all share the same level of commitment. The purpose of this book is to help investors identify the best-in-class in relation to ESG, both overall and particularly from a carbon perspective.

The absence of legislation, or even agreed terminologies, around what constitutes a sustainable/ESG or 'green' investment makes decision making difficult for investors. Given the importance of investor confidence in relation to green claims, the

Australian regulators ASIC and ACCC have made 'greenwashing', when a company overstates its green credentials, a top priority.

Aside from regulatory changes, investors are demanding more from companies in relation to ESG. Arguably, it has been investors who have driven the ESG investing mandate and the legislators who are catching up. Investors are increasingly seeking to invest in line with their personal values. While they still seek a return on their investment, they care *how* this return is generated.

The problem with ESG investing to date has been a lack of objective standards. The industry is still maturing, so while the data is improving, it is still not robust or completely reliable. Further, the lack of standardisation has given rise to many different methodologies, which makes it hard to compare companies and confidently sort the good from the great. On top of all of this, ESG is very broad, which is likely why the Australian government have been focusing on one specific aspect, climate, via mandatory climate related financial disclosures.

While decarbonisation and other environmental issues are perhaps the major theme in ESG investing, it also encompasses social issues — from workers' rights, diversity and inclusion to modern slavery and good governance. Essential to a company's overall success, good governance considers issues such as board composition and competency, executive remuneration, ethical policies and a social licence to operate.

While this book considers all ESG elements it has leaned into the E, given climate change–related initiatives have been an area of focus in Australia. Mandatory climate reporting requirements set to kick off via a phased approach from 1 July 2024 for large businesses, many of which are ASX-listed companies. The Australian Institute of Company Directors have advised their members that this is the biggest change to corporate reporting in a generation.

I have selected top ESG stocks from among ASX 300 companies, starting with overall ESG risk then drilling down into each individual ESG pillar. I began by looking at these companies' current overall ESG risk attributes and their ESG momentum: are they reducing their environmental, social and governance risks through improved management approaches? It is important to note that these metrics are necessarily subjective since the lack of regulatory standards can make it difficult to obtain objective data. If the data is not available, it has been estimated. Methodologies are explained, but their application can differ between companies, countries and researchers. Given that decarbonisation is the principal focus both domestically and offshore, carbon has been considered as a standalone metric. Overall carbon risk, emissions and carbon intensity as well as exposure to fossil fuels have been examined to help clarify specific risks to decarbonisation. Carbon data is obtained on a lagged basis.

What are the entry criteria?

Morningstar separates ASX 300 companies into the following 11 sectors: Basic Materials, Communication Services, Consumer Cyclical, Consumer Defensive, Energy, Financial Services, Healthcare, Industrials, Real Estate, Technology and Utilities.

Strict criteria have been applied for inclusion in *Top Stocks - Ethical, Sustainable, Responsible*. All companies must be included in the ASX 300 index, which comprises Australia's 300 largest stocks. Smaller companies are excluded because there is typically not enough consistent data available to make a thorough assessment.

The companies selected are the best-in-class within their sector. These companies typically have relatively low ESG risks, a strong pathway to decarbonisation, robust and transparent ESG reporting, and strong governance.

Assessments have been made primarily through the use of Morningstar Sustainalytics ESG data and other data sources such as company reports. Morningstar Sustainalytics is a leading independent ESG and corporate governance research firm that has been providing investors with ratings and analytics data for more than 30 years.

INTRODUCTION

I have divided the companies listed on the Australian Stock Exchange into their various sectors and selected the best-of-breed from each, acknowledging that different sectors have different ESG challenges and opportunities. In doing so I have sought to make the data consistent and comparable. For example, the financial services sector's challenges are different from those of the energy sector or the healthcare sector.

I have restricted the opportunity set to large-cap stocks as this is typically where the best sustainability data is available. Currently there is no regulatory requirement for companies to report on ESG metrics; however, most of the larger companies have the resources to enable them to report and those that operate globally often need to do so to meet mandatory ESG reporting disclosures and maintain global competitiveness.

Legislative changes in Australia are pending and we can expect to see staged mandatory reporting on ESG metrics, partly in relation to climate risk reporting, as soon as 2024. These changes will improve overall data and comparability, which will flow through to better data in both small- and large-cap sectors over time.

Some of the data is provided on a lagged basis; carbon emissions, for example, captures the 2021 fiscal year.

Unlike typical financial assessment we are looking at stocks purely through a sustainability lens. To obtain a more complete picture, investors are encouraged to consider the financial fundamentals of these companies, which are outlined in the companion book, Martin Roth's annual *Top Stocks*.

Head

At the head of each entry is the company name, its three-letter ASX code and its website address.

Market capitalisation

The estimate of the value of the business by multiplying the number of shares outstanding by the current price of the share (mil). Market cap was captured as of 30 November 2023.

Morningstar sectors

The Morningstar Global Equity Classification Structure classifies by equity sector and industry, based on the business activities which best reflect each company's largest source of revenue and income. This helps determine relative performance among industry peers.

Morningstar Sustainalytics peer group classification

Morningstar Sustainalytics assigns each ASX company to one of 42 peer groups, which allows for more meaningful peer comparability.

Environmental risk score

This measures the degree to which a company's economic value may be at risk due to environmental factors. Scores are between 0 and 100, with 100 being the worst. Most scores ranged between 0 and 25. I used the following simple scale for assessment: a score below 8.33 received a tick (✓); a score between 8.34 and 17.67 received a dash (–); a score above 17.68 received a cross (X).

Social risk score

This measures how much a company's economic value may be at risk due to social factors. Scores are between 0 and 100, with 100 being the worst, although most scores ranged between 0 and 25. I used the following simple scale for assessment: a score below 8.33 received a tick; a score between 8.34 and 17.67 received a dash; a score above 17.68 received a cross.

Governance risk score

This measures the degree to which a company's economic value may be at risk due to governance factors. Scores are displayed between 0 and 100, with 100 being the worst (although most scores ranged between 0 and 25). I used the following simple scale for assessment: a score below 8.33 received a tick; a score between 8.34 and 17.67 received a dash; a score above 17.68 received a cross.

ESG risk rating assessment

This is a visual representation of the ESG risk on a 1–5 scale. Stocks with five tabs are most desirable as they exhibit the lowest ESG risks, while those with one tab are the riskiest from an ESG perspective.

ESG risk classification

A company's risk is classified as *negligible, low, medium, high* or *severe*. ESG risks materialise unpredictably depending on fluctuating conditions. No predictions relating to financial or share price impacts — or the time horizon of such impacts — are intended to be implied by these risk categories. Rather, it attempts to measure the degree to which a company's economic value is put at risk by ESG factors, taking into account what risks management can and can't control.

ESG risk exposure score

This measures the degree to which a company's economic value may be materially driven by relevant ESG factors. It considers exposure to specific material risks within the industry and how well the company is managing those risks, on a scale from 0 (best) to 100 (worst).

This assessment is relative to all the individual stocks in the book. All stocks are ranked from highest to lowest risk; the higher the risk exposure score, the greater the risk. The entire cohort was captured, ranked then split into thirds. Companies facing the highest risks were scored 34.70–76.50 and given a cross; medium risk scored 26.40–33.00 and were given a dash; lowest risk scored 17.10–26.35 and were given a tick.

ESG risk rank universe

An assessment of a company's risk score relative to the entire global listed stock universe is expressed as a ranking. At the time of writing there were 15 491 stocks in the peer group globally.

ESG excess risk exposure score

This measures the difference between the company's exposure score and its sub-industry exposure score. The excess exposure score is subtracted from the company's exposure score. The company's exposure is desirable if it falls below the sub-industry's exposure score. A score above 0 shows that the company's exposure is above the sub-industry's exposure.

Assessment: The assessment has a binary outcome. A score below 0 means the company had less exposure than its sub-industry average so received a tick; a company with a score above 0 had more exposure so received a cross.

ESG risk compared to sub-industry peers

The company's ESG risk is subtracted from the average ESG risk for sub-industry peers. A negative number indicates that the company's ESG risk is less than the average of its peers. This is calculated by subtracting the company's ESG risk score from the average sub-industry ESG risk score.

Assessment: It is a binary outcome. Companies with lower ESG risk compared to their average sub-industry peers, depicted by a negative number, received a tick; companies with a higher score than their sub-industry peers received a cross.

ESG risk beta

This assesses the degree to which a company's risk exposure differs from its sub-industry peers' exposure. A score above 1 demonstrates that the company is more volatile and riskier than its peers; below 1 means the stock is less risky than its peers.

Assessment: Above 1 received a cross; exactly 1 received a dash; below 1 received a tick.

ESG risk score momentum

The year-on-year absolute change in ESG risk is measured by comparing the current score with the historical score for 12 months before on a rolling basis. It is calculated by subtracting the current ESG risk score from the ESG risk score from 12 months ago. A negative number shows positive or improving ESG momentum.

Assessment: Comparing ESG risk year on year, a negative figure shows reducing ESG risk so attracted a tick; a positive figure shows increasing ESG risks so attracted a cross. Zero attracts a dash.

ESG risk management score

This measures a company's handling of ESG risks across issues. The score ranges from 0 (no evidence of management) to 100 (very strong management). The overall management score is calculated by adding the weighted corporate governance management score to the sum of all weighted issue management scores, such as assessments of management policy commitments related to an ESG risk, programs designed to implement those policy commitments, the availability of quantitative performance data measuring how well the programs have met stated targets, and how well a company is managing its involvement in related ESG controversies.

Assessment: Dividing the range into thirds, companies were assessed using the following ranges: 0–33 received a cross; 34–67 received a dash; 68–100 received a tick.

ESG risk management classification

Risk management classification captures a company's management of ESG risks as weak, average or strong.

Assessment: I relied on Morningstar Sustainalytics classification of *weak, average* and *strong*. Weak management received a cross; average management received a dash; strong management received a tick.

ESG risk exposure classification

This denotes the overall ESG risk exposure assigned by Morningstar Sustainalytics. A company's overall exposure score was assigned to one of three categories in the ESG risk rating: low exposure (0–34.99 points), medium exposure (35–54.99 points) or high exposure (55–100 points).

Assessment: Low exposure received a tick, medium exposure received a dash and high exposure a cross.

ESG risk management score momentum

The change in absolute terms of the ESG risk management score is captured by comparing the current score to the historical score 12 months before on a rolling basis. A negative number shows deteriorating management of ESG momentum.

Assessment: If the company's management of ESG risks deteriorated year on year, the scores are negative. Negative scores received a cross, positive scores that captured improving management of ESG risks year on year received a tick. Zero received a dash.

Company controversies

An ESG controversy case is defined as either an event or an ongoing situation in which company operations and/or products allegedly have a negative environmental, social or governance impact. Topics include business ethics, society and community, environmental operations, environmental supply chain, products and services, employees, social supply chain, customers, governance and public policy.

Assessment: The level of company controversies relied on Morningstar Sustainalytics' classifications of 0–5. Those rated 0 (none) and 1 (low) received a tick; rated 2 (moderate) and 3 (significant) received a dash; rated 4 (high) and 5 (severe) received a cross.

Carbon overall risk score

A company's overall score is calculated as the difference between exposure and its management of the risk. A score of 0–10 represents *negligible* to *low risk*; 10.01–29.99 is medium risk; 30–49.99 is high risk; 50 or above is severe risk.

Assessment: Negligible or low risk receives a tick; medium risk received a dash; high or severe risk received a cross.

Carbon emissions

Carbon emissions are classified into three scopes. Scope 1 are direct company emissions, emissions that occur in their operations owned or controlled by the company; scope 2 are indirect company emissions from energy purchased; and scope 3 emissions are all other indirect upstream and downstream emissions not captured by scope 2 generated from the value chain. As the company is indirectly responsible for these emissions this can make them hard to account for. Examples of scope 3 emissions include emissions generated through use of a company's products or services, the transportation of the products to customers or the disposal products. Scopes 1, 2 and 3 emissions are measured in metric tonnes CO_2e. Of those in the ASX cohort for which we have data, the highest was 549 200 000 and the lowest 23.70 metric tonnes CO_2e.

Carbon fossil fuels level of involvement

To help in assessment of risk, a simplified tiered scale measures a company's dependence on fossil fuels based on a percentage of revenues. The level of involvement is ranked from zero to 5. Companies with zero have no fossil fuel involvement and those with a score of 5 have significant involvement.

Assessment: Companies with score of zero and 1 receive a tick, companies with score 2 and 3 a dash, and companies with 4 or 5 a cross.

Carbon fossil fuels level of involvement range

These are calculated as an aggregate percentage of involvement in fossil fuels (the sum of involvement in thermal coal extraction, thermal coal power generation, oil and gas generation, oil and gas production, and oil and gas product and services).

Assessment: Companies with 0 to 4.9 per cent receive a tick, 5 to 9.9 per cent and 10 to 24.9 per cent a dash, and 25 to 49.9 per cent and 50 to 100 per cent a cross.

Carbon intensity scopes 1, 2 and 3

This calculates total emissions across all scopes over revenue (USD). The range in ASX companies where data is available ranges from 0 to 30 090.01 metric tonnes CO_2e per million USD revenue.

Assessment: This assessment was relative to all stocks in the book. Stocks were ranked from highest to lowest emissions. The higher the emissions the less desirable and the greater the transition risk. The entire cohort was captured, ranked then split into thirds. The highest emitters, were between 419.93 and 30 090.01 in metric tonne Co_2e per Mil USD revenue, received a cross. The next group, which ranged from 57.72 to 414.01 received a dash. The lowest emitters, which ranged from 1.55 to 42.52, received a tick.

Company commentary

Each company commentary begins with a brief introduction to the company and its activities, followed by highlights of its sustainability aspirations and results as at 30 September 2023.

DEFINITIONS

AASB   Australian Accounting Standards Board — an independent government agency that develops, issues and maintains accounting standards in Australia. The *Corporations Act 2001* mandates the use of Australian accounting standards in the preparation of financial reports

APCO   Australian Packaging Covenant Organisation — a not-for-profit organisation leading the development of a circular economy for packaging in Australia

APPEA   Australian Petroleum Production and Exploration Association — represents Australia's oil and gas exploration and production industry to policy makers, regulators and the community

ARENA   Australian Renewable Energy Agency — an independent agency of the Australian Government tasked with managing Australia's renewable energy programs

ASI   Aluminium Stewardship Initiative — promotes sustainable processes through the value chain

ASRS   Australian Sustainability Reporting Standards — based on ISSB standards IFRS S1 and IFRS S2. These new standards are expected to apply to annual reporting periods from 1 July 2024

CACNSO   Climate Active Carbon Neutral Standard for Organisations — a certification standard for measuring and managing GHG emissions in order to achieve carbon neutrality

CEFC   Clean Energy Finance Corporation — Australian Government–owned green bank that facilitates flows of finance into the clean energy sector

CEMARS   Certified Emissions Measurement and Reduction Scheme — an internationally recognised carbon emissions measurement and reduction scheme for large organisations

CLC	Australian Climate Leaders Coalition—a group of corporate CEOs who support the Paris Agreement commitments and setting public decarbonisation targets
CO2e	Carbon dioxide equivalent —a measurement to compare the impact of GHG emissions contribution to climate change
EP 100	A global initiative whose mission is to accelerate energy efficiency through energy smart businesses
Fugitive emissions	The unintended or unaccounted release of pollutants into the atmosphere, typically occurring during production. These emissions can have varying harmful impacts to the environment depending on what the emissions are and the frequency and volume of pollutants released into the atmosphere.
GHG	Greenhouse gas emissions —includes carbon dioxide, which accounts for an estimated 75 per cent of emissions, methane, nitrous oxide, hydrofluorocarbons, perfluorocarbons and sulfur hexafluoride
GHG Protocol	Greenhouse Gas Protocol—provides standards for business and governments to ensure that they are appropriately accounting for and managing climate warming emissions
GICS	Global Industry Classification Standard—a standard for assigning companies to a specific economic sector and industry group that best defines its business operations
GRESB	Global Real Estate Sustainability Benchmark—industry-led organisation that provides actionable and transparent ESG data to financial markets
GRI	Global Reporting Initiative—a set of sustainability reporting standards that reflect best practice for organisations when reporting environmental, social and economic impacts
ICMM	International Council on Mining and Metals—a CEO-led leadership organisation committed to improving sustainable development in the mining and metals industry
IEA	International Energy Agency—Paris-based intergovernmental organisation that provides policy recommendations, analysis and data on the global energy sector

IFRS	International Financial Reporting Standards—a set of accounting rules for the financial statements of public companies intended to make them consistent, transparent and easily comparable
IFRS S1	General requirements for disclosure of sustainability-related financial information
IFRS S2	Climate-related disclosures
IGCC	Investor Group on Climate Change—a collaboration by Australian and New Zealand institutional investors focused on the impacts of climate change on investment
IIRF	International Integrated Reporting Framework (IIRF)—used to connect financial statements and sustainability-related financial disclosures
IPCC	Intergovernmental Panel on Climate Change—UN body tasked with advancing scientific knowledge and informing governments about climate change
Ipieca	International Petroleum Industry Environmental Conservation Association—global oil and gas industry association focused on advancing environmental and social performance across the energy transition
IRMA	Initiative for Responsible Mining Assurance—considered international best practice standard for responsible mining providing third-party verification.
ISCA	Infrastructure Sustainability Council of Australia—seeks to generate social, environmental and economic returns by advancing sustainability in infrastructure planning, procurement, delivery and operation
ISSB	International Sustainability Standards Board—an independent body that develops the IFRS Sustainability Disclosures, a comprehensive global baseline of sustainability disclosure standards
MECLA	Materials Embodied Carbon Leaders Alliance—an alliance of industry, university and government organisations working together to drive reductions in embodied carbon in the building and construction industry

NABERS National Australian Built Environment Rating System—provides simple and reliable comparable sustainability measurement across all building sectors

NGER National Greenhouse and Energy Reporting—a framework for reporting and disseminating company information about GHG emissions, energy production and energy consumption

NGFS Network for Greening the Financial System—a network of central banks and financial supervisors focused on accelerating the scaling up of green finance

NZAMI Net Zero Asset Managers Initiative—aims to galvanise the asset management industry to commit to a goal of net zero emissions

PCAF Partnership of Carbon Accounting Financials—enables financial institutions to assess and disclose greenhouse gas emissions associated with financial activities and begin their journey towards decarbonisation

RE100 Global corporate renewable energy initiative to accelerate change towards zero carbon electricity grids globally by 2040

RIAA Responsible Investments Association Australasia—a network of people and organisations dedicated to responsible investing and a sustainable financial system in Australia and Aotearoa New Zealand

Safeguard mechanism The Australian government's policy for reducing emissions via setting baselines on GHG emissions aligned to the government's GHG reduction targets of 43 per cent below 2005 levels by 2030 and net zero by 2050

SASB Sustainability Accounting Standards Board—a non-profit organisation that develops sustainability accounting standards and helps companies disclose relevant sustainability information to their investors

SBTN Science Based Targets Network—a corporate engagement program to help organisations set science-based targets in the sustainability space

TCFD Task Force on Climate-related Financial Disclosures—a framework to help organisations more effectively disclose climate-related risks

TNFD   Taskforce on Nature-related Financial Disclosures—a risk management and disclosure framework to help organisations and financial institutions to identify, assess, manage and report on nature-related dependencies, impacts, risks and opportunities

UN Global Compact   Global initiative to encourage businesses to commit to sustainable and socially responsible policies

UN PRI   Principles of Responsible Investment—United Nations–supported network of financial institutions working together to incorporate ESG issues into investment analysis and decision making

UN SDGs   United Nations Sustainable Development Goals—a collection of 17 interlinked objectives designed to serve as a 'shared blueprint for peace and prosperity for people and the planet, now and into the future'

XRB   External Reporting Board—develops and issues reporting standards on accounting, audit and assurance and climate for New Zealand organisations

PART I
THE COMPANIES

1. Basic materials

This sector comprises companies that are involved in utilising natural resources and commodities through extraction/mining, refining and processing materials. These metals and minerals and other essential commodities are important in the development of essential goods and services required for a transition to a low-carbon economy.

Basic materials can cover the following activities:

- exploration, production and distribution of energy resources, such as natural gas, and fossil fuels, such as oil and coal

- mining of minerals and metals, including gold, copper and ores

- manufacturing and distribution of chemicals and chemical products

- logging and manufacturing of materials from forestry, such as paper manufacturing

- production of construction materials, including steel, cement and bricks.

On the face of it, this sector may not look like a good fit for a responsible investing portfolio; however, lithium mining provides just one example of an essential component in the race to decarbonisation and the electrification of everything. Lithium is used in batteries required to run electric vehicles as well as battery storage for renewable energy sources and other consumer electronics such as smartphones, laptops and digital cameras. It is also used in medical devices, and in aircraft and satellites. Australia is one of the world's leading lithium producers and demand for lithium is expected to remain elevated given its contribution to the clean energy transition. This is an example of how nuanced responsible investing can be. There are trade-offs that have to be considered.

The demand for materials to support decarbonisation goes beyond lithium to include copper, nickel, chromium, zinc and other rare earth minerals. Wind turbines, solar panels, electric vehicles, batteries, energy storage, and carbon capture and storage are all examples of products that need inputs from minerals mining.

The biggest beneficiaries of the nineteenth-century gold rushes were the people selling mining equipment, from shovels to shoes. Sustainable investors should consider seeking out companies that are providing inputs into the net zero transition, such as mining of lithium and cobalt for batteries, and copper and aluminium for wind turbines.

Australia's largest company by market capitalisation, BHP, sits within this sector, as do other household names such as Rio Tinto, Fortescue Metals, Oz Minerals and Iluka Resources. Not surprisingly, given that we are a resource-rich nation and exporter of commodities, the basic materials sector has historically been a significant component of the ASX.

Some companies operating in this sector are taking significant steps to improve their environmental impact. They are looking to reduce their carbon footprint by being more energy efficient, using renewable energy, and investing in new and emerging technologies such as green hydrogen and ammonia in an attempt to minimise environmental impacts. However, steel production is hard to abate as it is energy intensive, and achieving a forward-looking net zero goal requires the commercial success of emissions-reducing emerging technologies.

Responsible miners need to minimise the destruction of wildlife habitats, reduce deforestation impacts and switch to chemicals that are less environmentally harmful than those traditionally used. As local regulation improves, reporting of climate-related impacts will become mandatory.

The other component is ensuring companies have a social licence to operate by taking into account all stakeholders and engaging with them to ensure alignment with ESG standards.

Unfortunately, some companies with solid ESG ratings have had to be excluded due to a lack of comprehensive data, while Newcrest Mining was excluded due to its takeover by US-headquartered Newmont Corporation.

BHP Group Limited

ASX code: BHP www.bhp.com

Market capitalisation:	$234 482 million
Sector:	Basic materials
Morningstar Sustainalytics peer group classification:	Diversified Metals Mining

Environmental risk score		Social risk score		Governance risk score	
15.28	–	8.39	–	4.16	✓

View: Supporting a low-carbon transition with caveats, BHP has been reducing its carbon intensity by offloading its fossil fuel assets and investing in renewables.

History/background

BHP is a diversified natural resources company focused predominantly on mining and metals. Founded in 1885 as the Broken Hill Proprietary Company, it is now the largest stock on the ASX as measured by market capitalisation. Headquartered in Melbourne, it is a global company with operations in many countries. BHP is one of the world's largest iron ore producers and is also involved in copper production.

Historically, it has been a big player in oil and gas exploration and production, which precluded it from being included in responsible investment portfolios. Recently BHP made a strategic decision to divest fossil fuel assets from many of its oil and gas assets, which were acquired by Woodside Petroleum in a deal worth approximately AU$40 billion. BHP made the decision to divest as it transitions its business towards low carbon. The company sought to sell its high-polluting Mt Arthur thermal coal mine in NSW, which is due to be decommissioned in 2030, but ended up holding onto it as the costs of regenerating the site to its former condition (a legal requirement) was estimated at US$700 million, which likely reduced buyer interest. In October 2023 BHP flagged the potential to convert the site to pumped hydro or solar farming.

Continuing with its fossil fuel divestment, BHP has also recently announced it will sell its Queensland-based Blackwater and Daunia metallurgical coal mines, in which it has a 50 per cent share, to Whitehaven Coal. However, this plan is controversial since it does nothing to reduce GHG emissions. Activists prefer mine closures and regeneration of sites over divestment through sales or, as a minimum, the sales process should require purchasers to adhere to Paris-aligned climate commitments to help with future GHG reductions.

ESG performance

BHP is an example of a company that may not look compelling at face value but is making a commitment to transform its business by prioritising sustainability, particularly seeking to improve environmental impacts within its operations. The data shows positive momentum in reducing ESG risks. BHP's goal is to achieve net zero emissions for scopes 1 and 2 by 2050, which may include some use of carbon credits. It defines its goal as 'to seek an outcome for which there is no current pathway'. It has an interim target of reducing operational GHG emissions by at least 30 per cent by FY30 from an FY20 baseline. A target is defined as 'an intended outcome … subject to certain assumptions or conditions'. Scope 3 ambitions are less definitive. They pursue the goal of net zero scope 3 by 2050 but outcomes are uncertain. Rather, by FY50 they target net zero GHG from shipping and net zero operational GHG emissions from their direct suppliers. By FY30 they aim to reduce GHG emissions intensity by 30 per cent in their steel making through investing in new technologies to reduce GHG emissions, particularly in its high carbon emitting businesses. The significant divestment from several fossil fuel assets is a clear commitment to decarbonisation. As a result, it is drawing the interest of a number of sustainable investors seeking to invest in companies that generate 5 per cent or less revenue from fossil fuel involvement. Before divestment BHP generated between 10 per cent and 24.9 per cent of its revenue from fossil fuel assets.

In the past BHP has faced challenges relating to ESG issues, such as negative environmental impacts relating to its mining activities, poor community relations and worker safety violations. The failure of a tailings dam in Brazil that polluted the Doce River was just one of its environmental disasters.

BHP's management of ESG risks is assessed as strong. It ranks highly against sub-industry peers and has significantly lower ESG risks than the average. Its total scopes 1, 2 and 3 carbon emissions are relatively high; however, this data is from 2021, prior to its fossil fuel divestments. Given that BHP is on a clear decarbonisation pathway, we can expect that carbon emissions will reduce significantly over time, and that this will be captured when the data refreshes.

Finally, when considering unmanaged ESG risks, BHP's highest risk is environmental, which is not surprising given its primary activity is mining; its lowest risk is governance. Overall, the ESG risks are quite low; however, most companies' ESG scores fall below a maximum threshold of 25; BHP's ESG risk scores across all three pillars fall well within those bounds. BHP is a signatory to the UN Global Compact and ICMM.

ESG risks	ESG measured	Assessment	Result
ESG exposure	ESG risk rating assessment	▮▮▮□	—
	ESG exposure risk classification	Medium	—
	ESG risk exposure score	68.10	X
	ESG excess exposure score	(3.90)	✓
	ESG risk score momentum	1.33	X
ESG sub-industry risk	ESG sub-industry rank	17/184	✓
	ESG risk compared to sub-industry peers	(16.43)	✓
	ESG risk beta	0.95	✓
Management of ESG risk	Management of ESG risks score	67.07	✓
	Classification of management of ESG risks	Strong	✓
	ESG risk management score momentum	(1.63)	X
Company controversy	Level of company controversy exposure	High	X
	Notable ESG Issues	Emissions, effluents and waste	

Carbon emissions	Measured risks	Assessment	Result
	Carbon overall risk	Medium	—
	Carbon overall risk score	18.94	—
	Carbon total emissions, scopes 1, 2 and 3	417 500 000	X
	Carbon level of involvement	1	✓
	Level of fossil fuel involvement	0%–4.9%	✓
	Carbon intensity, scopes 1, 2 and 3	6982	X

BlueScope Steel Limited

ASX code: BSL   www.bluescope.com

Average market capitalisation:	$9306.31 million
Sector:	Basic materials
Morningstar Sustainalytics peer group classification:	Steel

Environmental risk score		Social risk score		Governance risk score	
12.77	–	11.50	–	5.36	✓

View: BlueScope demonstrates a serious commitment to decarbonisation, providing detailed reporting and consideration of risks and opportunities across various climate change scenarios.

History/background

BlueScope Steel is amongst the biggest manufacturers of steel products used in the construction, manufacturing and automotive industries. Based in Australia, it operates in 16 countries. One of its competitive advantages is its metal coating and painting products, used by the construction industry. Colorbond pre-painted coated steel and Zincalume, a zinc aluminium alloy coated steel product, are considered innovative, as the protective coating enhances durability, is aesthetically pleasing and renders steel more resistant to corrosion.

The company exemplifies successful vertical integration as it sources the raw materials from which it manufactures the steel products it distributes. Its effective supply chain management results in timely delivery to its customers.

ESG performance

BlueScope has undertaken a number of sustainability initiatives around energy efficiency, waste reduction and steel recycling. It estimates 92 per cent of its GHG emissions are from iron and steel making. It has reduced its energy consumption in its own operations by using more efficient processes and equipment. For example, BlueScope intends to build an electric arc furnace at its Glenbrook site in New Zealand under a co-investment agreement with the NZ Government, which will reduce New Zealand's scopes 1 and 2 emissions by 45 per cent.

BlueScope is also using renewable energy sources such as solar power generation to reduce usage of fossil fuels and reduce its carbon footprint. It has a goal to achieve net zero by 2050 across scopes 1 and 2. The net zero goal comes with a caveat: achievement requires several components to fall into place, such as commercially viable new and emerging reduced emission technologies in the steel-making process, and access to reliable and affordable renewable energy and hydrogen. It has an interim target to reduce GHG emissions by 30 per cent by 2030 based on 2018 levels.

It also reports its activities transparently with reference to the GRI Standards, TCFD, SASB for iron and steel producers and UN SDGs. It has explored a range of climate-related scenarios to determine the potential implications for BlueScope, and these insights facilitate its risk management assessment. Further, it has outlined a credible pathway to decarbonisation although, while appreciating there are challenges in accessing reliable data, it would be useful to see scope 3 emissions incorporated in the plan.

Finally, it is looking at emerging technologies such as natural gas and hydrogen Direct Reduced Ironmaking (DRI) for less carbon-intensive iron ore processing, and has allocated funds to support emergent advances in the iron and steel-making industry related to net zero transition. Further endorsement of its commitment is the role of Chief Executive Climate Change, which allows laser-like focus at the executive level on climate strategy and reduction of emissions across the business. It is a signatory to the UN Global Compact.

ESG risks	ESG measured	Assessment	Result
ESG exposure	ESG risk rating assessment		—
	ESG exposure risk classification	Medium	—
	ESG risk exposure score	63.45	X
	ESG excess exposure score	1.45	X
	ESG risk score momentum	(1.69)	✓
ESG sub-industry risk	ESG sub-industry rank	17/157	✓
	ESG risk compared to sub-industry peers	(8.91)	✓
Management of ESG risk	Management of ESG risks score	58.60	✓
	Classification of management of ESG risks	Strong	✓
	ESG risk management score momentum	6.54	✓
Company controversy	Level of company controversy exposure	Moderate	✓
	Notable ESG issues	Carbon – own operations	

Carbon emissions	Measured risks	Assessment	Result
	Carbon overall risk	Medium	—
	Carbon overall risk score	18.83	—
	Carbon total emissions, scopes 1, 2 and 3	23 240 000	X
	Carbon level of involvement	0	✓
	Level of fossil fuel involvement	0%	✓
	Carbon intensity, scopes 1, 2 and 3	2461.78	X

Fortescue Metals Group Limited

ASX code: FMG
www.fortescue.com

Market capitalisation:	$76 943.33 million
Sector:	Basic materials
Morningstar Sustainalytics peer group classification:	Steel

Environmental risk score		Social risk score		Governance risk score	
10.36	–	7.56	✓	4.12	✓

View: Fortescue is leading the way in decarbonisation in the steel subsector, spending serious capital on researching innovative tech, though this is not without risk.

History/background

Fortescue Metals is in the business of mining, processing and exporting iron ore and is one of the largest iron ore producers globally (iron ore is a key ingredient in the production of steel). Its competitive advantage is in its low-cost iron ore production. It has been able to mine and process iron ore efficiently; this, coupled with its rail and port infrastructure, makes transportation cost effective and reliable.

Its chairman and founder, Andrew 'Twiggy' Forrest, has embraced decarbonisation and in particular has been a vocal proponent of green hydrogen. Fortescue's website claims the company is 'leading the green industrial revolution' via technologies that will enable the production of green iron and steel.

ESG performance

Fortescue plans to achieve 'real zero' emissions for scopes 1 and 2 by 2030. Real zero means no fossil fuels and, ideally, no carbon offsets. On top of this, it aims to achieve scope 3 net zero emissions by 2040.

This ambition has not been without controversy. Several senior executives, including the CEO, resigned in 2023 amid speculation that their departures might be linked to the costs associated with transitioning the company to a low carbon one, including the costs associated with exploring new technologies via a subsidiary company, Fortescue Energy, which includes green hydrogen projects. Green hydrogen denotes the way the hydrogen is produced. If renewable energy sources are utilised in hydrogen production, it is labelled green. The grand plan is to convert green hydrogen into ammonia for ease of storage and transportation. Fortescue hopes to use green hydrogen and green ammonia on its large-haul mining trucks and shipping fleet.

The new technologies behind renewable energy sources are the backbone of delivering green hydrogen and ammonia. While these alternative energy sources are not yet being used commercially, they are developing. Fortescue in partnership with Liebherr are undertaking green hydrogen truck trials and a retrofitted train that is partially using ammonia as an energy source is being tested on Fortescue's rail network. In addition, trials are due to start on a modified diesel ship engine powered by ammonia.

Decarbonisation isn't cost-free. Fortescue's board has agreed to a US$6.2 billion plan to decarbonise the company, with the expectation that this approach will bring greater long-term value to shareholders.

Fortescue is about to embark on a double materiality assessment as required by the GRI Standards, which may shape the areas it will focus on in the future.

The company reports transparently on a voluntary basis across a range of reporting standards including GRI, ICMM, TCFD and the UN SDGs. It also uses a range of datapoints to measure and benchmark its performance as it relates to ESG. It is a signatory to the UN Global Compact.

Fortescue's ambitions are high, its reporting is comprehensive and transparent, and it is a leading voice on decarbonisation. However, given steel making is an energy-intensive activity, the data from 2021 shows its carbon emissions are high, second highest in the cohort behind BHP and ahead of South32. If it can make the green technologies work, it would make a significant difference to its GHG emissions. It's putting serious capital behind green iron and steel. It is one to watch.

ESG risks	ESG measured	Assessment	Result
ESG exposure	ESG risk rating assessment	▓▓▓░░	—
	ESG exposure risk classification	Medium	X
	ESG risk exposure score	61.95	X
	ESG excess exposure score	2.95	X
	ESG risk score momentum	(2.89)	✓
ESG sub-industry risk	ESG sub-industry rank	4/157	✓
	ESG risk compared to sub-industry peers	(16.5)	✓
	ESG risk beta	1.05	X
Management of ESG risk	Management of ESG risks score	71.12	✓
	Classification of management of ESG risks	Strong	✓
	ESG risk management score momentum	6.49	✓
Company controversy	Level of company controversy exposure	Moderate	✓
	Notable ESG issues	Carbon – own operations	

Carbon emissions	Measured risks	Assessment	Result
	Carbon overall risk	Medium	—
	Carbon overall risk score	10.60	—
	Carbon total emissions, scopes 1, 2 and 3	249 620 000	X
	Carbon level of involvement	0	✓
	Level of fossil fuel involvement	0%	✓
	Carbon intensity, scopes 1, 2 and 3	11 394.15	X

Incitec Pivot Limited

ASX code: IPL   www.incitecpivot.com.au

Market capitalisation:	$5671.30 million
Sector:	Basic materials
Morningstar Sustainalytics peer group classification:	Diversified Chemicals

Environmental risk score		Social risk score		Governance risk score	
16.23	–	6.93	✓	4.87	✓

View: Incitec takes a comprehensive approach to managing ESG risks well and produces transparent and detailed reporting.

History/background

Incitec Pivot has a global presence across two main business lines: production and distribution of industrial chemicals and fertilisers by the Incitec Pivot fertilisers business and production and distribution of explosives, primarily used in mining to assist with excavation, via the Dyno Noble business. The chemicals produced are mainly used in mining, treatment of water and manufacturing. Fertilisers are used in agriculture to improve crop yields. The fertiliser business demand is linked to commodity markets success.

The explosives business helps in mining key resources that are inputs in a renewable energy future. It is linked to demand for inputs into renewable energy infrastructure and battery metals mining, such as lithium, copper and cobalt. The diversification of the two main business lines helps provide stability for the business as it is not reliant on one product or sector. Its main direct competitor in Australia is Orica.

ESG performance

Incitec Pivot is committed to decarbonisation and plans to pursue a GHG net zero pathway through short-, mid- and long-term goals for scopes 1 and 2. After being named in 2018 by the Climate Action 100+ activist group as a company that needed to do better, it implemented a number of positive changes including establishing a climate change policy with board oversight, establishing a decarbonisation and energy transition steering committee, chaired by the CEO, and appointing a chief strategy and sustainability officer to lead its decarbonisation efforts, as well as linking short- and long-term remuneration incentives to the achievement of climate goals.

Outlined in its 2023 Climate Change report are its emissions-reduction targets. Its long-term goal is to deliver net zero by 2050; by 2030 it aims to achieve a 42 per cent reduction in scope 1 and 2 emissions off a FY20 baseline. Its short-term goals are reducing emissions by 5 per cent by 2026 against the FY20 baseline. Scope 3 ambitions are missing. This is because it is completing its scope 3 mapping process to understand its 'cradle to grave' emission factors. Hopefully these will be incorporated into its emissions-reduction ambitions in the near future. It is using its climate-related scenario analysis to help inform its emissions-reduction activities, which include increased use of renewable energy for ammonia production, replacing fossil fuels and, via the formation of strategic partnerships with Singapore's Keppel Infrastructure and Temasek Holdings, determining if it can produce green ammonia commercially. The success of emissions-reduction technologies such as renewable or green hydrogen in the form of ammonia, carbon capture and storage and nitrous oxide abatement are important components in achieving future decarbonisation goals.

Further, it has a commitment to zero harm, covering safety and environmental management. The company supports a just transition to a sustainable future. To that end it seeks to continue to evolve its manufacturing facilities in order to use water and energy more efficiently and reduce GHG emissions through energy efficiency abatement and the exploration of new technologies such as green hydrogen.

Incitec Pivot has a raft of sustainability policies and reporting available on its website covering modern slavery, human rights, a supplier code of conduct and climate change. It has also begun tackling aspects of scope 3 emissions via a supplier due diligence process to determine risks around modern slavery and human rights and has been undertaking supply chain mapping to better understand supplier risk, particularly at the smaller, tail end of its supply chain for its explosives business. It is a signatory to the UN Global Compact.

Incitec Pivot's ESG momentum is positive. It is well below its average sector peer in outright ESG risk and its management of ESG risks is strong. While its greatest ESG risks are environmental, it is proactively addressing these risks.

ESG risks	ESG measured	Assessment	Result
ESG exposure	ESG risk rating assessment	▮▮▮▯	—
	ESG exposure risk classification	Medium	—
	ESG risk exposure score	61.70	X
	ESG excess exposure score	7.70	X
	ESG risk score momentum	(0.68)	✓
ESG sub-industry risk	ESG sub-industry rank	18/64	✓
	ESG risk compared to sub-industry average	(5.81)	✓
	ESG risk beta	1.14	X
Management of ESG risk	Management of ESG risks score	60.71	✓
	Classification of management of ESG risks	Strong	✓
	ESG risk management score momentum	0.57	✓
Company controversy	Level of company controversy exposure	Moderate	✓
	Notable ESG issues	Emissions, effluent and waste	

Carbon emissions	Measured risks	Assessment	Result
	Carbon overall risk	Medium	—
	Carbon overall risk score	21.09	—
	Carbon total emissions, scopes 1, 2 and 3	9 690 020	X
	Carbon level of involvement	0	✓
	Level of fossil fuel involvement	0%	✓
	Carbon intensity, scopes 1, 2 and 3	3038.61	X

Lynas Rare Earths Limited

ASX code: LYC   www.lynasrareearths.com

Average market capitalisation:	$6187.68 million
Sector:	Basic materials
Morningstar Sustainalytics peer group classification:	Diversified Metals Mining

Environmental risk score		Social risk score		Governance risk score	
9.42	–	7.59	✓	6.18	✓

View: Lynas specialises in mining materials that are utilised in decarbonisation infrastructure and has a commitment at board level to reduce GHG emissions aligned to the Paris Agreement.

History/background

Lynas Rare Earths is a mining company with headquarters in Australia and operations in Malaysia. The rare earths it mines are used in a number of goods and services that are well placed to support a decarbonised future, such as wind turbines and electric vehicles.

Lynas states on its website that it was 'established as an ethical and environmentally responsible producer of rare earth materials and is the world's only significant producer of separated rare earth materials outside of China'. Importantly, Lynas is able to track the materials it produces, from mine to end product.

ESG performance

Lynas is a signatory to the UN Global Compact and reports using the GRI sustainability reporting guidelines and TCFD as well as ISO Standards 9001, 14001 and 45001. It supports the GHG objectives of the Paris Agreement and seeks to reduce energy use within its operations by reducing fossil fuel use (typically diesel) and increasing the use of renewable energy sources. However, while it aims to deliver net zero GHG emissions by 2050, details are lacking in terms of what activities it will undertake to make this happen. It is also not clear which scopes are included although given they are still in the process of evaluating a variety of scope 3 measures, it is likely to include only scopes 1 and 2. There does not seem to be an interim emissions-reduction pathway in place either; an emissions-reduction pathway helps with credibility in achieving net zero. It is also unclear whether it has set a baseline year for emissions-reduction targets. Lynas reference the Minerals Council of Australia being committed to net zero by 2050 and that its membership commits it to this goal.

In 2023, however, it withdrew from the science-based targets initiative because it needed to report within a two-year time frame. The guidance it required from the chemical industry is not due to be published until 2024, which is outside of that commitment. This problem appears to be driven by an information gap rather than a commitment issue.

Lynas has a strong focus on health and safety and seeks to play its part in combating climate change. ESG issues are overseen by the board and are the responsibility of executives. Short-term incentives incorporate ESG milestones such as reductions in GHG emissions, strategic planning, and health and safety.

The company's key ESG material risks have been aligned with UN SDGs, identified, prioritised and mapped on a materiality matrix, complementing its risk management practices. Five material issues were identified; one of those was climate change and environment. It was the highest rated stock in the sector for positive ESG momentum, which captures improvement in ESG risks year on year. It is third best on its company ESG risk assessment compared to its sub-industry peers, demonstrating low ESG risk comparatively.

ESG risks	ESG measured	Assessment	Result
ESG exposure	ESG risk rating assessment		—
	ESG exposure risk classification	Medium	—
	ESG risk exposure score	61.25	X
	ESG excess exposure score	(7.55)	✓
	ESG risk score momentum	(9.31)	✓
ESG sub-industry risk	ESG sub-industry rank	6/184	✓
	ESG risk compared to sub-industry peers	(21.06)	✓
	ESG risk beta	0.89	✓
Management of ESG risk	Management of ESG risks score	68.20	✓
	Classification of management ESG risks	Strong	✓
	ESG risk management score momentum	16.06	✓
Company controversy	Level of company controversy exposure	Moderate	✓
	Notable ESG issues	Community relations	

Carbon emissions	Measured risks	Assessment	Result
	Carbon overall risk	Medium	—
	Carbon overall risk score	14.64	—
	Carbon total emissions, scopes 1, 2 and 3	517 198.85	—
	Carbon level of involvement	0	✓
	Level of fossil fuel involvement	0%	✓
	Carbon intensity, scopes 1, 2 and 3	1442.17	X

South32 Limited

ASX code: S32

www.south32.net

Market capitalisation:	$13 950.12 million
Sector:	Basic materials
Morningstar Sustainalytics peer group classification:	Diversified Metals Mining

Environmental risk score		Social risk score		Governance risk score	
13.21	–	8.34	–	4.06	✓

View: South32 is repositioning for net zero but is less ambitious than some of its peers.

History/background

South32 is a diversified mining and metals company with global operations, headquartered in Australia, created out of BHP in 2015 as a separate entity. It mines a variety of commodities including alumina, aluminium, metallurgical coal, nickel, copper, silver, lead, bauxite and manganese. A number of these materials are important inputs in decarbonisation infrastructure such as battery production for renewable energy storage and the powering of electric vehicles.

ESG performance

Like a number of its peers, it has made a commitment to sustainability and seeks to deliver sustainable mining practices by embracing technological advances to improve resource efficiency and reduce GHG emissions. The company places a strong emphasis on climate change, GHG emissions, and the health and safety of its workers. It supports the goal of the Paris Agreement, but despite its best intentions its goals cannot be relied on as there are currently no pathways to deliver them. However, its targets are more meaningful as there are already one or more pathways available to deliver. The medium-term target is to reduce its operational emissions by 50 per cent by FY35 from a FY21 baseline.

Over time it has changed its portfolio by divesting from some of its carbon-intensive and lower performing businesses and acquiring business with better alignment to a transitioning economy, including copper and low-carbon aluminium. However, approximately 90 per cent of its operational carbon emissions come from four operations, which is where it is focusing its attention. Its decarbonisation pathway for own operations is made up of near-term, medium-term and long-term goals. Near-term activities consist of efficiency gains, such as reducing fugitive emissions. Medium-term activities largely involve a transition to lower carbon / renewable energy sources. Longer-term activities include adopting new technology solutions such as green hydrogen and improved processing technologies, such as inert anodes, which have the potential to reduce emissions from aluminium production. Scope 3 reduction relies on partnerships with customers and suppliers to support and codesign emissions-reduction programs, engagement with industry to collaborate on decarbonisation, and supporting technology innovation to manage emissions in the value chain. It is working with a handful of customers and suppliers to reduce GHG emissions. Its near-term focus is better accounting for the quantum of scope 3 GHG emissions in its value chain.

On governance its chief sustainability officer and sustainability committee support the board in identifying and managing material risks, and advise the risk and audit committee on sustainability risks. Key executives are also accountable for sustainability strategy and reporting.

South32 reports in accordance with the GRI Standards 2021, and is aligned to the TCFD as well as the ICMM Mining Principles and Position Statements. It is a member of ICMM. It is seeking to deliver reporting in alignment with the IFRS Foundation's SASB standard for the metals and mining industry. It also produces an annual modern slavery report.

It is a UN Global Compact signatory. Its Moza Aluminium operation has a provisional ASI certification and it is a member of ResponsibleSteel, an organisation that developed global standards and certification of responsible steel sourcing and production.

Its production of metallurgical coal used in the steel-making process could cause this company to be screened out by sustainable investors. However, it may meet the threshold for those who will accept exposure limited to less than 5 per cent of South32's revenue based on 2021 data.

ESG risks	ESG measured	Assessment	Result
ESG exposure	ESG risk rating assessment		—
	ESG exposure risk classification	Medium	—
	ESG risk exposure score	72.55	X
	ESG excess exposure score	0.55	X
	ESG risk score momentum	1.67	X
ESG sub-industry risk	ESG sub-industry rank	10/184	✓
	ESG risk compared to sub-industry peers	(18.65)	✓
	ESG risk beta	1.01	X
Management of ESG risk	Management of ESG risks score	73.33	✓
	Classification of management ESG risks	Strong	✓
	ESG risk management score momentum	0.95	✓
Company controversy	Level of company controversy exposure	Moderate	✓
	Notable ESG issues	Occupational health and safety	

Carbon emissions	Measured risks	Assessment	Result
	Carbon overall risk	Medium	—
	Carbon overall risk score	23.19	—
	Carbon total emissions, scopes 1, 2 and 3	136 100 000	X
	Carbon level of involvement	1	✓
	Level of fossil fuel involvement	0%–4.99%	✓
	Carbon intensity, scopes 1, 2 and 3	25 280.78	X

Mineral Resources Limited

ASX code: MIN   www.mineralresources.com.au

Market capitalisation:	$11 939.55 million
Sector:	Basic materials
Morningstar Sustainalytics peer group classification:	Diversified Metals Mining

Environmental risk score		Social risk score		Governance risk score	
10.68	–	6.54	✓	4.24	✓

View: MinRes has made an impressive commitment to ESG, particularly in its use of several third-party data sources to benchmark its ESG performance and identify areas of future focus.

History/background

Mineral Resources (MinRes), with headquarters in Western Australia, was founded in 2006 and is involved in services and operations within the mining and minerals industry.

It identifies four core segments: mining services, iron ore, lithium and energy. Its mining services provide pit to port solutions for key clients along with manufacturing and maintenance of mining equipment. It mines and exports iron ore. Already a top five producer, it looks to improve output while maintaining low-cost production. It also mines and exports lithium, and is seeking full vertical integration from pit to battery. In its energy segment, it aims to decarbonise by replacing fossil fuels with renewables for MinRes business.

ESG performance

MinRes notes the importance of generating shareholder value while maintaining a social licence to operate through protecting the environment and making a positive contribution to the communities in which it operates.

Its ambition is to deliver net zero operational emissions in scopes 1 and 2 by 2050. It plans on achieving this through reducing diesel fuel, replaced by renewable energy sources, electrification of equipment and transport, energy storage and the adoption of new technology. However, due to expansion and construction activities its scope 1 emissions grew by 11 per cent in FY23. Its decarbonisation pathway includes a 50 per cent reduction in operational emissions by FY35 from a FY22 baseline. It's in the process of understanding its scope 3 emissions, so scope 3 are yet to be incorporated in its net zero ambitions.

MinRes has considered a range of future climate scenarios to help it assess the climate-related risks and opportunities in its business. It has also undertaken materiality assessments and mapped issues in order of importance to MinRes in a matrix. Of the 10 issues identified as having very high materiality, two are related to the environment, climate change and managing environmental impact. It has also aligned its most material impacts to relevant UN SDGs.

It reports in accordance with the GRI Standards 2021 and in alignment with the TCFD. It has joined the UN Global Compact and has begun the self-assessment process for IRMA verification for its Wodgina operations. For a number of years it has been reporting in line with SASB and the SDGs. It plans to report in line with the ISSB standards that are expected to come into effect in mid 2024. Its comprehensive reporting was recognised with a gold award for excellence in its sustainability reporting at the Australasian Reporting Awards (ARA) in 2023.

It has established a sustainability committee, which includes some very experienced members, to help inform the board's decision making and oversight as they relate to sustainability issues.

It uses a variety of ESG ratings agencies' data to benchmark and assess its performance against that of its peers. It also provides some interesting case studies on some of its successful ESG projects.

ESG risks	ESG measured	Assessment	Result
ESG exposure	ESG risk rating assessment	▓▓▓░░	—
	ESG exposure risk classification	Medium	—
	ESG risk exposure score	65.45	✓
	ESG excess exposure score	(3.55)	✓
	ESG risk score momentum	(8.50)	✓
ESG sub-industry risk	ESG sub-industry rank	3/184	✓
	ESG risk compared to sub-industry peers	(22.79)	✓
	ESG risk beta	0.95	✓
Management of ESG risk	Management of ESG risks score	74.26	✓
	Classification of management of ESG risks	Strong	✓
	ESG risk management score momentum	15.85	✓
Company controversy	Level of company controversy exposure	Moderate	✓
	Notable ESG issues	Emissions, effluent and waste	

Carbon emissions	Measured risks	Assessment	Result
	Carbon overall risk	Medium	—
	Carbon overall risk score	11.92	—
	Carbon total emissions, scopes 1, 2 and 3	1 149 772.47	X
	Carbon level of involvement	1	✓
	Level of fossil fuel involvement	0%–4.99%	✓
	Carbon intensity, scopes 1, 2 and 3	419.93	X

Vulcan Energy Resources Limited

ASX code: VUL   www.v-er.eu

Market capitalisation:	$433.62 million
Sector:	Basic materials
Morningstar Sustainalytics peer group classification:	Specialised Chemicals

Environmental risk score		Social risk score		Governance risk score	
4.86	✓	7.40	✓	4.51	✓

View: Vulcan's zero-carbon lithium process is still maturing but its research and development to date is impressive.

History/background

Vulcan Energy is a lithium and renewable energy producer with big ambitions that include decarbonising lithium production. It is dual listed on the Australian and Frankfurt stock exchanges. Its aim is to become the world's first net zero integrated lithium and renewable energy provider.

The company's innovative lithium extraction process, 'Zero Carbon Lithium™', uses geothermal energy wells to keep the process carbon neutral. The process allows for co-production of geothermal energy at scale with the excess sent back to the grid to provide heating and/or renewable energy to local communities. The proprietary alumina-based adsorption approach also reduces water consumption as the need for large evaporation ponds in the process is significantly reduced.

Vulcan has been working on this novel approach since 2018 and after a phase 1 definitive feasibility study (DFS) is moving towards the production phase expected to commence in 2026. A Minviro lifecycle assessment conducted from its DFS results suggests a climate change impact even better than net zero—a negative carbon impact. Vulcan has also received a conditional non-binding letter of support from Export Finance Australia for up to AU$200 million to finance phase 1 of the Zero Carbon Lithium™ project, which is scheduled to take place after completion of the bridging study and will coincide with German funding. Other in-principle support is coming from France, Italy and Canada. Consultant Environmental Resources Management has completed an Environmental and Social Impact Assessment (ESIA) for phase 1, which is a requirement for obtaining green finance and provides third-party validation of the approach.

ESG performance

As a result of the more stringent sustainability reporting regime in Europe, the quality of information supplied by Vulcan is high. For example, it provides a separate TCFD report, reports in line with GRI Standards and provides a corporate governance statement. It also undertakes a materiality assessment utilising expertise from global consultancy firm ERM.

Electric vehicle demands for lithium have led to European manufacturers signing binding agreements with five high-quality companies—Stellantis, Volkswagen, Renault, Umicore and LG Energy Solution—to shore up supply of critical raw materials. This has resulted in Vulcan's five-year plan of lithium production being fully committed.

The Australian operation's GHG emissions were certified by Climate Active and carbon credits were purchased to bring the operations to net zero certification. Vulcan is compliant with the Australasian code for reporting of exploration results. Executive remuneration is linked to sustainability metrics. Vulcan is a signatory to the UN Global Compact.

Vulcan's ESG scores are extraordinarily good. It is rated well by Morningstar Sustainalytics, attracting a low assessment for its overall ESG risks, the second best rating category available. It also has an exceptionally low ESG risk beta—the lowest out of all the companies listed in this book. Its ESG risk is also falling year on year. It has the third highest positive ESG momentum of all the stocks listed in this sector.

ESG risks	ESG measured	Assessment	Result
ESG exposure	ESG risk rating assessment	▨▨▨▨▢	✓
	ESG exposure risk classification	Low	✓
	ESG risk exposure score	32.95	✓
	ESG excess exposure score	(19.05)	✓
	ESG risk score momentum	(8.24)	✓
ESG sub-industry risk	ESG sub-industry rank	4/142	✓
	ESG risk compared to sub-industry peers	(14.49)	✓
	ESG risk beta	0.63	✓
Management of ESG risk	Management of ESG risks score	52.56	✓
	Classification of management of ESG risks	Strong	✓
	ESG risk management score momentum	25.04	✓
Company controversy	Level of company controversy exposure	None	✓
	Notable ESG issue	Human capital	

Carbon emissions	Measured risks	Assessment	Result
	Carbon overall risk	Low	✓
	Carbon overall risk score	4.46	✓
	Carbon total emissions, scopes 1, 2 and 3	2246.97	✓
	Carbon level of involvement	0	✓
	Level of fossil fuel involvement	0%	✓
	Carbon intensity, scopes 1, 2 and 3	No data	n/a

De Grey Mining Limited

ASX code: DEG   www.degreymining.com.au

Market capitalisation:	$2138.80 million
Sector:	Basic materials
Morningstar Sustainalytics peer group classification:	Gold

Environmental risk score		Social risk score		Governance risk score	
0.16	✓	5.00	✓	10.15	–

View: With the ESG capabilities of the Hemi mine yet to be determined, more concrete plans and metrics around De Grey's decarbonisation efforts are needed.

History/background

De Grey Mining was founded in 2002 as a multi-commodity explorer of base and precious metals within the Pilbara region of Western Australia. It has a large range of exploration tenements in the region. However, since finding large gold deposits near the surface at Hemi in the Pilbara the company is now focused squarely on the Hemi Gold Project. The size, quality, location and closeness to the surface means the mining potential is substantial with a low strip ratio using a low-cost open pit mining method. There is critical infrastructure already in place where the gold deposits have been found, which has added to its appeal. There is not a lot of publicly available information on this company.

ESG performance

In its annual report it declares that responsible management of ESG elements is central to its business success. It states it is aligned with ICMM and is implementing the 10 principles of the UN's SDGs. However, it is not yet a member of ICMM, and it has not signed up to the UN Global Compact.

De Grey says it adheres to the TCFD, which is part of its climate-related planning. It has an ESG policy which, although it appears to be at a high level, lacks necessary detail—science-backed targets, for example, or a clear commitment or pathway to net zero.

De Grey's Hemi mine is targeted to begin its first gold production in 2026 and the company has indicated it may be a low-carbon project due to the planned use of renewable energy and electric mobile equipment instead of diesel.

It has provided a basic scenario analysis for the Hemi mine and its design considers a variety of ESG issues including processing, energy supply, and storage of tailings and other mine waste. Assessments include emissions intensity and ways to reduce emissions relative to baseline assumptions, and work undertaken to date has taken into account ecological and hydrological as well as social impact and heritage assessments. Each part has been mapped to ICMM and TCFD principles based on an expectation that De Grey will set ESG targets when the project is more developed. Little detail is publicly available, however. Its intentions are positive but actions are where the rubber meets the road, so it will need to be monitored over time. The carbon emissions data referenced in the tables, based on Morningstar Sustainalytics estimates rather than on what the company has reported, seems positive.

Other positive developments include the creation of an ESG subcommittee of the board and an ESG working group to help with implementation. De Grey engaged a third party to help undertake a gap analysis to identify areas that will need attention but it is not clear whether this was a materiality assessment, what gaps were identified or the nature of future priorities. Greater transparency and more reporting on its ESG plans would be a great step forward.

The company has signed a native title mining agreement with the Kariyarra people in relation to developing and operating the mine. It promises employment and includes a management protocol to minimise negative impacts to Kariyarra cultural heritage.

De Grey Mining is assessed as having low risk in terms of ESG issues and it also receives a low ESG risk exposure score. Its environmental risk is assessed as the second lowest in the basic materials cohort, just behind Deterra Royalties. Compared to its peers, its ESG risk is low; however, its management of ESG risks is assessed as only average.

ESG risks	ESG measured	Assessment	Result
ESG exposure	ESG risk rating assessment		✓
	ESG exposure risk classification	Low	✓
	ESG risk exposure score	22.50	✓
	ESG excess exposure score	(0.50)	✓
	ESG risk score momentum	No data	n/a
ESG sub-industry risk	ESG sub-industry rank	5/87	✓
	ESG risk compared to sub-industry peers	(21.99)	✓
	ESG risk beta	0.98	✓
Management of ESG risk	Management of ESG risks score	32.94	X
	Classification of management of ESG risks	Average	–
	ESG risk management score momentum	No data	
Company controversy	Level of company controversy exposure	None	✓
	Notable ESG issues	Human capital	

Carbon emissions	Measured risks	Assessment	Result
	Carbon overall risk	Negligible	✓
	Carbon overall risk score	0	✓
	Carbon total emissions, scopes 1, 2 and 3	177.45	✓
	Carbon level of involvement	0	✓
	Level of fossil fuel involvement	0%	✓
	Carbon intensity, scopes 1, 2 and 3	6772.90	X

Sims Limited

ASX code: SGM

www.simsmm.com

Market capitalisation:	$2585.15 million
Sector:	Basic materials
Morningstar Sustainalytics peer group classification:	Facilities Maintenance

Environmental risk score		Social risk score		Governance risk score	
8.12	✓	6.48	✓	3.53	✓

View: With sustainability at the heart of all it does, Sims manifests impressive ambition, reporting and transparency yet is not resting on its laurels.

History/background

Sims Limited is a global company with three business divisions:

- Sims Metal specialises in metals recycling. Buying and processing scrap metal such as steel, copper and aluminium is its core business.

- Sims Lifecycle Services is a leading provider in IT asset and cloud infrastructure reuse, redeployment and recycling.

- Sims Resource Renewal has designed a process to manage and reuse Automotive Shredder Residue (ASR).

Sims is a large-scale recycler that refurbishes or recycles waste materials to make new products. The company's mission is to contribute to a world without waste and it sees itself as a leader in the circular economy. Recycling reduces the need to mine new raw materials, which are finite and carbon intensive to mine and process; recycling is a net positive for the environment. It estimates it avoided 12.4 tonnes of CO_2e emissions through its recycling efforts in the FY23.

ESG performance

Sims provides extensive ESG information including a climate report (aligned to TCFD), a sustainability report, a sustainability data book and a modern slavery statement. It has developed a clear pathway to net zero. It aims to be carbon neutral by 2030 and to achieve net zero by 2050 for scopes 1 and 2. It is aligning with science-based targets for scopes 1 and 2 emissions. However, scope 3 is where the bulk of its emissions lie, particularly for its core business, Sims Metals, which contributes

96 per cent of the total value chain emissions via marine freight and secondary processing of metal. It acknowledges that this needs to be addressed and has been engaging with its value chain to obtain more data relating to scope 3 emissions.

Its business strategy is aligned to three UN SDGs: decent work and economic growth, climate action, and responsible consumption and production.

Among its ESG achievements to date: 84 per cent of electricity consumption is via renewable sources. It has lowered its scopes 1 and 2 emissions by 32 per cent from its FY20 baseline, mostly through the decarbonisation of its electricity supply. The next focus will be replacing diesel mobile equipment with electric alternatives.

Sims undertakes regular materiality assessments to identify key issues and rank them in order of importance to the business and maps them to a materiality matrix. Emerging topics such as biodiversity and water stewardship have been captured as areas for future consideration. The process is aligned to international best standards via the GRI framework. Reporting is transparent and detailed. It is a UN Global Compact signatory.

ESG risks	ESG measured	Assessment	Result
ESG exposure	ESG risk rating assessment		✓
	ESG exposure risk classification	Low	✓
	ESG risk exposure score	37.20	X
	ESG excess exposure score	0.20	X
	ESG risk score momentum	(1.08)	✓
ESG sub-industry risk	ESG sub-industry rank	8/77	✓
	ESG risk compared to sub-industry peers	(5.29)	✓
	ESG risk beta	1.01	X
Management of ESG risk	Management of ESG risks score	55.92	–
	Classification of management of ESG risks	Strong	✓
	ESG risk management score momentum	2.72	✓
Company controversy	Level of company controversy exposure	Moderate	–
	Notable ESG issues	Community relations	

Carbon emissions	Measured risks	Assessment	Result
	Carbon overall risk	Low	✓
	Carbon overall risk score	8.22	✓
	Carbon total emissions, scopes 1, 2 and 3	574 588.95	–
	Carbon level of involvement	0	✓
	Level of fossil fuel involvement	0%	✓
	Carbon intensity, scopes 1, 2 and 3	132.43	–

Deterra Royalties Limited

ASX code: DRR   www.deterraroyalties.com

Market capitalisation:	$2622.10 million
Sector:	Basic materials
Morningstar Sustainalytics peer group classification:	Steel

Environmental risk score		Social risk score		Governance risk score	
0.14	✓	4.67	✓	7.13	✓

View: Deterra has good intentions, but its ESG information and reporting are scant and need to evolve.

History/background

Deterra Royalties, based in Perth, manages a portfolio of royalty assets across a range of mining projects and commodities owned and operated by third parties. A relatively new enterprise, it began operations as an independent listed entity in November 2020, created through a demerger from Iluka, who has retained a 20 per cent ownership. Deterra is seeking to add to its portfolio to increase growth and diversification.

ESG performance

The business is royalties based and therefore does well on ESG metrics. It has the lowest environmental risk score in the *Top Stocks* basic materials cohort, yet ultimately investors are indirectly buying mining exposure. Deterra does well if the areas in which it owns royalties are mined successfully. Of the six royalties it holds, three are currently producing: an iron ore operation and two mineral sands operations.

It has established a range of ESG-relevant policies, including climate and human rights policies. It has issued a modern slavery statement and has formulated ESG due diligence criteria, which is a starting point to understanding ESG risk and opportunities. It is a member of the UN Global Compact.

Its extremely succinct climate change policy was adopted by the board in 2022. It acknowledges the scientific evidence for climate change, declares the company's support for the objectives of the Paris Agreement and committed to net zero GHG emissions for its own operations by 2022. However, the bulk of emissions are not its own operations but rather within the operations it invests into.

ESG metrics do not seem to be front and centre. There is no materiality assessment, identification of key material ESG risk and opportunities, or detailed sustainability information or reporting. This needs to change.

ESG risks	ESG measured	Assessment	Result
ESG exposure	ESG risk rating assessment		✓
	ESG exposure risk classification	Low	✓
	ESG risk exposure score	22.00	✓
	ESG excess exposure score	0	✓
	ESG risk score momentum	(1.94)	✓
ESG sub-industry risk	ESG sub-industry rank	1/157	✓
	ESG risk compared to sub-industry peers	(26.6)	✓
	ESG risk beta	1.00	–
Management of ESG risk	Management of ESG risks score	47.12	–
	Classification of management of ESG risks	Average	–
	ESG risk management score momentum	9.06	✓
Company controversy	Level of company controversy exposure	None	✓
	Notable ESG issues	Human capital	

Carbon emissions	Measured risks	Assessment	Result
	Carbon overall risk	Negligible	✓
	Carbon overall risk score	0	✓
	Carbon total emissions, scopes 1, 2 and 3	81 002.10	–
	Carbon level of involvement	0	✓
	Level of fossil fuel involvement	0%	✓
	Carbon intensity, scopes 1, 2 and 3	760.66	X

Concluding remarks

Generally, companies operating in this sector are looking at how they can decarbonise, recognising that small changes can make a big difference in this high-emitting sector. It is encouraging to see how much innovation is occurring, such as zero-carbon lithium or green hydrogen in the production of steel. If these innovations bear fruit, it will be a game changer for the decarbonisation pathway. Yet there are no guarantees these innovations will work at scale, so there are risks as companies race to tackle the decarbonisation challenge.

Some innovations are more mature, and already in production. Vulcan plans to begin operations on its Zero Carbon Lithium Project in 2026. Green hydrogen is still in development.

On an absolute ESG risk basis, Deterra, De Grey, Vulcan and Sims all rated as low risk. Arguably, Sims is the least risky as it has been recycling scrap metals for 100 years. The rest of the basic materials cohort were assessed as medium risk.

Incitec and BHP were assessed as having the highest environmental risks in the cohort; BlueScope Steel had the highest social risk followed by BHP and South32, while De Grey and Deterra had the highest governance risks. This corresponded to the management of ESG risks. Deterra Royalties and De Grey Mining were assessed as average in this area and all others were assessed as strong.

On carbon risk, De Grey and Deterra rated best, with no carbon exposure. South32 had the highest carbon risk but this was still assessed as medium. On scopes 1, 2 and 3 total carbon emissions BHP produced the most (followed by Fortescue and South32) and was the highest out of the entire cohort in this book. (See Part 2 table, J. Carbon Emissions scopes 1, 2 and 3 for more detail.)

2. Communication services

The communication services sector includes telecommunication services, wireless telecom networks, media and entertainment services, and internet providers.

Demand for digital communications during the COVID pandemic caused an uptick in energy consumption. With many companies continuing to support full or hybrid remote working arrangements, demand is expected to remain elevated compared to pre-COVID levels.

Entertainment companies, broadcasters and publishing industries face several significant sustainability challenges.

The film industry has a significant carbon footprint and needs to address a range of other issues, including liveable wages, gender equality, and responsible production and consumption. As one recent example, the successful 2023 Writers Guild of America strike in Hollywood related to pay, health and retirement benefits, and safeguards for employees around the threat to their livelihoods posed by artificial intelligence.

Broadcasters face unique sustainability challenges, not least the carbon footprint associated with distributing and streaming video content. Some companies are seeking to become greener primarily by becoming more energy efficient.

The practices of responsible publishing include responsible sourcing of paper, management of their supply chain and being energy efficient in their own operations.

To summarise, the sustainability challenges for companies in the communication services sector include the need to reduce their carbon footprint, manage energy consumption, address the environmental impact of their operations and manage their supply chain.

EVT Limited

ASX code: EVT

www.evt.com

Market capitalisation:	$1761.70 million
Sector:	Communication services
Morningstar Sustainalytics peer group classification:	Movies and Entertainment

Environmental risk score		Social risk score		Governance risk score	
0.12	✓	8.17	✓	7.63	✓

View: With a lack of clarity around decarbonisation and large gaps in TCFD reporting, EVT's sustainability efforts disappoint.

History/background

EVT Limited is an Australian company that operates in the entertainment, hospitality and leisure industries. The company owns, operates and manages Event Cinemas, hotels and resorts, ski runs, and mountain bike and hiking trails. Event Cinemas include Vmax, Gold Class and 4DX. It owns Rydges Hotels & Resorts, Thredbo ski resort, a travel agency and a rewards program.

The company was formed in 1913 as Union Theatres and Australasian Films, which became Australia's biggest film company of the era. During the war years, the group helped shape the national identity of the time through producing films and connecting audiences with the experience of cinema.

EVT's competitive advantage lies in its ability to provide cutting-edge experiences using the latest technology and to help customers stay connected with everything that's new. EVT also offers Elevate Perks, which provides team members and their families with a great range of discounts across EVT experiences.

ESG performance

On sustainability EVT has three main areas of focus and seven specific goals:

1. sustainable design

   Goal 1. Obtain NABERS ratings for owned property.

   Goal 2. Obtain certifications for new builds and designs with a target for green star +5.

2.   sustainable practices and procurement

Goal 3. Reduce environmental impact of packaging across the group and manage waste sustainably.

Goal 4. Reduce consumption of energy and natural resources, and purchase renewable energy.

3.   transparency and reporting

Goal 5. Respond to climate risks and opportunities with TCFD reporting.

Goal 6. Raise awareness of environmental initiatives.

Goal 7. Strengthen implementation of goals through collaborative partnerships.

The group does not provide a separate sustainability report, although it discusses sustainability in the annual report. It acknowledges that the business is exposed to risks associated with climate change. As one example, physical risk and a reliance on natural snowfall at its Thredbo resort could increase the cost of insurance or, conversely, underinsurance of assets. Further, there are obligations in the way it manages its operations—specifically, sewage treatment and water licence requirements at Thredbo. Transition risk includes the potential impact on its business in relation to carbon pricing.

EVT appears to have no net zero ambitions or carbon reduction targets. This is disappointing and out of step with its peers. It's especially perplexing given one of its business units, Thredbo Resorts, is heavily impacted by climate change. Its annual report outlines some basic carbon reporting, which shows scope 1 and 2 emissions approximately 20 per cent lower in FY23 compared to FY19. However, it is not clear what activities it has been undertaking to reduce carbon emissions. It references energy efficiency initiatives, including replacing plant and equipment with newer, more efficient alternatives and increased use of renewables, but it lacks more granular data and a pathway of activities it plans to undertake.

Part of the problem is that without a carbon reduction target, there is a lack of specificity around carbon reduction initiatives. It provides no reporting on scope 3, which remains a work in progress. FY23 saw the group assess scope 3 boundaries, and FY24 should see the emissions review begin. If we are serious about limiting global warming, every company needs to make specific commitments to carbon reduction urgently. On commitment and reporting EVT is well behind most companies showcased in this book.

Thredbo has obvious vulnerabilities due to climate change; for its peak winter season it relies on consistent natural snowfall, but the right weather conditions have become less dependable. There are technologies that could support the resort, such as snow-making technology, but water is a key input here. While this is encouraging, its hard to imagine a scenario where summer demand would be high enough to offset lower revenues generated in winter due to declining snowfalls and a subsequently shorter ski season.

It has completed scenario analysis on climate-related risks across only two scenarios, where most companies undertake a range of scenarios. The company plans for a materiality assessment in FY24. FY23 saw the company undertake a TCFD gap analysis, which will also inform the potential material risks to the business.

EVT is not a signatory to the UN Global Compact, neither are its sustainability capabilities validated by any third-party organisation. It publishes minimal sustainability information and there is no mention in its reporting of alignment to SDGs. While it acknowledges climate science, it has yet to commit to specific targets, actions or a credible pathway to decarbonisation. The business does not have specific sustainability policies and shows no evidence that executive pay is aligned to sustainability performance. There is a lot to work on.

ESG risks	ESG measured	Assessment	Result
ESG exposure	ESG risk rating assessment		✓
	ESG exposure risk classification	Low	✓
	ESG risk exposure score	24.30	✓
	ESG excess exposure score	0.30	X
	ESG risk score momentum	(0.71)	✓
ESG sub-industry risk	ESG sub-industry rank	20/82	✓
	ESG risk compared to sub-industry peers	(1.63)	✓
	ESG risk beta	1.01	X
Management of ESG risk	Management of ESG risks score	36.50	–
	Classification of management ESG risks	Average	–
	ESG risk management score momentum	3.11	✓
Company controversy	Level of company controversy exposure	None	✓
	Notable ESG risk	Data privacy and security	

Carbon emissions	Measured risks	Assessment	Result
	Carbon overall risk	Negligible	✓
	Carbon overall risk score	0	✓
	Carbon total emissions, scopes 1, 2 and 3	128 651.87	–
	Carbon level of involvement	0	✓
	Level of fossil fuel involvement	0%	✓
	Carbon intensity, scopes 1, 2 and 3	306.61	–

SEEK Limited

ASX code: SEK   www.seek.com.au

Market capitalisation:	$8459.15 million
Sector:	Communication services
Morningstar Sustainalytics peer group classification:	HR Services

Environmental risk score		Social risk score		Governance risk score	
0.13	✓	8.12	✓	3.35	✓

View: Its comprehensive sustainability framework, detailed reporting and target of net zero across all scopes by 2030 put SEEK in a leading position among its peers.

History/background

Founded in Melbourne in 1997, SEEK was created to make it easier for candidates and companies hiring to connect by moving print newspaper job ads online. It is now the largest global online employment marketplace with a presence in Australia, New Zealand, Hong Kong, Southeast Asia, Brazil and Mexico. It also has a minority investment in employment services in other countries including China and South Korea.

Its advantage lies in its ability to leverage data and technology to provide insights and resourceful solutions. The company offers a range of products and services across its different business departments:

- SEEK Employment—job search and recruitment services for job seekers and employers

- SEEK Learning—online courses and training programs for job seekers and professionals

- SEEK Volunteer—volunteering opportunities for job seekers and professionals

- SEEK Business—business and franchise opportunities for entrepreneurs and business owners

- SEEK Insights—offers data and insights into the job market and employment trends.

ESG performance

SEEK's sustainability framework distinguishes the following:

- Social impact—via SEEK data and insights, publishing employment reports including the Advertised Salary Index to help support government policy and programs in Australia

- People—diversity and inclusion, an engaged workforce, health safety and wellbeing

- Human rights—fair hiring, online safety and security, modern slavery

- Environment—climate resilience, minimising environmental impact

- Responsible business—ethical conduct and responsible business practices

- Data and cyber—cybersecurity, data privacy, data trust and AI.

It's hardly surprising that the S in ESG features prominently for SEEK given the core of its business is recruitment of people. As part of its due diligence, in FY23 it undertook to scan the job ads on their platforms in the Asia Pacific region and escalated 10 per cent of them into a manual review process, which resulted in its excluding and closing hirer accounts and removing thousands of job ads from its platform.

In FY23 SEEK undertook modern slavery audits on cleaning contractors, a handful of which were required to improve policies and procedures.

SEEK obtained carbon neutral certification from Climate Active for its Australian and New Zealand business in 2021 and for global operations in 2022. It is aiming for net zero with a pathway that includes FY25 targets. It has undertaken a climate scenario analysis.

SEEK reports in alignment with TCFD and several UN sustainable development goals: SDG 8 decent work and economic growth, SDG 5 gender equality, SDG 13 climate action and SDG 17 partnerships. In FY23 it completed its climate scenario analysis and developed a social impact framework. Aspirations for FY24 include external verification of sustainability disclosures. It seeks a 40 per cent reduction from the 2022 baseline across all scopes by FY25 as a credible step towards net zero by 2030.

Its comprehensive reporting is in line with GRI, SASB and TCFD. It will be adopting ISSB reporting standards and seeking external verification of its sustainability performance data. It will also expand its ESG metrics for material ESG risks and opportunities and align these with its business strategies.

Its initial materiality assessment in 2019 uncovered human rights as a material topic, particularly in Asia, and climate change continues to be a material topic. FY23 saw the company revise its assessment to identify six key material areas, as captured in the sustainability framework already outlined.

The board, through the audit and risk management committee, is responsible for ESG risks. The board assesses material ESG risks and opportunities and approves ESG reporting topics. The MD and CEO have responsibility for management of the business, which includes ESG risks, and the CFO is responsible for reporting of ESG risks based on information validated by subject matter experts and evidence. The SEEK risk management framework has been revised to incorporate climate change, which is a regular item on board meeting agenda. On sustainability, SEEK is impressive, although its overall ESG momentum is deteriorating, and the data shows the company is becoming more exposed to ESG risks compared to the previous year. Simultaneously, Seek are improving their management of ESG risks year on year.

ESG risks	ESG measured	Assessment	Result
ESG exposure	ESG risk rating assessment	▮▮▮▮☐	✓
	ESG exposure risk classification	Low	✓
	ESG risk exposure score	21.00	✓
	ESG excess exposure score	0	—
	ESG risk score momentum	0	—
ESG sub-industry risk	ESG sub-industry rank	23/61	—
	ESG risk compared to sub-industry peers	(1.12)	✓
	ESG risk beta	1.00	—
Management of ESG risk	Management of ESG risks score	48.23	—
	Classification of management ESG risks	Average	—
	ESG risk management score momentum	(1.75)	X
Company controversy	Level of company controversy exposure	Low	✓
	Notable ESG risk	Data privacy and security	

Carbon emissions	Measured risks	Assessment	Result
	Carbon overall risk	Negligible	✓
	Carbon overall risk score	0	✓
	Carbon total emissions, scopes 1, 2 and 3	13 482	✓
	Carbon level of involvement	0	✓
	Level of fossil fuel involvement	0%	✓
	Carbon intensity, scopes 1, 2 and 3	24.18	✓

News Corp DR

ASX code: NWS

www.newscorp.com

Market capitalisation:	$19 264.84 million
Sector:	Communication services
Morningstar Sustainalytics peer group classification:	Publishing

Environmental risk score		Social risk score		Governance risk score	
0.02	✓	4.74	✓	6.72	✓

View: News Corp has been considering sustainability for longer than most and has therefore progressed further than most of its peers.

History/background

News Corp DR is a global media and information services company that operates in the United States, Australia and the United Kingdom. The company's businesses include news and information services, book publishing, digital real estate services, and cable network programming. News Corp DR was created in 2013 when News Corporation split into two separate publicly traded companies, 21st Century Fox and the new News Corp. The former was acquired by the Walt Disney Company in 2019 and renamed the Fox Corporation, which is listed on the NASDAQ.

The old News Corp was established in 1980 by Rupert Murdoch as a holding company for News Limited. News Limited was founded in 1923 in Adelaide by James Edward Davidson. The company has since grown to become a media conglomerate that owns several businesses and brands. These include: *The Australian* and the *Herald Sun* newspapers; REA Group, a digital property advertising company listed on the ASX; Dow Jones, a global provider of news and business information; the book publisher HarperCollins; Realtor.com, a US real estate website; the *New York Post* newspaper; and Foxtel, a pay-TV, broadband and streaming service.

ESG performance

On sustainability News Corp is quite advanced. Its Global Environmental Initiative, which has been running since 2013, looks to 'reduce, engage and source responsibly'. It hopes to achieve net zero carbon emissions across all scopes by 2050 (or earlier), an ambition that has been reviewed and validated against the SBTi corporate net zero standard. Meantime it seeks to reduce net zero emissions by 65 per cent against the FY16 baseline by FY30.

It has a net zero pathway plan that covers operational and supply chain emissions. Its supplier code of conduct sets out expectations across ethics and compliance, human and labour rights, health and safety, and sustainability, which includes targets to reduce GHG emissions, use renewable energy and manage waste. Despite this, scope 3 emissions increased in FY22 by 11 per cent due to both supplier emissions and corporate investments. Its aim is to reduce scope 3 by 25 per cent by FY30 from the FY21 base year.

To achieve these targets it plans to decarbonise its operations through energy efficiency gains such as converting to LED lights, energy efficient air compressors and better insulation. Supply chain emissions reductions are important as they make up the bulk of the company's emissions. It is undertaking a program of supplier engagement, aided by membership of the CDP supply chain program, which helps identify supplier-specific emissions factors and will help it more accurately capture scope 3 emissions. It is also investing in renewable energy and transitioning to renewable energy in its operations. It will seek to mitigate remaining emissions, probably via carbon offsets.

In its own operations it recycles all newsprint waste at its print centres. FY22 saw 77 per cent of its paper sourced from certified suppliers; it aims that by FY25 100 per cent will be from certified sources.

News Corp comprehensive reporting is aligned to GRI, SASB and TCFD frameworks. It understands where its risks and opportunities lie and where it needs to focus its efforts. It has a range of environmental policies in place, including global waste management and paper source policies and the News Corp environmental policy and supplier code of conduct.

On governance, oversight of ESG matters ultimately rests with the board. However, there is centralised management of ESG issues through the ESG steering committee, which is made up of senior leadership, as well as the ESG governance committee, comprising subject matter experts in ESG areas of focus. This committee also implements ESG strategy and monitors emerging issues. FY22 saw the incorporation of ESG metrics into executive compensation.

ESG risks	ESG measured	Assessment	Result
ESG exposure	ESG risk rating assessment		✓
	ESG exposure risk classification	Low	✓
	ESG risk exposure score	21.30	✓
	ESG excess exposure score	1.30	X
	ESG risk score momentum	0.23	X
ESG sub-industry risk	ESG sub-industry rank	10/59	✓
	ESG risk compared to sub-industry peers	(2.21)	✓
	ESG risk beta	1.07	X
Management of ESG risk	Management of ESG risks score	48.04	—
	Classification of management ESG risks	Average	—
	ESG risk management score momentum	(0.84)	X
Company controversy	Level of company controversy exposure	Moderate	—
	Notable ESG risk	Business ethics	

Carbon emissions	Measured risks	Assessment	Result
	Carbon overall risk	Negligible	✓
	Carbon overall risk score	0	✓
	Carbon total emissions, scopes 1, 2 and 3	2 491 010.00	X
	Carbon level of involvement	0	✓
	Level of fossil fuel involvement	0%	✓
	Carbon intensity, scopes 1, 2 and 3	266.19	—

Nine Entertainment Co. Holdings Limited

ASX code: NEC

www.nineforbrands.com.au

Market capitalisation:	$3149.61 million
Sector:	Communication services
Morningstar Sustainalytics peer group classification:	Broadcasting

Environmental risk score		Social risk score		Governance risk score	
0.12	✓	9.01	−	7.24	✓

View: As new kids on the block, with no emissions data and no clarity around sustainability, Nine is just beginning its ESG journey.

History/background

Nine Entertainment Co. Holdings Limited is a publicly listed Australian mass media company with holdings in radio and television broadcasting, publishing and digital media. The company's history dates back to the 1950s. Originally called TCN-9, on September 16, 1956, it broadcast Australia's first-ever TV program, *This Is Television*. In 2018 the company merged with Fairfax Media, expanding its brands and investments across television, video on demand, print, digital, radio and real estate classifieds.

Some of the products and services offered by Nine Entertainment are:

- Nine Network—a free-to-air television network that broadcasts a range of programs including news, sports and entertainment

- 9Now—a video-on-demand, catch-up TV service that carries the main and multichannels of the Nine Network

- Stan—an Australian subscription streaming service

- *The Sydney Morning Herald*—a major daily tabloid newspaper

- *The Age*—a major daily newspaper published in Melbourne

- *The Australian Financial Review*—a business-focused daily newspaper

- 9Honey—a digital platform for women

- Pedestrian—a digital platform for Millennials

- Domain Group (majority investment)—a real estate web portal.

ESG performance

Information on sustainability wasn't easy to find for this company. Its website includes a corporate responsibility component, which, it states, encompasses people, community, governance and environment. Its approach appears to focus on the social and governance elements of ESG, although even there it's light on details and data.

In FY21 the group undertook an ESG materiality assessment to identify the material topics of importance to its stakeholders. This identified six material issues to prioritise:

1. Facilitating trusted journalism

2. Consumer data security and privacy

3. Community engagement and contribution

4. Carbon footprint accounting—print and operations

5. Diversity and inclusion

6. ESG disclosure and transparency.

It does not produce a sustainability report and while some ESG activity is captured in its annual reports, it is limited. This company seems to be far behind its peers on its ESG journey.

There is no carbon data, no alignment to SDGs and no climate scenario assessments, and neither is its reporting aligned to global standards such as GRI, SASB or TCFD. Further, there are no commitments to net zero targets and no pathway to or acknowledgement of science-backed targets. The website does present an ESG policy, which was adopted by the board in July 2022. Some high-level information is offered. In January 2023 Nine appointed South Pole to help with its GHG accounting and goal setting. Once this work has been undertaken it will be in a better position to consider whether it is able to set science-based targets, provide reporting to stakeholders and adopt a net zero roadmap.

In the meantime Nine has joined Sustainable Screens Australia as a foundation member to support the establishment of Albert in Australia. Albert is an industry-backed organisation that supports the film and television industry to reduce the environmental impact of its productions.

Nine claims it provides senior sustainability representation across the industry and regularly reviews industry initiatives. The scope and contribution of these activities is unclear. It further points out that its mastheads contribute to sustainability conversations.

There really isn't much here to make an assessment on, so it is surprising to find how well Nine rates on Morningstar sustainability metrics.

ESG risks	ESG measured	Assessment	Result
ESG exposure	ESG risk rating assessment	▮▮▮▮▯	✓
	ESG exposure risk classification	Low	✓
	ESG risk exposure score	24.95	✓
	ESG excess exposure score	0.95	X
	ESG risk score momentum	(0.56)	✓
ESG sub-industry risk	ESG sub-industry rank	33/63	−
	ESG risk compared to sub-industry peers	0.13	X
	ESG risk beta	1.04	X
Management of ESG risk	Management of ESG risks score	35.16	−
	Classification of management ESG risks	Average	−
	ESG risk management score momentum	2.34	✓
Company controversy	Level of company controversy exposure	Moderate	−
	Notable ESG risk	Product governance	

Carbon emissions	Measured risks	Assessment	Result
	Carbon overall risk	Negligible	✓
	Carbon overall risk score	0	✓
	Carbon total emissions, scopes 1, 2 and 3	267 880.87	−
	Carbon level of involvement	0	✓
	Level of fossil fuel involvement	0%	✓
	Carbon intensity, scopes 1, 2 and 3	156.67	−

Concluding remarks

A mixed bag represents this sector. News Corp and SEEK are well advanced on their sustainability journeys and provided detailed information with a clarity of approach including net zero commitments across scopes 1, 2 and 3. This alone was impressive, as many companies are yet to incorporate scope 3 into their net zero commitments. SEEK has plans for 2030 delivery while News Corp is aiming for 2050 or earlier. News Corp's commitments have been validated by a credible third party, which adds to their substance.

EVT and Nine Entertainment disappointed. Nine is not even on the field yet and supplied very limited information to work with. It has a lot of work ahead. EVT is doing marginally better and at least supplied some data, but its lack of decarbonisation commitments is discouraging.

On individual ranking in their industry subsectors News Corp rated highest, coming in 10th out of 59 peers, followed by EVT, then SEEK with Nine coming in last.

Interestingly, all four were assessed as average in management of ESG risks in their business, but SEEK and News Corp had the highest scores and demonstrated better management of ESG risks. Nine scored the lowest.

News Corp's notable ESG issue was business ethics; for SEEK and EVT it was data privacy and security, whereas Nine's is product governance.

On sustainability and activities to reduce their carbon footprint, News Corp and SEEK were standouts in the communication sector.

3. Consumer cyclical

These stocks are associated mainly with discretionary consumer spending and should do well when economic times are robust. Typically, consumer cyclical goods are nice-to-have rather than essential. Companies captured in this sector include household names like Wesfarmers, Amcor, Harvey Norman and JB Hi-Fi. Subsectors include fashion goods, media, cars and automotive parts, hotels, restaurants, and leisure and consumer services. Given that these are goods that consumers can live without, businesses in this sector can suffer when economic times are tough.

Sustainability challenges that affect this sector include supply chain issues such as the responsible sourcing of materials around manufacturing processes, safe working conditions, reasonable wages, child labour and modern slavery. An extreme illustration of the failings of these issues came to light in 2012 when a factory fire in Dhaka, Bangladesh, caused the deaths of more than a hundred, mainly female, workers who were trapped on the upper floors when a fire broke out in a ground-floor warehouse. This tragic event highlighted unsafe working conditions common in garment factories throughout the developing world. Large international brands saw they had a role to play here and agreed to better supply-chain standards. Safety standards were improved and enshrined in legislation that saw some limited advances in worker rights and safety standards.

Another sustainability focus is the environmental impact of fast fashion which encourages the practice of wearing an item of clothing only a few times before consigning it to landfill. In Australia some 200 000 tonnes of clothing/textiles end up in landfill every year. The focus is now on creating products with longer life cycles.

The sustainability of operations around the use of electricity and water and waste management practices are further issues. Textile production, for example, is water intensive and a major source of greenhouse gas emissions, and the chemicals and dyes used are often highly pollutive. Producers are increasingly turning to sustainable fabrics as alternatives to conventional materials such as cotton, which uses large amounts of water and chemicals in both the growing and production phases.

Within this sector we found 18 companies that exhibited low ESG risk, although none received the top rating of negligible risk. Eight of the companies, including Myer, Lovisa and Nick Scali, were missing some data so were removed from the data set. Tabcorp, a company that specialises in gambling and entertainment services, was also omitted for ethical reasons.

JB Hi-Fi Limited

ASX code: JBH

www.jbhifi.com.au

Market capitalisation:	$5230.54 million
Sector:	Consumer cyclical
Morningstar Sustainalytics peer group classification:	Electronics Retail

Environmental risk score		Social risk score		Governance risk score	
3.60	✓	7.55	✓	4.04	✓

View: JB Hi-Fi has made some clear commitments to sustainability and its momentum is positive.

History/background

JB Hi-Fi is a widely recognised electronics retailer operating in Australia and New Zealand. Apart from its own branded stores it also operates The Good Guys chain of white goods and consumer electronics stores.

The company was established in 1974 by John Barbuto (JB), who opened the first store in Keilor East, Victoria, with the aim of delivering a range of specialist hi-fi equipment and recorded music at Australia's lowest prices. He sold the business in 1983.

Over the years many additional stores have been opened. In 2000 JB Hi-Fi was purchased by senior management and private equity with a view to going national. A few years later it was listed on the ASX. JB Hi-Fi is one of Australasia's largest and fastest growing retailers of home entertainment and is known for its competitive pricing and value for money.

Its products include:

- consumer electronics such as smartphones, laptops, televisions, home audio equipment, speakers and headphones

- home appliances such as fridges and washing machines

- entertainment such as video games and gaming consoles

- recorded music and audio including CDs and vinyl records.

JB's competitive advantage is the low prices it achieves through its bulk purchasing power. Cost-conscious consumers see the store as offering value. It also offers great customer service and support both instore and online. It taps into consumer trends to offer products that align with consumer demand, ensuring it remains relevant in a fast-paced sector.

ESG performance

The company focuses on health and safety for employees and customers, and for communities through workplace giving. Its ethical sourcing policy sets minimum standards and expectations across the supply chain in relation to labour conditions, health and safety, and environmental management. It actively pursues climate action and product waste and recycling initiatives.

In its annual sustainability report, JB Hi-Fi outlines these efforts in more detail, including an instore soft plastics recycling initiative and a free instore e-waste recycling service for customers. According to JB Hi-Fi, electronic waste is responsible for 70 per cent of toxic chemicals found in landfills and waterways and, in Australia, is growing up to three times faster than municipal waste.

JB Hi-Fi actively pursues supplier engagement, risk assessment and ESG due diligence. It added 107 suppliers to its engagement activities in FY23. Those assessed as high risk environmentally, socially or ethically are added to a watch list for monitoring.

The company seeks to reduce scopes 1 and 2 emissions to net zero by 2030. JB reports that scopes 1 and 2 emissions have declined by 14.47 per cent compared to its FY20 baseline year. It has achieved this by a combination of behavioural change, energy efficiency upgrades such as phasing in LED lights and the use of renewables. To that end it has been installing solar power generators in some stores: as of FY23, 25 stores, or about 11 per cent of its 218 stores across Australia and New Zealand, have solar power generators. It has approval from landlords to install solar power generators across a further eight stores. It is making ongoing improvements in sustainable packaging.

The company assesses its climate-related material and physical transition risks as per TCFD recommendations, and is working towards developing and refining its scope 3 emission estimates. It undertakes an annual review on the material risks and opportunities from climate change and incorporates this into its strategic planning. To that end it has considered a variety of climate change scenarios and the likely risk or opportunity of each for the business.

The company's sustainability plan provides a framework to support the integration of sustainability into the business. The sustainability team provides biannual updates to the audit and risk management committee, which reports to the board. Sustainability initiatives form part of executive variable reward plans, including net zero objectives, ethical sourcing, waste management, sustainable packaging and workplace giving.

Carbon intensity is significant (albeit estimated) in scope 3, so it will be important to report on scope 3 and reduce these emissions going forward. JB Hi-Fi should incorporate scope 3 into its net zero ambitions, as this is where the bulk of the company's emissions occur.

ESG risks	ESG measured	Assessment	Result
ESG exposure	ESG risk rating assessment		✓
	ESG exposure risk classification	Low	✓
	ESG risk exposure score	25.8	✓
	ESG excess exposure score	(1.20)	✓
	ESG risk score momentum	0.29	X
ESG sub-industry risk	ESG sub-industry rank	7/34	✓
	ESG risk compared to sub-industry peers	(2.66)	✓
	ESG risk beta	0.96	✓
Management of ESG risk	Management of ESG risks score	44.62	–
	Classification of management of ESG risks	Average	–
	ESG risk management score momentum	3.38	✓
Company controversy	Level of company controversy exposure	Low	✓
	Notable ESG issues	Data privacy and security	

Carbon emissions	Measured risks	Assessment	Result
	Carbon overall risk	Low	✓
	Carbon overall risk score	7.10	✓
	Carbon total emissions, scopes 1, 2 and 3	7 405 984.67	X
	Carbon level of involvement	0	✓
	Level of fossil fuel involvement	0%	✓
	Carbon intensity, scopes 1, 2 and 3	1132.65	X

Premier Investments Limited

ASX code: PMV   www.premierinvestments.com.au

Market capitalisation:	$3893.98 million
Sector:	Consumer cyclical
Morningstar Sustainalytics peer group classification:	Retail Apparel

Environmental risk score		Social risk score		Governance risk score	
2.33	✓	9.83	–	6.35	✓

View: Premier acknowledges ESG issues but a dearth of policies, commitment and reporting compared to others suggests they are not given a high priority.

History/description

Premier Investments, headquartered in Australia, has been listed on the ASX since 1987. It owns and operates a portfolio of well-known brands that include Smiggle, Peter Alexander, Just Jeans, Portmans, Dotti and Jay Jays. Its appeal to different demographics is a perceived competitive advantage. The company has a range of traditional bricks-and-mortar stores in six countries as well as a global online presence.

Premier Investments' commitment to ethical and responsible business practices is distilled into four pillars:

- People—health and safety, diversity, equality and inclusion

- Partners—an ethical sourcing program that includes visiting and engaging with factories overseas to mitigate modern slavery risks. The company uses a range of tools to audit and monitor risks, including EiQ and Sentinel.

- Planet—mitigating its environmental impact by reducing energy and resources (for example, ensuring new stores use LED lighting and phasing out plastic shopping bags)

- Product—switching to responsibly sourced materials in apparel, such as recycled polyester.

This commitment is supported by the board and is a strategic focus of the executive team.

ESG performance

Although Premier produces a modern slavery report, this is mandatory for a business this size. It dedicates a number of pages in its annual report to its sustainability philosophy and approach, but it doesn't produce a sustainability report. It does produce a short, eight-page report that outlines its commitment to sustainable and responsible business practices. It covers people, community, environment, and product and ethical sourcing. It outlines some of its practices at a high level. It would be great to see more granular detail. It is not a signatory to the UN Global Compact, its reporting on ESG is far from comprehensive, and it has made no net zero commitment. It doesn't report its carbon emissions either, although its carbon footprint is estimated as low.

ESG risks	ESG measured	Assessment	Result
ESG exposure	ESG risk rating assessment	▮▮▮▮▯	✓
	ESG exposure risk classification	Low	✓
	ESG risk exposure score	26.55	✓
	ESG excess exposure score	(0.45)	✓
	ESG risk score momentum	0.30	X
ESG sub-industry risk	ESG sub-industry rank	53/82	–
	ESG risk compared to sub-industry peers	1.01	–
	ESG risk beta	0.98	✓
Management of ESG risk	Management of ESG risks score	33.52	–
	Classification of management of ESG risks	Average	–
	ESG risk management score momentum	4.77	✓
Company controversy	Level of company controversy exposure	Moderate	✓
	Notable ESG issues	Data privacy and security	

Carbon emissions	Measured risks	Assessment	Result
	Carbon overall risk	Negligible	✓
	Carbon overall risk score	0	✓
	Carbon total emissions, scopes 1, 2 and 3	127 329.65	✓
	Carbon level of involvement	0	✓
	Level of fossil fuel involvement	0%	✓
	Carbon intensity, scopes 1, 2 and 3	120.25	–

Wesfarmers Limited

ASX code: WES www.wesfarmers.com.au

Market capitalisation:	$59 757.56 million
Sector:	Consumer cyclical
Morningstar Sustainalytics peer group classification:	Home Improvement Retail

Environmental risk score		Social risk score		Governance risk score	
4.81	✓	7.16	✓	3.44	✓

View: Wesfarmers incorporates sustainability standards in its day-to-day operations with robust and transparent reporting.

History/description

Wesfarmers is a conglomerate of diversified businesses that spans several industries and a large number of well-known retail brands, including Bunnings, Kmart, Target and Officeworks. Recently it has added a healthcare division through the acquisition of Australian Pharmaceutical Industries, which includes Priceline, Soul Patterson Chemists and Clear Skin clinics.

Other more recent business lines include the new data and digital division OneDigital. This includes Catch marketplace and the OnePass program, which Wesfarmers will be able to leverage across its retail assets to provide customers with a seamless omnichannel experience. It also owns the customer loyalty program Flybuys, a real estate retail property trust with 74 properties mostly leased to Bunnings, a 50 per cent share in a financial services business and a softwood sawmill.

Its industrial interests span the production of chemicals, energy and fertilisers. It also supplies industrial and safety products such as tools, workwear and equipment through its Blackwoods brand. Its energy interests include liquified natural gas operations and a joint venture in lithium production.

ESG performance

Wesfarmers has made a commitment to sustainability across its businesses. It undertakes an annual materiality assessment of each business division; this is important because the diverse nature of the businesses it operates means each will have different materiality priorities. This process enables Wesfarmers to identify the key issues facing stakeholders in its various businesses. Once a material issue has been prioritised and validated, it is assessed externally by a third party before it is presented to the executive team and to the audit and risk committee for discussion. Finally, it is passed to the board for approval.

In FY23 the top 10 Wesfarmers material sustainability issues were:

1. climate resilience

2. ethical sourcing and human rights

3. health, safety and wellbeing

4. data and cybersecurity

5. governance, compliance, conduct and ethics

6. people development, diversity and inclusion

7. circular economy (recycling)

8. advancing reconciliation

9. product quality, safety and standards

10. economic and community contributions.

Wesfarmers' sustainability disclosures align with the Global Reporting Initiative (GRI) Standards, UN Sustainable Development Goals and TCFD recommendations. It is a signatory to the UN Global Compact and provides detailed information on how it incorporates the 10 principles in its businesses.

Wesfarmers recognises climate change as a key material risk and has outlined a pathway to net zero for scopes 1 and 2 emissions. It anticipates meeting scope 1 commitments through implementing new technology solutions, notably for ammonia production, which is responsible for approximately half of all the group's scope 1 emissions. For scope 2, it is improving energy efficiency, for example by phasing in LED lighting and renewable energy sources.

It applies an internal shadow price on carbon so financial decisions reflect all costs, including environmental costs. This, in turn, should support emission-efficient decisions. It has undertaken climate scenario analysis to help identify opportunities and threats. It has also begun engagement work across the value chain in relation to reducing scope 3 emissions and is building an understanding of how the TNFD framework links directly to climate resilience.

Wesfarmers has established policies on climate and modern slavery and reports transparently to a high standard. Executive remuneration is linked to performance on various ESG issues.

ESG risks	ESG measured	Assessment	Result
ESG exposure	ESG risk rating assessment		✓
	ESG exposure risk classification	Low	✓
	ESG risk exposure score	27.35	✓
	ESG excess exposure score	1.35	X
	ESG risk score momentum	2.04	X
ESG sub-industry risk	ESG sub-industry rank	16/45	—
	ESG risk compared to sub-industry peers	(1.11)	✓
	ESG risk beta	1.05	X
Management of ESG risk	Management of ESG risks score	47.84	—
	Classification of management of ESG risks	Average	—
	ESG risk management score momentum	0.55	✓
Company controversy	Level of company controversy exposure	Moderate	✓
	Notable ESG issues	Data privacy and security	

Carbon emissions	Measured risks	Assessment	Result
	Carbon overall risk	Low	✓
	Carbon overall risk score	6.45	✓
	Carbon total emissions, scopes 1, 2 and 3	31 760 930	X
	Carbon level of involvement	2	X
	Level of fossil fuel involvement	5%-9.9%	✓
	Carbon intensity, scopes 1, 2 and 3	1281.46	X

Super Retail Group Limited

ASX code: SUL   www.superretailgroup.com.au

Market capitalisation:	$3136.73 million
Sector:	Consumer cyclical
Morningstar Sustainalytics peer group classification:	Automotive Retail

Environmental risk score		Social risk score		Governance risk score	
0.11	✓	7.28	✓	3.19	✓

View: Super Retail is the highest ranked company in the Morningstar Sustainalytics sub-industry automotive retail, though there is more work to do, particularly on scope 3.

History/description

Super Retail Group operates in the leisure and sporting goods, auto accessories and outdoor retail sectors. Its most recognisable brands include Supercheap Auto, BCF, Macpac and Rebel.

ESG performance

It provides a sustainability report on its website and has various sustainability policies in place including a modern slavery statement, a responsible sourcing policy and a raft of other governance protocols. It reports to both mandatory and voluntary standards, including adherence to the GRI standards and aligning to TCFD recommendations. The Sustainability Accounting Standards Board (SASB) provides a framework of key materiality issues for different sectors; it is also guided by the Sustainable Development Goals (SDGs). Super Retail undertakes a materiality assessment by engaging with a wide range of stakeholders to help identify and monitor key ESG risks. It has also undertaken scenario analysis to evaluate the potential risks and opportunities across three different scenarios for its business.

Its main areas of priority are team, community, responsible sourcing, circular economy and climate. Within these focus areas are 12 goals linked to measurable targets. Two of the goals are development of a decarbonisation road map and to enhance climate-related disclosures. Further, the company aims to achieve net zero emissions across scopes 1 and 2 by 2030 for Australian and New Zealand stores, distribution centres, offices and operations within its direct control. The activities it will undertake to achieve this are energy efficiency measures and investing in renewable energy. For its scope 1 and 2 emissions, 97 per cent come from scope 2, via electricity usage in its retail stores, distribution centres and offices. While scope 1 emissions are low, they have been rising. It has flagged the use of carbon offsets for the scope 1 emissions that it is unable to reduce.

In FY23 it reduced its scopes 1 and 2 emissions by 11.4 per cent on FY22 and against its FY17 baseline by 23.6 per cent. The reduction is due to grid decarbonisation via renewables with an aim to use 100 per cent renewable energy by FY30 and the continuation of its energy efficiency measures, including LED lighting, solar, intelligent controllers and air conditioning improvements. Missing is comprehensive scope 3 information. It has flagged the intent to identify scope 3 emissions and determine how to reduce them. These need to be added to its decarbonisation road map for completeness. It has also established working groups to help manage some of the more challenging issues such as emissions, waste, a circular economy, and diversity and inclusion. What reporting it does is transparent and comprehensive.

On governance, risks including ESG risks are captured and managed within the risk management policy and risk and compliance framework, partially informed by sustainability materiality assessment. FY23's goal focused on improving climate-related disclosures because they pose a material risk to its business. The board is responsible for approving the sustainability framework and goals, monitoring risks and the implementation of the sustainability program, supported by board committees. A new board committee has been established, risk and sustainability, and the former audit and risk committee will become the audit committee. The two committees will be involved in ESG reporting, disclosure and assurance.

It is a signatory to the UN Global Compact and provides scopes 1 and 2 data to the clean energy regulator annually. It is also a member of APCO and Supercheap Auto is a member of the Electric Vehicle Council.

ESG risks	ESG measured	Assessment	Result
ESG exposure	ESG risk rating assessment		✓
	ESG exposure risk classification	Low	✓
	ESG risk exposure score	18.20	—
	ESG excess exposure score	(0.80)	✓
	ESG risk score momentum	0.17	X
ESG sub-industry risk	ESG sub-industry rank	1/49	✓
	ESG risk compared to sub-industry peers	(3.45)	✓
	ESG risk beta	0.96	✓
Management of ESG risk	Management of ESG risks score	43.16	—
	Classification of management of ESG risks	Average	—
	ESG risk management score momentum	(0.97)	X
Company controversy	Level of company controversy exposure	Moderate	✓
	Notable ESG issues	Product governance	

Carbon emissions	Measured risks	Assessment	Result
	Carbon overall risk	Negligible	—
	Carbon overall risk score	0	—
	Carbon total emissions, scopes 1, 2 and 3	62 750.00	✓
	Carbon level of involvement	0	✓
	Level of fossil fuel involvement	0%	✓
	Carbon intensity, scopes 1, 2 and 3	24.78	✓

Amcor PLC

ASX code: AMC www.amcor.com

Market capitalisation:	$20 707.05 million
Sector:	Consumer cyclical
Morningstar Sustainalytics peer group classification:	Metal and Glass Packaging

Environmental risk score		Social risk score		Governance risk score	
13.55	–	0.88	✓	3.18	✓

View: Amcor is an early mover in sustainability and considered a global leader in responsible packaging.

History/description

Amcor is a global leader in developing and producing responsible packaging across a range of industries including food and beverages, personal care, healthcare, home care and industrial applications. It is dual listed on the ASX and the NYSE. The business is split into four divisions: flexibles packaging, rigid packaging, speciality cartons and closures. The bulk of sales in FY23 came from flexible packaging (68 per cent) and rigid packaging (22 per cent).

Sustainability is front and centre of its value proposition and competitive advantage. In 2018 it committed to ensuring that all its products are recyclable, reusable or compostable by 2025. It may be controversial for some investors that the company provides packaging to the tobacco industry via its business unit Amcor Speciality Cartons. This business unit contributed 7 per cent to FY23 sales.

Amcor's paper-making activities date back to the 1860s. Due to business growth and diversification beyond paper, its original name, Australian Paper Manufacturers (APM), was changed to Amcor in 1986. In 2014 Amcor demerged its packaging distribution business into a separate business called Orora, which is also listed on ASX.

ESG performance

As an early adopter, Amcor has integrated ESG across the business. It produces a comprehensive annual sustainability report.

The corporate sustainability team defines the strategy, sets targets and maps the implementation of outcomes. Amcor's board provides guidance and input into sustainability strategy as an important component of risk management. It also has sustainability teams and functional leaders at business group level. These three groups are represented in Amcor's sustainability leadership council, which meets monthly to help drive the company's sustainability strategy forward. As the company's sustainability commitment evolves, the number of positions directly related to sustainability grows across the business, including in R&D, commercial procurement, HR, health and safety and operations. Sustainability performance metrics are built into science, technology and innovation (STI) for certain teams and key executives.

The company has committed to science-based targets for achieving net zero emissions by 2050. Its goal is to reduce GHG emissions by 60 per cent by FY30 against a 2006 baseline. FY23 saw a 40.2 per cent reduction in GHG so it is on track. Its area of focus now is increasing the use of renewable energy. It has also submitted its net zero proposal to SBTi for validation. GHG emissions are tracked quarterly, and results are reviewed by the management team and the board.

Amcor has considered three climate-change scenarios, as developed by NGFS, and the corresponding risks and opportunities of each. The scenario analysis process was undertaken in FY22 aided by external consultants. Across all three scenarios considered it uncovered a mix of transition and physical risks. It has addressed the potential impact of each and provided actions to mitigate.

In FY23 the bulk of Amcor's scope 3 greenhouse gas (GHG) emissions was related to raw material purchases. This equated to 90 per cent of the scope 3 footprint and 75 per cent of total carbon footprint. So scope 3 reduction efforts are focused on supplier collaboration in reducing emissions from raw materials. It is working on obtaining better GHG data from its suppliers, which will allow for clarity in decision making and reporting as well as aid with engagement and, ultimately, GHG reductions. It is also formalising its expectations for suppliers, which goes beyond the provision of verified GHG data to requiring a comprehensive roadmap for delivering ambitious long-term, science-based targets for GHG reductions. For strategic and critical suppliers, Amcor seeks commitment to a supplier code of conduct or evidence that it meets the requirements of its own internal code of conduct. It also has a requirement for EcoVadis sustainability compliance in order to assess performance and identify any area of risk.

It participates with a number of industry bodies to reduce plastic pollution and is also involved in policy advocacy relating to recycling and waste management.

An annual materiality assessment ensures it engages widely with stakeholders to help define and prioritise material issues. It has identified a number of significant issues including climate change, GHG emissions, energy management, biodiversity and deforestation.

The company maps its performance using a variety of sustainable reporting frameworks including GRI, SASB and TCFD. In fact, it has been reporting aligned to GRI standards for 12 years. It assesses progress against CDP modules for climate change, water security and forest annually, which allows it to measure its environmental impact on each. It also uses business sustainability ratings company EcoVadis to assess and monitor the corporate social responsibility of its global operations.

It has identified the most material SDGs for Amcor. Globally, it is a member of many organisations, mostly related to packaging; locally, it is a member of the Australian Packaging Covenant and the Great Barrier Reef Foundation. Interestingly, it is not a signatory to the UN Global Compact.

ESG risks	ESG measured	Assessment	Result
ESG exposure	ESG risk rating assessment		✓
	ESG exposure risk classification	Low	✓
	ESG risk exposure score	34.70	✓
	ESG excess exposure score	2.70	X
	ESG risk score momentum	1.73	X
ESG sub-industry risk	ESG sub-industry rank	25/67	−
	ESG risk compared to sub-industry peers	(0.96)	✓
	ESG risk beta	1.08	X
Management of ESG risk	Management of ESG risks score	53.48	−
	Classification of management of ESG risks	Strong	✓
	ESG risk management score momentum	(0.02)	X
Company controversy	Level of company controversy exposure	Low	✓
	Notable ESG issues	E&S Impact of Products and Services	

Carbon emissions	Measured risks	Assessment	Result
	Carbon overall risk	Medium	−
	Carbon overall risk score	12.56	−
	Carbon total emissions, scopes 1, 2 and 3	11 787 788	X
	Carbon level of involvement	0	✓
	Level of fossil fuel involvement	0%	✓
	Carbon intensity, scopes 1, 2 and 3	916.55	X

Harvey Norman Holdings Limited

ASX code: HVN   www.harveynormanholdings.com.au

Market capitalisation:	$4896.81 million
Sector:	Consumer cyclical
Morningstar Sustainalytics peer group classification:	Electronics Retail

Environmental risk score		Social risk score		Governance risk score	
4.18	✓	8.31	✓	5.86	✓

View: Late to the sustainability party and not as evolved as other featured companies, Harvey Norman is arguably doing no more than the bare minimum.

History/description

Harvey Norman is an Australian-based company with a focus on the retail of, primarily, household and electrical goods. Locally, it operates under a franchise system. Other brands owned by the company include Domayne and Joyce Mayne. It offers an omnichannel approach for customers via retail bricks-and-mortar, online, mobile and social media.

Its overseas operation uses a different business model: company-operated stores. Harvey Norman has retail stores in New Zealand and Ireland and a controlling interest in Pertama Holdings, which trades as Harvey Norman in Singapore and Malaysia. It also operates a handful of stores in Slovenia and Croatia.

In addition, Harvey Norman has a property portfolio that consists largely of some of the complexes in which the company operates in Australia, New Zealand and Slovenia.

ESG performance

Sustainability has evidently not been a key priority, and the company is likely to be playing catchup when climate reporting becomes mandatory.

Harvey Norman does not produce a standalone sustainability report and has no dedicated section on its website, although its annual report devotes a number of pages to the company's sustainability efforts. It recognises that its approach to sustainability is maturing and acknowledges it has more work to do.

The company anticipates the release of its inaugural climate statement in FY24, ahead of expected changes in government reporting requirements in FY25. To date its climate reporting has been disappointing. Publicly, it has provided no climate change scenario risk modelling, no net zero pledges and no commitment to decarbonisation pathways. Further, it has yet to release its scope 1, 2 or 3 emissions and is not reporting in line with TCFD or GRI recommendations.

In 2022 it outlined a sustainability framework, which consists of three pillars:

- People—diversity and inclusion, employee health and safety, community engagement and sponsorship, and data security and privacy

- Places—minimising environmental impact through waste management and the circular economy, climate change impact and resilience, energy use and emissions

- Products—safe and sustainable packaging (targeting the removal of plastics and polystyrene, but with no time frame or metrics provided) and human rights (but with no details concerning measuring and monitoring). It is not clear what action it would take if a supplier failed to meet a required standard.

It does produce a modern slavery report but, given the company's size, this is a legal requirement.

Tellingly, it produces higher ESG risk than the average in the sector, although its carbon risk is assessed as low and it has no direct fossil fuel involvement.

It is not a signatory to the UN Global Compact. Its limited engagement in sustainability and lack of transparency, reporting and commitments are disappointing.

ESG risks	ESG measured	Assessment	Result
ESG exposure	ESG risk rating assessment		✓
	ESG exposure risk classification	Low	✓
	ESG risk exposure score	25.90	✓
	ESG excess exposure score	(1.10)	✓
	ESG risk score momentum	0.73	X
ESG sub-industry risk	ESG sub-industry rank	19/34	—
	ESG risk compared to sub-industry peers	0.52	X
	ESG risk beta	96	✓
Management of ESG risk	Management of ESG risks score	31.43	—
	Classification of management of ESG risks	Average	—
	ESG risk management score momentum	3.83	✓
Company controversy	Level of company controversy exposure	Moderate	✓
	Notable ESG issues	Human capital	

Carbon emissions	Measured risks	Assessment	Result
	Carbon overall risk	Low	✓
	Carbon overall risk score	9.75	✓
	Carbon total emissions, scopes 1, 2 and 3	419 199.12	✓
	Carbon level of involvement	0	✓
	Level of fossil fuel involvement	0%	✓
	Carbon intensity, scopes 1, 2 and 3	137.82	✓

Eagers Automotive Limited

ASX code: APE   www.eagersautomotive.com.au

Market capitalisation:	$3439.90 million
Sector:	Consumer cyclical
Morningstar Sustainalytics peer group classification:	Automotive Retail

Environmental risk score		Social risk score		Governance risk score	
0.13	✓	9.61	–	4.41	✓

View: While it has not progressed as far as others, Eagers has set a decarbonisation plan in motion and is headed in the right direction.

History/description

Eagers Automotive is primarily involved in the ownership and operation of motor vehicle dealerships. It is the largest automotive retail group in Australia and New Zealand, with an estimated 11 per cent share of new vehicle sales. The company is a full-service offering across the sale of new and used vehicles, service, parts and the facilitation of consumer finance. The company has the following key business divisions:

- New vehicles — sells new vehicles

- Used vehicles — sells used vehicles

- Parts and accessories — distributes and sells parts, accessories and car care products

- Service — repairs and services vehicles

- Finance and insurance — facilitates finance and leasing of motor vehicles

- Property — owns property and investments.

The company was founded in 1913 and listed on ASX in 1957.

ESG performance

It does not produce a separate sustainability report, or even a sustainability section on the company's website, but it does address sustainability issues in its annual report.

It has adopted a three-pillar sustainability approach:

- People — attract and retain the best people

- Planet — climate change and the environment
- Performance — sustainable growth through robust risk management processes.

The main source of its scope 1 emissions are transport fuel, diesel, petrol and LPG. Scope 2 are from purchased electricity which has been decreasing due to energy efficiency gains, increased use of renewable energy and site consolidations. The majority of its operation GHG emissions come from heating, ventilation and air conditioning. Part of the solution has been installation of solar panels across multiple sites to help reduce GHG emissions. In addition it has been installing energy-efficient lighting and air conditioning, and using sensors and timing devices to reduce overall energy consumption. It has also set targets to increase the sale of electric vehicles. It is the preferred retail partner for new EV entrants into the market and it is diversifying by adding in an electric truck segment. It further supports electric vehicle transition through its finance division via novated leasing and fleet management.

The company aims to achieve carbon neutrality by 2025 across its Australian operation and by 2035 for global manufacturing sites, and net zero emissions across the value chain, including business and manufacturing operations, by 2050. It has a credible pathway to reducing carbon emissions by 50 per cent by 2030, off a 2013 baseline. Further climate-related risks are considered across strategic, operational, people, legal and social categories. The board considers climate and sustainability risks as relevant when setting performance objectives and undertaking capital expenditure, as well as when reviewing and guiding strategy.

It plans to source all electricity at production facilities from renewables by 2040.

Pleasingly, it utilises SASB reporting standards, has considered the TCFD and aligns its business to five SDGs. Although it lags behind some of its peers, and its management of ESG risks is assessed as merely average, it is on a positive trajectory. It would be great to see a formal materiality assessment and then an annual review to ensure the most significant ESG issues are identified and monitored.

Interestingly, from a carbon perspective it is assessed as having negligible risks, although scope 3, where it generates most of its emissions, is the big challenge and is yet to be addressed. Scope 3 relates primarily to the carbon emitted by customers' usage of cars once sold. With the global uptake of electric vehicles, that should decline naturally. The company anticipates that 50 per cent of new vehicles sold will be electric by 2030, rising to 100 per cent by 2040.

Eagers is not a signatory to the UN Global Compact.

ESG risks	ESG measured	Assessment	Result
ESG Exposure	ESG risk rating assessment	▣▣▣▣☐	✓
	ESG exposure risk classification	Low	✓
	ESG risk exposure score	20.10	✓
	ESG excess exposure score	1.10	X
	ESG risk score momentum	(0.26)	✓
ESG sub-industry risk	ESG sub-industry rank	28/49	–
	ESG risk compared to sub-industry peers	0.12	X
	ESG risk beta	1.06	X
Management of ESG risk	Management of ESG risks score	30.62	–
	Classification of management of ESG risks	Average	–
	ESG risk management score momentum	1.70	✓
Company controversy	Level of company controversy exposure	Moderate	✓
	Notable ESG issues	Product governance	

Carbon emissions	Measured risks	Assessment	Result
	Carbon overall risk	Negligible	✓
	Carbon overall risk score	0	✓
	Carbon total emissions, scopes 1, 2 and 3	366 733.35	✓
	Carbon level of involvement	0	✓
	Level of fossil fuel involvement	0%	✓
	Carbon intensity, scopes 1, 2 and 3	57.72	✓

Bapcor Limited

ASX code: BAP

www.bapcor.com.au

Market capitalisation:	$1826.04 million
Sector:	Consumer cyclical
Morningstar Sustainalytics peer group classification:	Distribution

Environmental risk score		Social risk score		Governance risk score	
4.38	✓	4.37	✓	3.70	✓

View: While Bapcor's journey to sustainability began relatively recently, it has already made great progress.

History/description

Bapcor is a specialist, vertically integrated operator in the automotive aftermarket industry, supplying parts, accessories, equipment and services. Approximately 80 per cent of its business is trade related. It operates in Australia, New Zealand and Thailand, and one of its key strategic priorities is to continue its expansion into Asia.

It classifies its business into four segments:

- Trade—automotive and truck replacement parts

- Specialist wholesale—brakes, clutches, suspension, turbochargers and shock absorbers

- Retail—integrated supply chain, distributing to a variety of retail stores that are a mix of company-owned, franchise and satellite stores. Autobarn, Autopro and Sprint are among the brands in this segment

- Service—auto service centres (Midas and ABS in Australia, and Battery Town and The Shock Shop in New Zealand).

The company was originally founded in 1971 as Burson Group. It was sold to a private equity manager in 2011 and listed on the ASX in 2014. It became Bapcor Group in 2015 and has been acquiring businesses on a fairly regular basis since 2015.

ESG performance

It dedicates a section of its website to community and sustainability and aims to deliver shareholder wealth and optimise business operations in a socially and environmentally positive way through integrating ESG into its business practices.

Bapcor articulates its ESG strategic framework, starting with values and code of conduct.

The company's ESG strategy has four pillars:

- human rights / modern slavery, ethical supply chain and procurement
- environmental sustainability, net zero emissions, waste management and packaging / circular economy
- good governance, health and safety, diversity and inclusion, culture and development, and privacy
- positive community impact, community engagement and fair tax contributions.

Although it has yet to produce a standalone sustainability report, it dedicates quite a few pages in its annual report to sustainability efforts and ambitions. It also lists sustainability as one of the key business risks it needs to manage.

The annual report outlines the company's work in assessing its carbon footprint in FY22. It uses 2023 as the baseline when committing to reduce scopes 1 and 2 emissions by 40 per cent by 2030 and 50 per cent by 2033. These advances will be driven by renewable energy procurement across the property portfolio and the decarbonisation of its fleet. It would be good to see this ambition incorporate scope 3 to fully capture all GHG emissions. That said, the bulk of emissions are estimated as almost evenly split between scopes 1 and 2, with the latter slightly higher. It has provided a reasonably detailed and credible roadmap to decarbonisation, including scenario analysis.

Bapcor's reporting recognises GRI standards and UN SDGs. It plans to undertake a formal materiality assessment in the future. The annual report provides some details of the company's approach to date and of future pathways. It is a member of the UN Global Compact.

ESG, and specifically climate risk, are overseen by the nomination, remuneration and environmental, social and governance committee. The board is provided with regular updates on ESG, and climate-related risks are integrated into enterprise risk management processes.

ESG risks	ESG measured	Assessment	Result
ESG exposure	ESG risk rating assessment	▮▮▮▮▯	✓
	ESG exposure risk classification	Low	✓
	ESG risk exposure score	19.75	✓
	ESG excess exposure score	(0.25)	✓
	ESG risk score momentum	(0.17)	✓
ESG sub-industry risk	ESG sub-industry rank	13/33	✓
	ESG risk compared to sub-industry peers	(0.93)	✓
	ESG risk beta	0.99	✓
Management of ESG risk	Management of ESG risks score	37.95	–
	Classification of management of ESG risks	Average	–
	ESG risk management score momentum	0.88	✓
Company controversy	Level of company controversy exposure	Low	✓
	Notable ESG issues	Carbon – own operations	

Carbon emissions	Measured risks	Assessment	Result
	Carbon overall risk	Medium	✓
	Carbon overall risk score	13.24	✓
	Carbon total emissions, scopes 1, 2 and 3	14 391	✓
	Carbon level of involvement	0	✓
	Level of fossil fuel involvement	0%	✓
	Carbon intensity, scopes 1, 2 and 3	11.14	✓

Concluding remarks

Overall, despite diversity among subsectors, Consumer Cyclical rated well on ESG metrics. Interestingly, all the companies in this sector apart from Amcor rated average for management of ESG risks. Bapcor had the lowest risk for controversies — assessed as having no risk at all — while JB Hi-Fi and Amcor were assessed as having low carbon exposure, with the rest of the cohort a notch higher, at moderate.

Four companies — Eagers, Premier Investments and Super Retail — were assessed as having no carbon risk exposure. Wesfarmers, Harvey Norman and JB Hi-Fi had low risk and Bapcor and Amcor medium risk.

On carbon emissions, looking at all three scopes, Wesfarmers had the highest, followed by Amcor and JB Hi-Fi. For all three companies, the bulk of their emissions come from scope 3. Only Wesfarmers, Amcor and Super Retail reported on their scope 3 emissions; for the rest of their cohort scope 3 emissions were assessed via estimations. Bapcor had the lowest emissions across all three scopes followed by Super Retail Group.

Wesfarmers was the only company in this sector with exposure to fossil fuels within its business interests. This impacted its environmental score, which ranked 19th highest across all the companies in the book, yet it was one of the better performing companies from a governance perspective, coming in at fifth place.

On overall ESG risk, Super Retail Group scored best followed by JB Hi-Fi then Wesfarmers. Bapcor also did better than average. Eagers had slightly elevated ESG risks compared to its peers.

Finally, Super Retail had the lowest overall ESG risk, ranking first out of 49 peers in the automotive retail subsector. JB Hi-Fi was next best, ranking seventh out of 34 peers in the electronic retail subsector globally.

4. Consumer defensive

This sector comprises companies that produce or distribute essential goods and services that consumers need on an ongoing basis. It includes a wide range of products including tangible items such as packaged foods and beverages, and non-food agricultural products, as well as intangible items such as consumer services. As these products and services are deemed necessities, these companies can expect a regular, stable demand even during times of economic stress.

Notable ESG issues in the sector are broad, covering human capital, human rights, supply chain, product governance, resource use, environmental and social impact of products and services, use and biodiversity (supply chain and 'carbon own operations'). Some examples of sustainability issues in this sector are:

- packaging waste. Engaged consumers notice a reduction in plastic packaging as companies look to embrace more sustainable packaging, such as recycled paper or compostable materials, or promotion of responsible disposal, such as glass bottle recycling.

- minimisation of food waste to conserve resources such as water and energy and transportation of food, reducing GHGs. Decreasing waste can also reduce food costs and avoid food being discarded in landfill.

- sourcing of sustainable raw materials and avoidance of materials with a harmful ecological impact, such as the use of palm oil and its impact on orangutan habitat

- sustainable agriculture that reduces negative impacts on biodiversity, water or soil pollution and is less carbon intensive. One interesting innovation in cattle farming is the introduction of a seaweed feed supplement to reduce methane emissions by up to 90 per cent.

For this sector I have chosen the companies with the lowest ESG risks. There are five; however, G8 Education was excluded due to lack of a comprehensive data set. Woolworths was excluded as it rates a notch higher than those selected as a medium risk. Ironically, Endeavour Group, which was spun out of Woolworths and has a range of negative ethical components, such as alcoholic drinks, hotels and poker machines, rated better overall on ESG risks than Woolworths.

Coles Group Limited

ASX code: COL

colesgroup.com.au

Market capitalisation:	$20 517.54 million
Sector:	Consumer defensive
Morningstar Sustainalytics peer group classification:	Food Retail

Environmental risk score		Social risk score		Governance risk score	
5.92	✓	8.67	–	3.06	✓

View: Coles Group's net zero ambitions don't yet take into account scope 3, which makes up the bulk of its emissions, but it is engaging with suppliers to start to address this significant gap.

History/background

Coles Group is one of the largest supermarket chains operating in Australia. It has a portfolio of leading retail brands including Coles Supermarkets, Coles Express, Liquorland and Vintage Cellars. Coles was founded by George James Coles who opened the first Coles variety store in Victoria in 1914. In the 1960s Coles opened Australia's first supermarket in Victoria with the vision of providing for all household needs in the one place. In 1983 the Flybuys loyalty program was launched. In 1985 the company acquired Myer Emporium, becoming Coles Myer. In 2004 Coles launched Coles Express service stations, and in 2006 it sold its holding in Myer. In 2007 Coles was acquired by Wesfarmers, and in 2018 Coles demerged from Wesfarmers, listing on the ASX as a standalone entity in 2018.

ESG performance

Its board oversees and approves the company's strategic direction, including its sustainability and governance polices and climate change impacts. The board is supported by the audit and risk committee, which measures the group's management of ESG risks and disclosures of nonfinancial and financial material risks.

The chief operations and sustainability officer reports regularly to the managing director and CEO, who in turn report to the board and the audit and risk committee on sustainability risks and commitments. Quarterly sustainability reporting is provided to the board.

FY23 saw a refresh of the sustainability steering committee charter and membership and a change to a bimonthly cadence for FY24. The steering committee will have key management oversight of Coles' sustainability strategy and performance going forward.

Coles undertakes an annual materiality assessment, informed by the GRI Standards and the UN Global Compact principles, and conforms to ISO 31000:2018 risk management guidelines. The latter process has identified 10 key interconnected ESG issues across stakeholders. Coles has mapped its sustainability strategy to nine of the 17 UN SDGs.

Various stakeholders identified Coles' number one material issue in FY23 to be climate change, including security of supply and business continuity. It has identified climate change as a key risk since FY19. Coles supports the Paris Agreement and is committed to decarbonisation and transition to net zero. To deliver on this commitment it needs to reduce emissions by energy management and the use of renewables.

Coles has built a pathway to decarbonisation and is developing a climate action roadmap that will incorporate short-, medium- and long-term actions to manage climate-related risks. It already has in place a number of GHG reduction commitments. Using FY20 as its baseline, it aims to reduce scopes 1 and 2 emissions by more than 75 per cent by the end of FY30. This target has been validated by a science-based target initiative and classified as aligned to limiting to 1.5 degrees Celsius. The FY20 baseline was recalculated to take into account the sale of the Coles Express business.

FY23 saw a 27.7 per cent reduction in emissions from FY22 and a 33.5 per cent reduction from baseline. It plans to deliver net zero scopes 1 and 2 emissions by 2050. However, by far the biggest source of GHG emissions for the group is scope 3, estimated to account for more than 90 per cent of Coles' emissions. Of that, 82 per cent are estimated to come from goods and services purchased. To tackle this, Coles has set supplier engagement targets based on how much Coles spends with suppliers: 75 per cent of the supplier spend will meet science-based targets by FY27.

Coles also expects to use 100 per cent renewable electricity by 2025 via solar and large-scale generation certifications. It has arrangements in place with renewable energy suppliers in Queensland, Victoria and New South Wales and its renewable energy purchases accounted for 45 per cent of total grid electricity consumption in FY23. Eighty-eight Coles stores have solar panels; another 20 stores will join them in FY24. Solar panels are also installed at a number of its distribution centres.

The second-biggest materiality issue is waste, and Coles' commitment is to divert 85 per cent of the group's solid waste from landfill by FY25. It is certainly on track, as 84 per cent of waste was diverted from landfill in FY23.

The third-biggest issue is plastics and packaging. Starting with its own brands, it has committed to having 100 per cent of its packaging reusable, recyclable or compostable by 2025. FY22 saw them at 94.6 per cent, but FY23 saw a decline of 10.8 per cent on the previous year, to 83.8 per cent, due to the suspension of the REDcycle soft plastics recycling program. Industry now deems all soft plastics as non-recyclable.

Coles has been a signatory to the UN Global Compact since 2019, and a member of the Australian Climate Leaders Coalition, the Carbon Market Institute, the Energy Users Association of Australia and the Electric Vehicle Council, among others.

Coles provides detailed, comprehensive reporting which includes a sustainability data pack. It has set ambitious GHG emissions-reduction targets founded on science-based targets and is on course to tackle its biggest GHG emissions, scope 3. Its commitments to ESG issues are broad and go well beyond the environment.

ESG risks	ESG measured	Assessment	Result
ESG exposure	ESG risk rating assessment	▓▓▓▓	✓
	ESG exposure risk classification	Low	✓
	ESG risk exposure score	41.00	X
	ESG excess exposure score	3.00	X
	ESG risk score momentum	(0.36)	✓
ESG sub-industry risk	ESG sub-industry rank	9/120	✓
	ESG risk compared to sub-industry peers	(7.53)	✓
	ESG risk beta	1.08	X
Management of ESG risk	Management of ESG risks score	60.70	—
	Classification of management of ESG risks	Strong	✓
	ESG risk management score momentum	0.94	✓
Company controversy	Level of company controversy exposure	Moderate	—
	Notable ESG issues	Human rights – supply chain	

Carbon emissions	Measured risks	Assessment	Result
	Carbon overall risk	Low	✓
	Carbon overall risk score	8.14	✓
	Carbon total emissions, scopes 1, 2 and 3	1 845 972	X
	Carbon level of involvement	0	✓
	Level of fossil fuel involvement	0%	✓
	Carbon intensity, scopes 1, 2 and 3	64.66	—

Endeavour Group Limited

ASX code: EDV   www.endeavourgroup.com.au

Market capitalisation:	$8829.53 million
Sector:	Consumer defensive
Morningstar Sustainalytics peer group classification:	Specialty Retail

Environmental risk score		Social risk score		Governance risk score	
4.46	✓	7.81	✓	5.46	✓

View: Endeavour has made an impressive start on the path to sustainability, but it urgently needs to reduce its scope 3 emissions, which constitute the lion's share of its total emissions.

History/background

Endeavour was previously part of the Woolworths Group but became a standalone entity in 2021 through a demerger. It operates within the retail and hotel segments. Endeavour Group assets include retail liquor sales, which includes well-known retail chain stores BWS and Dan Murphy's. It also has one of the largest portfolios of licensed hotels in the country, approximately 350 premises, and many of these hotels have gaming operations (poker machines). The company's purpose is expressed as 'creating a more sociable future, together'. It has achieved success through a combination of organic growth and strategic acquisitions.

ESG performance

Its approach to sustainability has three pillars:

- Planet—commitment to addressing climate change and reducing carbon footprint

- People—safe and inclusive workplaces

- Responsibility and community—responsible service of alcohol and gambling.

In its FY23 sustainability report it acknowledges that its sustainability program is in its early days. It supports the UN Global Compact, has linked its three pillars to relevant SDGs, and reports in line with GRI and TCFD. It aims to continue to improve its reporting to these standards and those issued by ISSB over time.

In FY23 it undertook a materiality assessment to identify and prioritise material ESG opportunities and issues that included broad stakeholder consultation. This comprehensive assessment covered 30 ESG topics based on the GRI Standards, the WEF-IBC stakeholder capitalism metrics framework, ASX corporate governance principles, SASB standards, and Australian regulatory requirements for liquor and gaming industries. The material topics identified were mapped to a materiality matrix and grouped under responsibility/governance, people and planet, essentially its three sustainability pillars. Stakeholders advised Endeavour that responsibility and compliance are their biggest issues.

Its ambition is to reduce emissions by adopting renewable energy, tracking supplier carbon emissions and encouraging suppliers to disclose scope 3 emissions. Another focus will be packaging: it will seek to collaborate with suppliers to introduce more sustainable packaging, including recycling and waste solutions. It has created sustainable packaging guidelines around the principles of reusable, recyclable and compostable to help stakeholders understand the company's commitment to improved packaging. Its climate change strategy incorporates validation of emissions, mapping operations against environmental obligations to understand the risks, and improving governance and compliance.

FY23 saw the group undertake a climate risk assessment to uncover physical and transition risks and opportunities. Climate commitments include net zero emissions for scopes 1 and 2 by 2050 and using 100 per cent renewable power for its own operations by 2030. Part of the work undertaken showed that 89 per cent of scopes 1 and 2 emissions come from electricity. It has operational control over 2000 facilities and has 144 sites with solar installations. It has also completed an LED light rollout and installed occupancy sensors that turn off lights when areas are unoccupied. More than half of Dan Murphy's stores have electronic shelf labelling, which reduces paper ticketing and waste. It has installed fast EV charging stations at a couple of regional Dan Murphy's stores, which are using 100 per cent renewable energy to help with EV uptake and reduce range anxiety! Endeavour is also undertaking work to better understand its material upstream and downstream scope 3 emissions categories and is focusing in particular on waste emissions.

The board provides direct oversight of its sustainability strategy. The people, culture and performance committee and the audit, risk management and compliance committee oversee progress and management of sustainability risks. The CEO and executive committee have responsibility for managing strategy and the various business units are responsible for implementing sustainability initiatives with the support of sustainability teams and working groups. Progress reports are delivered to the board quarterly. Further sustainability goals are incorporated into short-term and long-term incentives for eligible staff.

Endeavour is still in the early stages of its journey but has made reasonable progress. It has mapped out the areas it wants to focus on and has built out, and acted on, detailed plans. Ultimately, to make a positive impact it will have to account for and reduce scope 3 emissions, as the data indicates that these make up about 90 per cent of carbon emissions for the group.

ESG risks	ESG measured	Assessment	Result
ESG exposure	ESG risk rating assessment		✓
	ESG exposure risk classification	Low	✓
	ESG risk exposure score	26.35	✓
	ESG excess exposure score	0.35	X
	ESG risk score momentum	0.73	X
ESG sub-industry risk	ESG sub-industry rank	33/90	–
	ESG risk compared to sub-industry peers	(0.99)	✓
	ESG risk beta	1.01	X
Management of ESG risk	Management of ESG risks score	34.46	–
	Classification of management of ESG risks	Average	–
	ESG risk management score momentum	(1.75)	X
Company controversy	Level of company controversy exposure	Moderate	–
	Notable ESG issues	Human capital	

Carbon emissions	Measured risks	Assessment	Result
	Carbon overall risk	Medium	–
	Carbon overall risk score	11.37	–
	Carbon total emissions, scopes 1, 2 and 3	3 520 384.20	X
	Carbon level of involvement	0	✓
	Level of fossil fuel involvement	0%	✓
	Carbon intensity, scopes 1, 2 and 3	414.01	–

Metcash Trading Limited

ASX code: MTS

www.metcash.com

Market capitalisation:	$3536.96 million
Sector:	Consumer defensive
Morningstar Sustainalytics peer group classification:	Food Distribution

Environmental risk score		Social risk score		Governance risk score	
3.69	✓	7.89	✓	3.86	✓

View: Employing science-based targets, global frameworks and detailed reporting, Metcash has made impressive progress in improving its sustainability capabilities across its business.

History/background

Metcash is a wholesale distribution and marketing company that services and supplies independent retailers in Australia and New Zealand who operate across its three spheres:

- Food. Well-known brands of food business include IGA and Foodland.

- Hardware. Independent Hardware Group is Australia's largest home improvement wholesaler and includes well-known brands Mitre 10 and Home Hardware. Total Tools Holdings is the franchisor to professional tool retailers in Australia.

- Liquor. Its Independent Brands Australia network supplies well-known brands such as Cellarbrations, The Bottle-O and IGA Liquor. The company is the second-largest in the market, supplying approximately 90 per cent of independent liquor stores.

ESG performance

On sustainability Metcash applies three pillars: planet, people and community. It got off to a slow start but has been steadily elevating its commitments to sustainability. It released its inaugural standalone sustainability report in FY22. Sustainability is a part of its corporate vision and it has been improving its reporting and increasing its emissions-reduction ambitions.

On governance, overall responsibility rests with the board, which sets the company's strategy. Further support comes from the audit risk and compliance committee, the group leadership team and the ESG Council, which is chaired by the CEO and includes members of the group leadership team. The ESG Council meets quarterly. In addition, it has formed an energy steering committee to consider how the business can make energy efficiency gains. This committee is made up of leaders from risk and compliance, operations, facilities and sustainability, along with energy specialists from outside the organisation. Climate risk is incorporated in the corporate risk register.

Metcash plans to establish a board sustainability and risk committee. It is upping the ante on reporting, starting with alignment with the GRI Standards from FY23, adding in TCFD alignment in FY24 and adopting the ISSB standards when they are finalised. They are considering whether to adopt TFND reporting.

On climate change specifically, Metcash has assessed several climate warming scenarios aligned to the IPCC's Sixth Assessment Report of 2021 to help identify risks and opportunities to align with its strategic decision making. It has set reduction in emissions targets in line with the science-based targets methodology with a pathway to net zero. It has set its baseline emissions at FY20 and seeks to achieve a 10 per cent reduction of GHG emissions against that baseline by FY25. It aims for a 42 per cent reduction in scopes 1 and 2 by FY30 and net zero scopes 1 and 2 emissions by FY40 through energy efficiency projects and expansion of solar power at its distribution centres. Metcash also plans to achieve 100 per cent use of renewable energy by 2025.

It has been undertaking comprehensive work on scope 3 estimates using processes endorsed by the Climate Active Carbon Neutral Standard for Organisations. It has segmented its emissions into organisational, upstream and downstream, and the next stage is to determine the best ways to reduce these emissions. It estimates that 12.2 per cent of scope 3 emissions are organisational, with the remaining 87.8 per cent from upstream and downstream emissions.

Other focuses for Metcash are waste, packaging and recycling. It has a target of 80 per cent waste-to-landfill diversion by 2028. It is a member of APCO and is aiming for 100 per cent reusable, recyclable or compostable packaging.

Metcash has undertaken a materiality assessment to determine the greatest risk and opportunities for its business relating to GRI-aligned key topics, which were mapped to SDGs.

It has established a sustainable finance facility of $525 million, which has three key performance indicators:

- reducing emissions and increasing renewable energy use

- reducing waste to landfill and increasing upcycling and recycling

- employee wellbeing and safety.

Part of the requirement of this facility is validation via an external audit of national greenhouse energy reporting figures to track progress towards achieving its 2030 goal.

In sum, Metcash has provided comprehensive reporting and is making great progress towards fulfilling its sustainability ambitions.

ESG risks	ESG measured	Assessment	Result
ESG exposure	ESG risk rating assessment		✓
	ESG exposure risk classification	Low	✓
	ESG risk exposure score	26.60	✓
	ESG excess exposure score	(0.40)	✓
	ESG risk score momentum	(0.81)	✓
ESG sub-industry risk	ESG sub-industry rank	8/43	✓
	ESG risk compared to sub-industry peers	(2.59)	✓
	ESG risk beta	0.98	✓
Management of ESG risk	Management of ESG risks score	42.02	—
	Classification of management of ESG risks	Average	—
	ESG risk management score momentum	2.36	✓
Company controversy	Level of company controversy exposure	Low	✓
	Notable ESG issues	Human capital	

Carbon emissions	Measured risks	Assessment	Result
	Carbon overall risk	Low	✓
	Carbon overall risk score	8.73	✓
	Carbon total emissions, scopes 1, 2 and 3	186 754.79	—
	Carbon level of involvement	0	✓
	Level of fossil fuel involvement	0%	✓
	Carbon intensity, scopes 1, 2 and 3	17.79	✓

IDP Education Limited

ASX code: IEL   www.idp.com

Market capitalisation:	$6307.10 million
Sector:	Consumer defensive
Morningstar Sustainalytics peer group classification:	Consumer Services

Environmental risk score		Social risk score		Governance risk score	
0.11	✓	9.26	–	5.17	✓

View: IDP Education's ESG commitment is in its early stages but recent sustainability strategies, including the collection of data on scopes 1, 2 and 3, will help inform a climate action plan.

History/background

IDP Education is a global student placement service operating in more than 50 countries around the world. The company was founded in 1969 as a government agency, the Australian Asian Universities Cooperation Scheme (AAUCS), which was set up to deliver development assistance to universities operating in South-East Asia. Since those humble beginnings it has developed into a leading student recruitment company. In 1981 it changed its name to the International Development Program and in 1996 the company became wholly owned by 38 Australian universities. In 2006 the ASX-listed company SEEK took a 50 per cent stake in the company. It was listed on the ASX in 2015.

The business's key products and services are:

- Student Placement Services: IDP Education provides free education counselling and migration consultation to students who have an interest in studying abroad. It offers virtual counselling sessions and face-to-face counselling at its offices.

- IELTS: IDP Education is a co-owner of the International English Language Testing System (IELTS), along with the British Council and Cambridge Assessment. IELTS is the world's most popular English language proficiency test for study, work and migration.

- Hotcourses: In 2017 IDP Education acquired Hotcourses Group, which provides course information and marketing services to students, including a course search engine, course guides, student reviews and marketing services to education institutions to help them attract prospective students.

ESG performance

IDP does not have an evolved sustainability strategy. While it claims to have been engaged in numerous sustainability activities for years, only in FY23 has it actually sought to better define its sustainability strategy and set up a sustainability framework to allow for better integration. To galvanise its foundational work, it utilised a third party to undertake an ESG materiality assessment to pinpoint key opportunities and issues that would inform its future strategic direction. The process was guided by the GRI Standards, the ISSB guidelines and the UN's SDGs to help identify financial and societal impacts through double materiality measurement. The process identified 17 material topics that were prioritised and mapped to a materiality matrix. Those deemed most important included cybersecurity, cultural satisfaction and engagement, and business credibility and ethics.

IDP's sustainability strategy has three pillars:

- opportunity for all, including customers and clients, and inclusive culture and education to address social challenges

- trusted partnerships, responsible business, and respect for partners and suppliers

- environmental action, emissions reduction and resource management.

On climate change, IDP acknowledges that the bulk of its emissions come from scope 3 activities. It measures scopes 1, 2 and 3 emissions through a carbon inventory that aligns with the ISO 14064 greenhouse gas protocol and Australia's Climate Active Standard. It estimates that 86 per cent of the company's emissions come from scope 3. FY23 saw it develop a climate action plan for a pathway to net zero. Part of that plan involves building an emissions-reduction plan. Reduction opportunities will be identified by environment committees to be established across the region.

It plans to undertake a climate risk assessment in FY24, the findings of which will be used for long-term strategic planning. It is a signatory to the Climate Action Network for International Educators Accord, and it expects to collaborate with others in the sector.

Despite some good foundational work it has, as yet, made no firm sustainability commitments—no pathway to net zero, no decarbonisation goals based on science-backed targets, and no assessment of the risks and opportunities relating to a range of differing climate scenarios. It is not a signatory to the UN Global Compact. All this means IDP is well behind on its sustainability journey compared to other organisations operating in the consumer defensive sector.

ESG risks	ESG measured	Assessment	Result
ESG exposure	ESG risk rating assessment	▮▮▮▮☐	✓
	ESG exposure risk classification	Low	✓
	ESG risk exposure score	21.90	✓
	ESG excess exposure score	(1.10)	✓
	ESG risk score momentum	(0.52)	✓
ESG sub-industry risk	ESG sub-industry rank	49/150	✓
	ESG risk compared to sub-industry peers	(1.35)	✓
	ESG risk beta	0.95	✓
Management of ESG risk	Management of ESG risks score	34.90	–
	Classification of management of ESG risks	Average	–
	ESG risk management score momentum	2.49	✓
Company controversy	Level of company controversy exposure	Moderate	–
	Notable ESG issues	Product governance	

Carbon emissions	Measured risks	Assessment	Result
	Carbon overall risk	Negligible	✓
	Carbon overall risk score	0	✓
	Carbon total emissions, scopes 1, 2 and 3	23 890.38	✓
	Carbon level of involvement	0	✓
	Level of fossil fuel involvement	0%	✓
	Carbon intensity, scopes 1, 2 and 3	61.99	–

Concluding remarks

The companies chosen in this sector have generally made good progress on sustainability. All have undertaken ESG materiality assessments to determine the key ESG issues and have mapped them to a materiality matrix. All have used globally recognised frameworks such as the GRI Standards, although IDP Education has so far made no GHG reduction commitments on any of the scopes and is not yet on a pathway to decarbonisation. Metcash, Coles and Endeavour have scopes 1 and 2 reduction targets and are reporting their progress. Coles has gone a step further by having its decarbonisation plans validated by a science-based target initiative classified as aligned to 1.5 degrees Celsius.

But for all these companies, scope 3 reduction targets remain a work in progress. All are still in the phase of gathering scope 3 data and engaging with their supply chains. Again, Coles stood apart, having set science-based supplier engagement targets of 75 per cent by FY27. Given that scope 3 often contains the largest GHG emissions, this is an important area of improvement across the consumer defensive sector.

All four companies in this group were rated as having low ESG risk. Coles had in place the most robust sustainability policy and processes, but Endeavour and Metcash were also solid. IDP has a way to go to catch up with the level of detail supplied by others in this sector.

Coles was strong on management of ESG risks, with Metcash, IDP and Endeavour a notch lower. Coles, Metcash and IDP have improved ESG momentum year on year, but Endeavour's has deteriorated.

On GHG emissions, Endeavour produced the most across scopes 1, 2 and 3, significantly higher than peers at 3 520 384.20 metric tonnes CO2e based on estimations. Coles reported 1 845 972, and Metcash and IDP were significantly lower. All need to address scope 3 emissions going forward.

Coles and Endeavour were signatories to the UN Global Compact, which involves ongoing reporting obligations in line with the 10 principles. All companies map their activities back to the UN's SDGs.

When it comes to management of sustainability risks and opportunity, Coles is the standout in this sector. It's not only talking the talk but walking the walk. Endeavour comes a close second despite its controversial underlying business of retail alcohol sales and the operation of hotels. IDP, despite playing catchup, has a naturally efficient business model for ESG, so once it gets itself organised it could do even better on ESG metrics.

5. Energy

Electrical energy powers our world. To date we have predominantly relied on fossil fuels as our primary source of energy. However, burning fossil fuels comes at a cost. The scientific consensus is that emissions from fossil fuels are the primary contributor to global warming. A 2018 report from the UN's Intergovernmental Panel on Climate Change has established that 89 per cent of global GHG emissions come from fossil fuels. To try to combat global warming, 193 nations signed up to the historic Paris Agreement in 2015, establishing a united commitment to reduce GHG emissions to net zero by 2050.

As a net exporter of coal, oil and gas, Australia ranks among the highest carbon emitters in the world on a per capita basis, according to a 2019 report from Climate Analytics. It is not surprising, therefore, that low-carbon strategies and techniques to minimise fossil fuel exposure are becoming increasingly important to sustainability-focused investors in resource-rich Australia, particularly as the world is transitioning to a low-carbon economy.

The Australian large-cap listed market is highly skewed to fossil fuels. Twenty-two companies with fossil fuel exposures make up more than 20 per cent of the ASX 300 benchmark. Exposure is measured by revenue generated through involvement in thermal coal extraction, thermal coal power generation, oil and gas generation, oil and gas production, or oil and gas products and services. The structurally high exposure to fossil fuels in our market creates challenges for Australian investors. Underweighting or removing all exposure to fossil fuels limits investor choice and diversification benefits. The other option is to consider companies that currently have high carbon emissions and fossil fuel exposures but are committed to decarbonisation.

Decarbonisation is a dominant theme in ESG investing, and companies that are well placed to operate in a decarbonised world should have better long-term prospects. This puts the energy sector in a difficult position, as arguably they have the hardest path to travel. They need to transform their businesses expeditiously, reducing their reliance on fossil fuels and building out alternative renewable energy sources that are less carbon intensive.

On a positive note, the costs of renewables have been declining rapidly, making them more cost effective to set up than new fossil fuel production. Renewables already make up approximately 30 per cent of the total volume of electricity supplied to

Australia's National Electricity Market (NEM), and this figure is expected to rise year on year. Also, more than 3 million homes have rooftop solar, which means more than one in three Australian households are harnessing the benefits of the sun.

Regulations too are evolving, making higher emitters more accountable. For example, there are now more stringent mechanisms in place to ensure higher GHG emitters reduce their emissions year on year.

Not all energy companies are embracing the net zero challenge. While some are divesting and setting themselves up for success in the net zero economy, others are doubling down by buying up fossil fuel assets to make as much money as they can while they can.

Even when investing sustainably, the energy sector remains controversial. Some investors will argue that it has no place in the sustainable investor's portfolio. However, given the sector's outsized impact on overall carbon emissions, ultimately we need the energy sector to play a part. A number of companies are attempting to solve the complex problem of supplying reliable affordable energy while simultaneously reducing carbon output and generating returns for shareholders. Their success would be a big boost to Australia's net zero ambitions. Arguably, these companies should deliver good returns to investors because they are evolving and setting up for future success.

This sector rates poorly on ESG risk. The best-of-breed companies selected exhibit high ESG risks. This is out of step with all other sectors whose top companies typically boast low to negligible ESG risks. Of course, energy companies typically also face high carbon risks, although Origin Energy exhibits lower carbon risks than the rest.

Woodside Energy Group Limited

ASX code: WDS

www.woodside.com.au

Market capitalisation:	$58 861.24 million
Sector:	Energy
Morningstar Sustainalytics peer group classification:	Oil and Gas Exploration and Production

Environmental risk score		Social risk score		Governance risk score	
17.19	–	7.51	✓	6.21	✓

View: Woodside's ESG commitment is unclear as it continues to explore the development of new gas projects, which is at odds with decarbonisation ambitions.

History/background

Woodside Energy Group is a petroleum exploration and production company and Australia's largest independent company dedicated to oil and gas.

Woodside is an interesting case. While it ranks as one of the better operators in the sector, it shows little interest in moving away from fossil fuel exploration and production; rather, it is focusing on carbon capture as its primary decarbonisation tool. Its ESG risk rating encapsulates the high ESG risks associated with its operations.

Woodside has been exploring the development of new gas projects and buying oil and gas assets from other companies, which seems at odds with its stated commitment to the Paris Agreement. In the short term, its high exposure to oil and gas assets has paid off financially through the energy supply shock. Improved profitability may continue while the Russia–Ukraine war continues. But in the long term, high fossil fuel exposure and carbon intensity is risky given the global commitment to achieving net zero emissions by 2050. Woodside is flagged as having high exposure to stranded asset risk based on its current operations.

Further, the company faces regulatory pressures as Australia puts a price cap on domestic gas sales. It will be interesting to see the impact, if any, this has on Woodside's bottom line.

ESG performance

Woodside's actions seem at odds with its claimed commitment to decarbonisation and the use of renewables. Its climate transition plans capture only 10 per cent of its emissions, and it relies predominantly on carbon offsets. Carbon capture and offsets may have a role to play in decarbonisation, but the primary focus needs to be genuine carbon reduction. The obvious solution is to pursue alternative renewable energy sources.

Woodside's management of climate risk is poor year on year; however, its excess exposure score is below the average for its sub-industry peers in oil and gas exploration and production. It ranks quite highly on an ESG basis compared with its sub-industry peers and is assessed as having positive momentum in managing ESG risks.

While it provides climate data aligned to TCFD, its membership and funding of the Australian Petroleum Production and Exploration Association (APPEA) seems at odds with its stated commitment to decarbonisation in line with the Paris Agreement. And its plan to pursue new oil and gas drilling opportunities through its stake in Trion belies its stated commitments to reducing GHG emissions.

Woodside says the UN's own climate science panel accepts that there are a range of energy transition pathways, that there will be continuing demand for oil as the world decarbonises, and that despite its new oil and gas projects it should still be able to achieve its climate targets. Technically, this may be true as the bulk of the GHG emissions will be created when the fossil fuels are burned (scope 3), and Woodside's targets only capture scopes 1 and 2. Further, Woodside uses offsets to help to mitigate its emissions. This is a good illustration of why all scopes must be captured if we are serious about carbon reduction. While offsets may have a role to play, they should never be the primary mechanism for reducing GHGs.

While the company is pledging to invest in renewable energy and low carbon, it is spending more on fossil fuel production.

ESG risks	ESG measured	Assessment	Result
ESG exposure	ESG risk rating assessment	▓▓ ▓ □ □ □	X
	ESG exposure risk classification	High	X
	ESG risk exposure score	69.35	X
	ESG excess exposure score	(1.65)	✓
	ESG risk score momentum	(0.71)	✓
ESG sub-industry risk	ESG sub-industry rank	18/169	✓
	ESG risk compared to sub-industry peers	(12.42)	✓
	ESG risk beta	0.98	✓
Management of ESG risk	Management of ESG risks score	65.04	✓
	Classification of management of ESG risks	Strong	✓
	ESG risk management score momentum	1.53	✓
Company controversy	Level of company controversy exposure	Moderate	X
	Notable ESG issues	Carbon – products and services	

Carbon emissions	Measured risks	Assessment	Result
	Carbon overall risk	High	X
	Carbon overall risk score	34.00	X
	Carbon total emissions, scopes 1, 2 and 3	81 878 000	X
	Carbon level of Involvement	5	X
	Level of fossil fuel involvement	50%–100%	X
	Carbon intensity, scopes 1, 2 and 3	11 530.49	X

Ampol Limited

ASX code: ALD

www.ampol.com.au

Market capitalisation:	$8157.08 million
Sector:	Energy
Morningstar Sustainalytics peer group classification:	Oil and Gas Refining and Marketing

Environmental risk score		Social risk score		Governance risk score	
19.37	X	10.27	−	4.92	✓

View: Ampol has made modest progress towards decarbonisation, but scope 3 emissions must be addressed.

History/background

The Australian petroleum company Ampol is the largest transport energy distributor and retailer in Australia, with more than 1900 Ampol-branded stations across the country. The company was founded in 1936 as the Australian Motorists Petrol Company and later became Ampol Petroleum Ltd. It was listed on the Australian Securities Exchange (ASX) in 1948.

Ampol's business units include:

- Fuels and Infrastructure. Ampol trades, imports and refines fuel, and manages complex supply chains across Australia, the Asia-Pacific region and the United States.

- In-store Retail. Ampol operates a vast network of stores across Australia that offer a range of products and services, including convenience items, food and coffee.

- Retail Support. Ampol's Retail Support team works to build and maintain operational excellence across every facet of the retail business.

- Corporate and Functional. Ampol's corporate team works to make things happen across its diverse business with flexibility and accountability.

Ampol's key products and services include:

- Fuel. Ampol sources crude oil and refined products from the global market and operates one oil refinery in Lytton, Queensland, which refines crude oil into petrol, biofuel, diesel, jet fuel and other specialty products such as liquid petroleum gas (LPG).

- Retail. Ampol operates a vast network of stores across Australia that offer a range of products and services, including convenience items, food and coffee.

ESG performance

Australia's largest transport energy distributor and retailer, Ampol has a mixed report card. While it has pledged to be net zero for its own operations by 2040, this covers only scopes 1 and 2 emissions. However, it does not capture scope 3, which is where the bulk of its emissions lie. To make a genuine impact on carbon emissions it needs a plan to tackle scope 3.

While carbon emissions are high, they are approximately half those of Woodside; however, Ampol's carbon emissions figures are based on estimations rather than being supplied via reporting.

Ampol's management of ESG risks is assessed as average but the risk management momentum score indicates improvements here, which is positive. Its high-risk ESG rating captures elevated ESG risks, and like others operating in this sector, its largest ESG risks are environmental.

The bulk of revenue generated by Ampol is through fuel and infrastructure assets. It is considering how it can play a part in the growing demand for electrification. Its own modelling predicts EVs will be the dominant mode of transport by 2050. It has launched a new charging brand, AmpCharge, and is adding EV power charging stations through a funding arrangement with the Australian Renewable Energy Authority and the NSW government at its service stations. The plan is to operate up to 500 EV charging bays by 2027. While these are positive developments, they are small steps in the overall company context.

ESG risks	ESG measured	Assessment	Result
ESG exposure	ESG risk rating assessment		X
	ESG exposure risk classification	High	X
	ESG risk exposure score	57.80	X
	ESG excess exposure score	(1.20)	✓
	ESG risk score momentum	1.70	X
ESG sub-industry risk	ESG sub-industry rank	35/92	✓
	ESG risk compared to sub-industry peers	(2.55)	✓
	ESG risk beta	0.98	✓
Management of ESG risk	Management of ESG risks score	47.79	–
	Classification of management of ESG risks	Average	–
	ESG risk management score momentum	3.10	✓
Company controversy	Level of company controversy exposure	Moderate	✓
	Notable ESG issues	Carbon – products and services	

Carbon emissions	Measured risks	Assessment	Result
	Carbon overall risk	High	X
	Carbon overall risk score	39.07	X
	Carbon total emissions, scopes 1, 2 and 3	41 894 877	X
	Carbon level of involvement	5	X
	Level of fossil fuel involvement	50%–100%	X
	Carbon intensity, scopes 1, 2 and 3	2666.93	X

Viva Energy Group Limited

ASX code: VEA　　　　　　　　　　　www.vivaenergy.com.au

Market capitalisation:	$4756.03 million
Sector:	Energy
Morningstar Sustainalytics peer group classification:	Oil and Gas Refining and Marketing

Environmental risk score		Social risk score		Governance risk score	
21.14	X	7.74	✓	4.77	✓

View: Viva's ESG approach is average, but its capability in managing ESG risks is strong.

History/background

Viva Energy Group is one of the larger transport energy distributors and retailers in Australia. It operates in the same industry subsector as Ampol. This Australian company owns the Geelong Oil Refinery and retails Shell-branded fuels across Australia under a licence agreement. It has been in operation for more than 120 years and plans to be a part of Australia's energy transition.

It is the second largest vertically integrated transport fuel supplier and pipeline owner in the country. It also owns and retails Liberty Oil and Westside Petroleum-branded service stations. In total, Viva Energy supplies a network of more than 1330 fuel outlets across Australia.

Viva generates retail sales income unrelated to fuels through its previous alliance with and now acquisition of the Coles Express retail division. Further diversification includes bitumen manufacturing and Viva are the exclusive supplier of Shell's aviation gasoline.

ESG performance

Viva Energy produces a sustainability report and supports the objectives of the Paris Agreement. It has net zero GHG emission goals across scopes 1 and 2 separated between its non-refining businesses, including retail, fuels, marketing, and supply and distribution, where it aims for net zero by 2030, and a 10 per cent reduction in emissions intensity for its Geelong refinery business, which is responsible for approximately 97 per cent of its scopes 1 and 2 emissions. The Australian Government safeguard mechanism creates an additional impetus to reduce emissions at the refinery. Viva's overarching ambition is to reach net zero by 2050 for scopes 1 and 2 for the overall group. It aims to achieve this by reducing company emissions through energy efficiency, using renewable energy through the purchase of large-scale generation certificates, and investing in renewable projects such as ultra-low sulphur gasoline and the new energies service station, which will be a publicly accessible hydrogen focused refuelling facility offering refuelling for heavy (buses and trucks) hydrogen fuel cell EVs.

In FY22 Viva Energy updated its most material scope 3 emission sources across upstream and downstream. It calculated the estimate with deference to the GHG protocol and the IPIECA methodology. The most material impact was the combustion of sold product, which equates for 90 per cent of downstream scope 3 emissions and 87 per cent of total GHG emissions. When upstream scope 3 emissions were taken into account scope 3 emissions totalled 96.4 per cent of GHG emissions for the group (excludes Viva Energy Polymers), which is why scope 3 must be included in GHG reduction goals.

It has undertaken a materiality assessment to help it prioritise sustainable risks and opportunities to focus on. The assessment uncovered that climate change and the energy transition were the most material topics.

It reports aligned to GRI standards and with consideration to SASB, ISSB and TCFD. It also provides a data supplement, which provides detailed sustainability information. Viva Energy is a founding member of the Australian Climate Leaders Coalition (CLC).

Viva Energy has high ESG risks, although it rates well on the management of those risks (assessed as strong). Not surprisingly given the industry it operates in, its highest ESG risk pertains to the environment. Its ESG risks are gaining momentum, with the company exhibiting slightly higher ESG risks year on year, which is something to watch.

ESG risks	ESG measured	Assessment	Result
ESG exposure	ESG risk rating assessment	▮▮☐☐☐	X
	ESG exposure risk classification	High	X
	ESG risk exposure score	58.85	X
	ESG excess exposure score	(0.15)	✓
	ESG risk score momentum	0.63	X
ESG sub-industry risk	ESG sub-industry rank	32/92	−
	ESG risk compared to sub-industry peers	(3.46)	✓
	ESG risk beta	1.00	−
Management of ESG risk	Management of ESG risks score	51.06	✓
	Classification of management of ESG risks	Strong	✓
	ESG risk management score momentum	(0.11)	X
Company controversy	Level of company controversy exposure	Low	✓
	Notable ESG issues	Carbon – products and services	

Carbon emissions	Measured risks	Assessment	Result
	Carbon overall risk	High	X
	Carbon overall risk score	40.16	X
	Carbon total emissions, scopes 1, 2 and 3	36 774 217	X
	Carbon level of involvement	4	X
	Level of fossil fuel involvement	25%-49.90%	X
	Carbon intensity, scopes 1, 2 and 3	3153.81	X

Beach Energy Limited

ASX code: BPT

www.beachenergy.com.au

Market capitalisation:	$3387.78 million
Sector:	Energy
Morningstar Sustainalytics peer group classification:	Oil and Gas Exploration and Production

Environmental risk score		Social risk score		Governance risk score	
21.76	X	7.68	✓	7.26	✓

View: There is cognitive dissonance in Beach Energy's forging ahead with gas exploration while aiming to reduce its carbon emissions.

History/background

Based in Adelaide, Beach undertakes oil and gas exploration. Beach Energy was founded in 1961 as Beach Petroleum NL and it listed on the stock exchange in 2003. It changed its name to Beach Energy Limited in 2009 to reflect its transition from a petroleum company to a diversified energy company. The company's key products include hydrocarbon products such as crude oil, natural gas and condensate, which are used to provide local and international energy and inputs for manufacturers of products, including lubricants, plastics, fabrics, fertilisers and paints.

Beach Energy operates production in a range of locations, however, only the Otway basin is 100 per cent Beach operated; all other sites it partially operates or has a non-operated interest. The company's stated competitive advantage lies in its ability to produce clean, affordable and reliable energy for the community while maintaining high standards of health, safety and environmental management.

ESG performance

Beach Energy has pledged to reduce scopes 1 and 2 emissions by 35 per cent by 2030 against an FY18 baseline and to reach net zero by 2050. It plans to reduce GHG emissions by reducing operational emissions through a fuel flare and vents program, which alone will reduce carbon emissions by approximately 18 000 tCO_2e (excluding Moomba CCS). It has also undertaken work to identify emissions-reduction opportunities at each operated asset, which will guide future emissions-reduction activities and capital allocation. In instances where they are not able to reduce emissions, they will utilise carbon offset certificates to meet emissions-reduction targets and safeguard mechanism obligations.

While the bulk of its emissions are scope 1 (its own operations), it would be useful to see the missing scope 3 emissions captured and their impact on the net zero commitment charted. To that end, Beach Energy is in the process of estimating its scope 3 emissions with help from an external consultant. Use of sold products is where the bulk of its scope 3 emissions occur, making up approximately 98 per cent of its scope 3 estimate. It will continue to work on improving its scope 3 reporting and plans to incorporate emissions reporting requirements in contracts across its value chain.

It believes natural gas is an important component of the energy transition to help maintain energy supply as the transition to renewables occurs. However, natural gas is a fossil fuel, primarily composed of methane, which has a global warming potential 84 times greater than carbon dioxide and when burned releases CO2. While it does typically produce less emissions than other fossil fuels, it is still a contributor to GHG emissions. There is ongoing debate on the role natural gas can perform in the energy transition as the 'least worst' fossil fuel, but extraction, transportation and use of natural gas all produce GHG emissions.

Beach Energy is considering new energy opportunities in the renewable energy market, which includes the development of a wind farm near its Kupe gas plant in New Zealand, purchasing offshore wind licences in the Gippsland basin, and hydrogen production and storage opportunities in the South Australian Otway Basin.

It has undertaken a materiality sustainability assessment to help identify key material topics for the business. The six identified were: diversity equity and inclusion, health and safety, community engagement and investment, Indigenous participation, greenhouse gas emissions and climate adaptation, and resilience and transition. It has also undertaken scenario analysis guided by IEA's 2022 World Energy Outlooks scenarios and the IPCC's climate scenarios to identify potential risks and opportunities. In FY23 it developed a GHG Management Plan to provide guidance of GHG emissions from Beach-operated facilities.

Like its competitors, Beach appears to see carbon capture and storage as a pathway to net zero. To that end, it is involved with the Moomba carbon capture and storage project through a joint venture arrangement with Santos. Meantime it is forging ahead with gas exploration and developments, such as the Otway offshore drilling program. This activity and its membership of APPEA seem at odds with its net zero ambitions, and this is concerning. It is exploring renewables and new energy opportunities including Santos clean fuels collaboration for hydrogen and CO2 imports, but it is early days. It is not a signatory to the UN Global Compact, but it is a member of Business for Societal Impact (B4SI), International Association for Public Participation (IAP2), Carbon Dioxide Cooperative Research Centre (CO2CRC), Future Energy Exports Cooperative Research Centre (FEnEx CRC), Australian Industry Greenhouse Network (AIGN), Supply Nation and Safer Together.

It reports in line with GRI standards, focusing in on topics with material impacts and linkages back to relevant SDGs.

ESG risks	ESG measured	Assessment		Result
ESG exposure	ESG risk rating assessment			X
	ESG exposure risk classification	High		X
	ESG risk exposure score	62.85		X
	ESG excess exposure score	(9.15)		✓
	ESG risk score momentum	(3.52)		✓
ESG sub-industry risk	ESG sub-industry rank	48/169		✓
	ESG risk compared to sub-industry peers	(6.63)		✓
	ESG risk beta	0.87		✓
Management of ESG risk	Management of ESG risks score	49.04		—
	Classification of management of ESG risks	Average		—
	ESG risk management score momentum	3.10		✓
Company controversy	Level of company controversy exposure	Low		✓
	Notable ESG issues	Carbon – products and services		

Carbon emissions	Measured risks	Assessment	Result
	Carbon overall risk	High	X
	Carbon overall risk score	42.81	X
	Carbon total emissions, scopes 1, 2 and 3	621 530.52	X
	Carbon level of involvement	5	X
	Level of fossil fuel involvement	50%–100%	X
	Carbon intensity, scopes 1, 2 and 3	542.59	X

Origin Energy Limited

ASX code: ORG　　　　　　　　　　　　　www.originenergy.com.au

Market capitalisation:	$14 195.44 million
Sector:	Energy
Morningstar Sustainalytics peer group classification:	Multi-utilities

Environmental risk score		Social risk score		Governance risk score	
22.26	X	9.30	–	5.29	✓

View: Origin has high ESG risks, but its investment in renewables, including renewable energy provider Octopus, is encouraging.

History/background

Origin Energy undertakes oil and gas exploration, generation and delivery and is one of the largest energy providers in Australia to residential, business and wholesale customers.

The business is broken up into the following segments:

- Energy markets. Origin Energy sells electricity and natural gas to residential, business and wholesale customers in Australia, New Zealand and around the Pacific. Origin is also involved in electricity trading—buying and selling electricity.

- Integrated gas. Origin Energy is involved in the exploration, production and sale of liquefied natural gas (LNG) and natural gas in Australia and overseas.

- Renewables. Origin Energy is committed to transitioning to renewable energy sources and has invested in wind, solar and battery storage projects.

- Corporate. This segment includes the company's corporate functions and support services.

Origin has demonstrated an interest in beefing up its renewable energy capacity and has exposure to wind, solar and hydrogen renewable energy sources. As of March 2022 renewable energy and storage account for more than 20 per cent of its total owned and contracted generation portfolio. Origin purchases wind power from various wind farms in NSW, South Australia and Victoria, installs solar panels and has numerous large-scale solar power purchase agreements in place. It has recently invested in solar power company Octopus. The sale of its share of the Beetaloo Basin JV gas development site in Northern Territory potentially frees up capital to make further investments in the renewable energy space.

ESG performance

Origin aims to be net zero across scopes 1, 2 and 3 emissions by 2050. It is targeting a 40 per cent reduction in scopes 1, 2 and 3 equity emissions intensity by 2030 off an FY19 baseline, which is aligned with the Paris Agreement. It also targets 20 million tonne reduction in absolute scope 1, 2 and 3 equity emissions by 2030. To achieve this it will reduce methane emissions that are occurring from venting and leaks, grow its renewables and storage capacity and invest in future fuels such as hydrogen. It will also help its customers to decarbonise by offering low-carbon products and via a portfolio of carbon credits to offset emissions.

In August 2022 it launched its Climate Transition Action Plan (CTAP), which outlines its short- and medium-term goals in reducing carbon emissions. Before the launch its net zero ambitions took into account only scopes 1 and 2. Incorporating scope 3 emissions is a positive development. Further, it plans to decommission its high-polluting Eraring coal power plant earlier than originally projected, possibly as soon as 2025. While it sees the need to exit coal-powered energy generation, it also sees the need to 'keep the lights on' during the transition, which means at times there may be fluctuations in energy production to meet market demands. That will then impact on emissions generated. Origin's scope 1 and 2 emissions increased by 4 per cent in FY23 as a result of increased energy generation led by market demand. Despite this it still believes it is on track for the medium- and long-term decarbonisation goals.

The CTAP considers a variety of climate scenarios to identify risks and opportunities. Origin also undertakes a materiality assessment on an annual basis; the findings inform its strategy and priorities. Eleven material topics were identified and grouped under customers, communities, planet, and our people and culture. However, Origin's continuing support of gas as a source of reliable energy during the energy transition is at odds with a net zero future. At the time of writing, Brookfield's Origin acquisition had set an interesting precedent as the Australian Competition and Consumer Commission (ACCC) has allowed a merger between the two companies despite its being likely to substantially reduce competition. The ACCC has granted the acquisition on the basis of reducing GHG emissions, with the expectation the merger will accelerate the availability of renewable energy solutions, thereby helping Australia's renewable energy transition, to the material benefit of all Australians.

Origin's strategic priorities include accelerating uptake of renewable energy and cleaner energy solutions in its energy portfolio and helping its customers decarbonise. Activities to help customers decarbonise include:

- Origin zero, for large business customers, includes renewable electricity, behind the meter connected to virtual power plant, EV fleet management solutions and data analytics to improve energy efficiency.

- Green power and climate active certified products. Origin has a range of products that are certified carbon neutral by Climate Active, essentially offsetting carbon emissions.

- Solar energy and battery storage. Origin is an approved seller of solar energy and installs solar systems on the roofs of residential homes and commercial buildings.

Origin has reported against the TCFD framework since 2018.

Origin's continuing membership of APPEA is a concern. It is not a member of the UN Global Compact.

ESG risks	ESG measured	Assessment	Result
ESG exposure	ESG risk rating assessment		X
	ESG exposure risk classification	High	X
	ESG risk exposure score	76.50	X
	ESG excess exposure score	14.50	X
	ESG risk score momentum	3.11	X
ESG sub-industry risk	ESG sub-industry rank	84/104	X
	ESG risk compared to sub-industry peers	6.79	X
	ESG risk beta	1.23	X
Management of ESG risk	Management of ESG risks score	55.61	✓
	Classification of management of ESG risks	Strong	✓
	ESG risk management score momentum	1.10	✓
Company controversy	Level of company controversy exposure	Moderate	✓
	Notable ESG issues	Carbon – products and services	

Carbon emissions	Measured risks	Assessment	Result
	Carbon overall risk	Medium	✓
	Carbon overall risk score	29.21	✓
	Carbon total emissions, scopes 1, 2 and 3	45 115 087	X
	Carbon level of involvement	5	X
	Level of fossil fuel involvement	50%-100%	X
	Carbon intensity, scopes 1, 2 and 3	5085.50	X

Concluding remarks

The stocks in this sector exhibited high ESG risks and would not make the top stock ESG list in any other sector. The featured stocks were relatively better than their peers, but they generally performed poorly when compared across all sectors.

On overall ESG risk Woodside led the field here, with the lowest ESG risk score of 72.59, This was still extremely high, but relative to others in the cohort it was the best performer. Woodside knows how to position itself, and considering actions undertaken by other companies, Origin, Ampol and Viva Energy seem better placed to transition to a net zero economy. For example, Origin's scope 3 greenhouse gas emissions were very low. As regulations improve, scope 3 will be taken into account in the future. Woodside is ahead of many by reporting on scope 3, which is positive, but as Woodside has the highest scope 3 emissions in the sector by a significant margin it is going to be an ongoing challenge as the transition to net zero unfolds.

Origin attracted the lowest overall carbon risk score in this cohort and also had the lowest overall carbon risk exposure. It was assessed as having medium carbon risk, with others in the cohort assessed as high.

On ESG risk exposures Beach Energy was the standout, having significantly less risk exposure than its subsector peers at 9.15. Interestingly, Woodside also did well but Origin disappointed, with substantially higher ESG risk exposure than its sub-industry peers. It is worth noting that within this cohort there were three different subsectors in operation, so these were not exact like-for-like comparisons:

- Oil and Gas Exploration and Production: Woodside and Beach
- Oil and Gas Refining and Marketing: Viva and Ampol
- Multi-utilities: Origin.

On ESG momentum in the management of ESG risks, Beach and Ampol were equal best followed by Woodside and Origin. Viva was the weakest. Origin did poorly on ESG risk exposure momentum, followed by Ampol, with Beach being the best in the cohort.

Origin had the highest environmental risk score. This captured unmanageable environmental risk exposure after taking into account the company's management of risk, although all companies in the cohort were closely bunched.

Woodside and Beach were exposed to carbon stranded asset risks. Woodside ranked as having the highest risk exposure, at 94.59, although Beach was close behind at 94.00. Stranded assets are effectively assets that can no longer be used. This has the potential to negatively impact their valuation; at worst, assets could even cross the ledger and become liabilities.

The energy sector is hard to abate and faces significant challenges during the transition to a decarbonised world, which will determine which companies are best placed to benefit from the transition. All in all, my money is on Origin. It has a clear pathway to decarbonisation and seems most prepared for the challenge.

6. Financial services

Australia's relatively sophisticated financial services sector, covering banking, insurance, superannuation and funds management, facilitates economic activities and contributing to the stable operation of the overall financial system. Banks have an important role to play as the provision of capital directly impacts the projects companies can undertake. The reality is it's going to cost money to transition the global economy to net zero, and public funding won't be enough. We need banks to step in.

Globally, 94 per cent of banks acknowledge that sustainability is a strategic priority. They are recognising that it makes commercial sense to embrace sustainability principles and that financing fossil fuels does not have great long-term prospects. Shareholders, including bank shareholders, are demanding more of the companies they invest in, and ESG considerations have become increasingly important.

Insurance companies provide protection against potential financial losses from natural disasters, accidents or other unforeseen events. Insurance companies are at the heart of climate change risk as they identify and mitigate risks such as extreme weather events triggering floods, bushfires and rising sea levels. The growing frequency of these events is heavily impacting underwriting activity, with some affected regions becoming too great a risk and therefore uninsurable.

Asset managers provide investment services and products to help individuals and companies manage their wealth. When considering ESG risks, governance issues have been the key focus in this sector, especially since the release of the findings of the 2017 royal commission into banking and financial services, which found widespread governance issues. The extent of these issues shook Australians' trust and damaged the reputations of these once credible institutions.

Operations of a number of large financial institutions were found to be underpinned by questionable ethics that encouraged institutions to focus on maximising profits at the expense of their clients. Unsurprisingly, given some of the practices exposed, business ethics featured prominently as a risk. While the public perception may have been that the banks largely got away with their misbehaviour, particularly as the fines imposed were relatively small compared to the outsized profits generated, the revelations served as a catalyst for change. As a result of the Commission's findings, a number of financial services board members and executives were stood down, and there were improvements to regulations and compliance procedures.

Product governance and data privacy and security are also notable material ESG risks in this sector.

The companies selected as top stocks in this sector were assessed as having low ESG risks overall. The cohort's weakest ESG scores were in the governance pillar.

Washington H. Soul Pattinson and Company Limited

ASX code: SOL

www.whsp.com.au

Market capitalisation:	$12 092.42 million
Sector:	Financial services
Morningstar Sustainalytics peer group classification:	Multi-sector Holdings

Environmental risk score		Social risk score		Governance risk score	
0.14	✓	3.04	✓	10.96	–

View: WHSP lags behind its peers on ESG, particularly for its own operations, and the overall increase in ESG risk is an issue to watch.

History/background

Washington H. Soul Pattinson (WHSP) is an Australian-based company that invests in a diversified pool of assets across a range of industries. It was founded in 1903 by Lewy Pattinson and listed on the ASX in 1903.

ESG performance

The company has policies on sustainable investment, climate change and human rights and produces an annual modern slavery statement. Its sustainable investment policy is inspired by UN PRI and TCFD, although WHSP is not a signatory, or formally committed, to these frameworks.

The corporate governance structure outlines roles and responsibilities. The board oversees ESG risk and opportunities, and in FY22 endorsed a separate strategy to further develop and document the company's approach to climate change and energy transition in particular. It undertakes climate change risk analysis and reports on scopes 1 and 2 emissions, although GHG emissions increased slightly in FY23. According to its annual report, more than 90 per cent of emissions related to electricity purchased; however, since FY22 100 per cent of energy used is now sourced from accredited green power generators. The company is on a carbon neutral pathway through the purchase of 50 tonnes of carbon credits. The use of green power and carbon credits resulted in scopes 1 and 2 being offset but it is not clear that this has been certified. It also references its commitment to decarbonisation by seeking out energy transition opportunities within its investment portfolio.

Future reporting will follow a TCFD framework, and WHSP's stated ambition is to be aligned with ISSB standards S1 and S2 on sustainability and climate disclosures as well as AASB standards, which it anticipates will come into effect in 2025. To that end it is identifying any gaps in processes so it can report to new guidelines. More generally, it would be good to see more detailed climate-related reporting including scope 3 emissions. It is not a signatory to the UN PRI or the UN Global Compact. All in all, its ESG data reporting metrics and commitments lack detail. This company is not leading the way.

ESG risks	ESG measured	Assessment	Result
ESG exposure	ESG risk rating assessment		✓
	ESG exposure risk classification	Low	✓
	ESG risk exposure score	23.70	✓
	ESG excess exposure score	(1.30)	✓
	ESG risk score momentum	2.82	X
ESG sub-industry risk	ESG sub-industry rank	32/68	–
	ESG risk compared to sub-industry peers	(0.39)	✓
	ESG risk beta	0.95	✓
Management of ESG risk	Management of ESG risks score	41.12	–
	Classification of management of ESG risks	Average	–
	ESG risk management score momentum	(3.10)	X
Company controversy	Level of company controversy exposure	None	✓
	Notable ESG issues	ESG integration financials	

Carbon emissions	Measured risks	Assessment	Result
	Carbon overall risk	Medium	–
	Carbon overall risk score	15.26	–
	Carbon total emissions, scopes 1, 2 and 3	676 088.86	X
	Carbon level of involvement	0	✓
	Level of fossil fuel involvement	0%	✓
	Carbon intensity, scopes 1, 2 and 3	646.35	X

National Australia Bank

ASX code: NAB

www.nab.com.au

Market capitalisation:	$88 631.32 million
Sector:	Financial services
Morningstar Sustainalytics peer group classification:	Diversified Banks

Environmental risk score		Social risk score		Governance risk score	
0.89	✓	9.07	–	9.79	–

View: NAB's approach to ESG goes beyond its own operations to responsible lending that considers ESG risk and opportunities in its supply chain.

History/background

The National Australia Bank was founded in 1858 primarily to serve the needs of the community during the goldrush, it was then called the National Bank of Australasia. It was a government-owned bank until it became a publicly listed company in 1980.

NAB is one of Australia's big four major banks. It offers an extensive range of banking services across retail, business and corporate and institutional markets. Its business units include:

- Banking services to individuals. This includes savings accounts, transaction accounts and term deposits. For individuals it offers home loans, personal loans and credit card services.

- Business banking. It offers business loans, finance, business accounts, and other products and services for business customers.

- Corporate and institutional banking. It provides corporate finance, treasury management, capital raising, debt structuring, funding solutions, trading and custodial services.

- Technology and digital. It develops and maintains NAB's technology infrastructure and digital platforms, including online banking.

- International operations. It supports customers across Australia, New Zealand, Asia, Europe and the US with foreign exchange, international money transfers and trade finance.

ESG performance

NAB's stated ambition is for its lending portfolio to align to net zero emissions by 2050. To that end it has set a range of decarbonisation targets for 2030 across several emission-intensive sectors, and it plans to add more sectors to decarbonisation targets next year.

NAB has been involved in managing ESG risk and opportunities for many years. In terms of sustainability, it is a signatory to the UN's environmental program finance initiative Principles for Responsible Banking. It aims to link all business activities back to an applicable SDG and the Paris Agreement. It reports comprehensively.

It has identified six priority Sustainable Development Goals:

- SDG 7 — affordable and clean energy
- SDG 8 — decent work and economic growth
- SDG 9 — industry, innovation and infrastructure
- SDG 11 — sustainable cities and communities
- SDG 13 — climate action
- SDG 15 — life on land.

Sustainability is built into its governance structures. Oversight of sustainability activities is the responsibility of the board. NAB also has a Sustainability Council, consisting of members of the executive leadership group, which monitors progress on sustainable goals.

NAB focuses on being a responsible lender. Its customer-related risk policies take into account ESG risks, going beyond its own operations to include the supply chain. It encourages suppliers to become signatories to the NAB group's supplier sustainability principles, which outlines sustainability requirements for suppliers working with the bank. These comprehensive principles cover corporate governance, workforce policies and human rights, work health and safety, environmental management, risk management, supply chain management, and community and supplier diversity.

On fossil fuel funding, NAB has provided guidance on funding activities across coal, oil and gas. It will not finance new thermal coal-mining projects, or new or material expansion of coal-fired power generation facilities, but it will finance metallurgical coal as an input into steel production, as to date there are no viable alternatives. It will also not directly finance greenfield gas extraction projects outside Australia. Within Australia it will consider directly financing greenfield gas exploration if it is considered important for energy security. It will not directly finance Arctic gas extraction production or pipeline projects and will not directly finance oil tar sands or ultra-deepwater oil and gas extraction. The wrinkle here is in the word *direct*. It would be good to remove this qualification.

Beyond this limited risk appetite for fossil fuel, it will not knowingly fund improper land acquisition, or businesses that do not adequately care for animals (it has an animal welfare principles document), or growing or manufacturing of tobacco-based products. It is a signatory to the UN's Tobacco-Free Finance Pledge.

NAB provides extremely detailed reporting on its ESG efforts, including in the annual report an ESG data pack, a modern slavery statement, and a climate report, with further details on its website. In 2022 it appointed a chief climate officer to support the transition to decarbonisation.

On climate risk, NAB is increasing its risk disclosures and is focused on reducing its own GHG emissions through reduction/avoidance, using carbon credits to offset residuals. It has been certified as carbon neutral by Climate Active Carbon Neutral Standard for organisations since 2010. It claims to fund more projects expanding renewable energy supply than any other Australian bank. Its total lending to power generation for renewables was 73.3 per cent in FY23. It also provides finance to clients seeking to reduce emissions through products such as green bonds. NAB is a member of the UN Global Compact, part of the Net-Zero Banking Alliance, the RE100, a global corporate renewable energy initiative that is committed to 100 per cent renewable energy, and the UN Global Compact's Think Lab on Just Transition.

ESG risks	ESG measured	Assessment	Result
ESG exposure	ESG risk rating assessment	▓▓▓▓☐	✓
	ESG exposure risk classification	Low	✓
	ESG risk exposure score	46.20	✓
	ESG excess exposure score	2.20	X
	ESG risk score momentum	(2.27)	✓
ESG sub-industry risk	ESG sub-industry rank	64/356	✓
	ESG risk compared to sub-industry peers	(6.95)	✓
	ESG risk beta	1.05	X
Management of ESG risk	Management of ESG risks score	60.20	–
	Classification of management of ESG risks	Strong	✓
	ESG risk management score momentum	4.23	✓
Company controversy	Level of company controversy exposure	Significant	X
	Notable ESG issues	Data privacy and security	

Carbon emissions	Measured risks	Assessment	Result
	Carbon overall risk	Low	✓
	Carbon overall risk score	5.24	✓
	Carbon total emissions, scopes 1, 2 and 3	131 586	–
	Carbon level of involvement	0	✓
	Level of fossil fuel involvement	0%	✓
	Carbon intensity, scopes 1, 2 and 3	8.56	✓

Magellan Financial Group Limited

ASX code: MFG   www.magellangroup.com.au

Market capitalisation:	$1346.90 million
Sector:	Financial services
Morningstar Sustainalytics peer group classification:	Asset Management and Custody Services

Environmental risk score		Social risk score		Governance risk score	
2.36	✓	7.45	✓	9.33	–

View: Once a mighty, market-leading firm, Magellan has fallen from grace, with a revolving door of CEOs, though it operates within a sector that has low ESG risks and itself scores well on ESG.

History/background

Magellan Financial Group is a Sydney-based asset manager formed in 2006 by Hamish Douglass and Chris Mackay, offering investors a range of financial products. It led the way in introducing active exchange traded funds onto the ASX. In February 2018 it acquired Airlie Funds Management an Australian equities fund manager to diversify the product suite, which was internationally focused. It also acquired its North American distribution partner Frontier Partners Group in 2018. Magellan was a home-grown runaway success story that dominated the funds management market with huge support, particularly for its global equities funds. Due to leadership turnover and some unfortunate investment decisions, there have been significant outflows.

ESG performance

Magellan signed the Net Zero Asset Managers Initiative in 2022 and is committed to supporting investing aligned to net zero GHG emissions by 2050. It publishes a stewardship strategy on climate-related risks and opportunities that outlines its approach to achieving this. It undertakes analysis on companies to determine a variety of climate-related metrics, including a company's climate-related targets and ambition to deliver net zero by 2050, whether or not it has a net zero pathway to emissions reductions in both the short and medium term, and finally they seek to identify a company's reporting with alignment to TCFD. If there is no alignment to net zero transition, Magellan will engage with the company, and if no improvements occur over time the escalation strategy could be divestment.

Magellan is recognised as a responsible investor by Responsible Investments Association Australasia, it is a UN PRI signatory (signed in 2012) and a member of the Investor Group on Climate Change (IGCC). As well as a climate stewardship strategy, it publishes a modern slavery statement, and policies on ESG and proxy voting. Its responsible investment principles outline the framework and process of ESG integration into its investment process and corporate governance.

Magellan launched specific sustainable strategies in 2016, which incorporated its own proprietary low-carbon overlay. However, its own business ESG reporting and commitments are sparse. It reports on scopes 1 and 2 emissions, but not yet scope 3 It references its travel agent capturing employee business travel, which forms a part of upstream scope 3 emissions. Beyond that there is no mention of the scale of the scope 3 emissions generated by travel. It has made no corporate net zero pledge; there is no materiality assessment, no scenario analysis and no mapping to SDGs. It is not reporting aligned to the TCFD framework or to GRI. Magellan's ESG momentum is currently negative. While it has low ESG risks, its ESG risk management is deteriorating. It nonetheless ranks very favourably within its sub-industry peer group on ESG risks.

Its carbon emissions are extremely low. It ranks well on all carbon metrics, and its operating business is assessed as having no exposure to fossil fuels.

ESG risks	ESG measured	Assessment	Result
ESG exposure	ESG risk rating assessment	▮▮▮▮▯	✓
	ESG exposure risk classification	Low	✓
	ESG risk exposure score	36.05	X
	ESG excess exposure score	(4.95)	✓
	ESG risk score momentum	1.55	X
ESG sub-industry risk	ESG sub-industry rank	39/397	✓
	ESG risk compared to sub-industry peers	(11.51)	✓
	ESG risk beta	0.88	✓
Management of ESG risk	Management of ESG risks score	49.11	—
	Classification of management of ESG risks	Average	—
	ESG risk management score momentum	(3.03)	X
Company controversy	Level of company controversy exposure	None	✓
	Notable ESG issues	Human capital	

Carbon emissions	Measured risks	Assessment	Result
	Carbon overall risk	Low	✓
	Carbon overall risk score	6.66	✓
	Carbon total emissions, scopes 1, 2 and 3	1958.60	✓
	Carbon level of involvement	0	✓
	Level of fossil fuel involvement	0%	✓
	Carbon intensity, scopes 1, 2 and 3	3.82	✓

QBE Insurance Group Limited

ASX code: QBE   www.qbe.com

Market capitalisation:	$22 961.48 million
Sector:	Financial services
Morningstar Sustainalytics peer group classification:	Property and Casualty Insurance

Environmental risk score		Social risk score		Governance risk score	
0.91	✓	8.46	–	9.90	–

View: QBE's underwriting efforts place it at the forefront of ESG risks, particularly around the impacts of climate change.

History/background

QBE is a general and reinsurance company headquartered in Sydney with operations around the world.

Insurers like QBE who obtain the bulk of their revenue from premiums generated from property and casualty insurance are arguably at the forefront of responses to climate change as they are dealing with its immediate effects now. This means the impacts of climate change have a direct impact on QBE's financial position and its underwriting process must assess risks and decide whether or not an asset is insurable. With more frequent extreme events such as floods and bushfires, its focus is hardly surprising. Insurers are choosing either not to insure assets that are too high risk or to increase premiums, which risks making insuring the asset unaffordable.

QBE focuses on setting its business up for success in the low-carbon economy and building out its pathways to transition.

ESG performance

ESG risks are explicitly linked to financial risks in this business, so they take them very seriously. QBE's overall ESG risks are assessed as low, and its environmental risks in particular are extremely low.

QBE's areas of focus are:

1. orderly and inclusive transition to net zero economy

2. sustainable and resilient workforce

3. growth through innovative, sustainable and impactful solutions.

QBE has a range of policies and reports relating to sustainability, including a group environmental policy and an environmental and social risk framework, as well as supplier sustainability principles. It produces an annual sustainability report. In 2022 it released a social disclosure supplement and it publishes a sustainability data book. It reports in line with TCFD.

QBE resigned from the Net Zero Asset Owner Alliance (NZAOA) in May 2023, although it continues to support the Insurance Council of Australia's 'Climate Change Roadmap: Towards a Net-Zero and Resilient Future'. QBE joined the UN-convened Net Zero Insurance Alliance and has pledged to contribute to limiting warming to 1.5 degrees by the end of 2100 through a Net Zero 2050 underwriting portfolio. It is a signatory to the UN PRI and of the UN Global Compact. It is also committed to the UN Environment Programme—Finance Initiative and Principles for Sustainable Insurance. It is part of RE100 and the IGCC, among others.

Within its investment portfolios it has committed to lifting its climate solutions investments to 5 per cent of the portfolio by 2025 and to reducing its developed equity portfolio by 25 per cent of scopes 1 and 2 carbon emissions. This may look promising, but it is very specific and covers only a small portion of its investments, the bulk of which are in defensive assets, cash and fixed interest. It would be nice to see greater ambition here.

It has committed its insurance and reinsurance underwriting portfolios to net zero GHG emissions by 2050.

Within its own operations it is reducing scopes 1 and 2 emissions, and has extended its commitment to containing its material scope 3 emissions. As part of its RE100 commitment, it plans to source 100 per cent of its electricity from renewables by 2030. It committed to starting the net zero engagement policy with its biggest suppliers in 2023 with the aim of setting targets by 2025.

All in all, QBE ranks very highly in its sub-industry, its low ESG risk placing it higher than many of its peers. It is managing ESG risks well, although not as well as it did in the previous 12 months.

ESG risks	ESG measured	Assessment	Result
ESG exposure	ESG risk rating assessment	▮▮▮▮▯	✓
	ESG exposure risk classification	Low	✓
	ESG risk exposure score	44.00	X
	ESG excess exposure score	3.00	X
	ESG risk score momentum	0.02	X
ESG sub-industry risk	ESG sub-industry rank	3/87	✓
	ESG risk compared to sub-industry peers	(8.11)	✓
	ESG risk beta	1.07	X
Management of ESG risk	Management of ESG risks score	59.31	—
	Classification of management ESG risks	Strong	✓
	ESG risk management score momentum	0.41	✓
Company controversy	Level of company controversy exposure	Moderate	✓
	Notable ESG issues	Product governance	

Carbon emissions	Measured risks	Assessment	Result
	Carbon overall risk	Low	✓
	Carbon overall risk score	2.17	✓
	Carbon total emissions, scopes 1, 2 and 3	26 690.00	✓
	Carbon level of involvement	0	✓
	Level of fossil fuel involvement	0%	✓
	Carbon intensity, scopes 1, 2 and 3	1.55	✓

NIB Holdings Limited

ASX code: NHF

Market capitalisation:	$3664.44 million
Sector:	Financial services
Morningstar Sustainalytics peer group classification:	Life and Health Insurance

Environmental risk score		Social risk score		Governance risk score	
2.02	✓	7.62	✓	9.55	–

View: Acquisitions have had a short-term impact on carbon emissions and net zero ambitions, but NIB seems to be ramping up its ESG commitments.

History/background

NIB was founded by BHP in the 1950s to provide health insurance to its Steelworks employees. From those humble beginnings it now provides health and travel insurance to more than 1.7 million members in Australia and New Zealand. It was the first Australian health insurer to list on the ASX in 2007 after it demutualised.

NIB has several business channels, including:

- Australian Residents Health Insurance. It provides affordable healthcare to Australian residents and helps them to better manage their health and wellbeing via products, services, programs and providers.

- GU Health. NIB's GU Health business is Australia's only established specialist corporate health insurer, providing health insurance plans to corporate groups.

- nib New Zealand. As the second largest health insurer in New Zealand, it provides a range of health insurance options for Kiwis and for New Zealand companies who want health insurance for their employees.

- Inbound Health Insurance. It provides health cover for students coming to Australia to study and workers migrating for employment (NIB Overseas Student Health Cover and Overseas Visitors Health Cover).

- nib Travel. Australia's third largest travel insurance distributor, nib Travel provides travel insurance for travellers.

- nib Thrive. This is nib Group's National Disability Insurance Scheme (NDIS) business, helping people living with disability and long-term health needs overcome their challenges and improve their quality of life.

ESG performance

NIB's sustainability strategy is based on five pillars:

- population health
- natural environment
- community spirit and cohesion
- leadership and governance
- people, culture and employment.

It maps its business activities back to eight SDGs.

NIB's board is ultimately responsible for oversight and the operation of the sustainability strategy, supported by the chief risk officer and the management sustainability committee. Chaired by the chief risk officer, the committee is responsible for oversight of the sustainability pillars and initiatives. The risk and reputation committee identifies and assesses material risks. It recommends ESG standards and practices, including climate-related risk management. ESG measurements are a part of short-term incentive plans for executives. The wider group scorecard has a sustainability metric that applies equally across all executives and employees related to the achievement of FY23 sustainability goals.

NIB maintains its climate-neutral certification through the purchase of carbon credits though it acknowledges that this alone is not sufficient to tackle its GHG emissions-reductions. It transitioned all controlled offices to 100 per cent renewable energy in FY21. It has also committed to achieving net zero in 2040 across all scopes. To help with that objective, it is encouraging suppliers to disclose their emissions at contract renewal.

Unfortunately, FY23 scopes 1 and 2 emissions have marginally increased (by approximately 2 per cent year on year), and scope 3 emissions were up 40 per cent due to business acquisitions. Although NIB has a very low exposure to carbon emissions, its scope 3 emissions make up the bulk of emissions reported. NIB has decided to delay validation of net zero, science-backed targets. Its FY23 annual report declares that it does not believe climate change risk is material in the short term.

In FY23 NIB published a climate-related disclosure report in which it outlined climate change scenario analysis across short-, medium- and long-term time frames, which considered both physical and transition risk as per the TCFD framework. The purpose of this analysis was to identify specific risks and opportunities within the business. The report also outlined its pathway to net zero emissions. Finally, it included future works, including:

- developing a climate action and resilience plan
- quantifying the costs of climate risks, assets and activities exposed to physical and transition risks
- developing a climate risk transition plan.

NIB produces a modern slavery statement, a responsible investment policy, a diversity and inclusion action plan, a supplier code of conduct and a reconciliation action plan.

It aims to have 25 per cent of its investment portfolio aligned to net zero science-based targets in line with the Paris Agreement by 2027, and 100 per cent by 2040.

NIB conducts regular ESG materiality assessments to identify key ESG opportunities and risks. FY22 assessment identified eight key material topics that it has mapped to its sustainability pillars. It is a signatory to the UN Global Compact.

ESG risks	ESG measured	Assessment	Result
ESG exposure	ESG risk rating assessment		✓
	ESG exposure risk classification	Low	✓
	ESG risk exposure score	42.00	X
	ESG excess exposure score	2.00	X
	ESG risk score momentum	(1.77)	✓
ESG sub-industry risk	ESG sub-industry rank	29/94	✓
	ESG risk compared to sub-industry peers	(4.09)	✓
	ESG risk beta	1.05	X
Management of ESG risk	Management of ESG risks score	57.47	—
	Classification of management of ESG risks	Strong	—
	ESG risk management score momentum	9.11	✓
Company controversy	Level of company controversy exposure	Low	✓
	Notable ESG issues	Product governance	

Carbon emissions	Measured risks	Assessment	Result
	Carbon overall risk	Low	✓
	Carbon overall risk score	6.56	✓
	Carbon total emissions, scopes 1, 2 and 3	6917.30	✓
	Carbon level of involvement	0	✓
	Level of fossil fuel involvement	0%	✓
	Carbon intensity, scopes 1, 2 and 3	3.63	✓

Challenger Limited

ASX code: CGF

www.challenger.com.au

Market capitalisation:	$4103.77 million
Sector:	Financial services
Morningstar Sustainalytics peer group classification:	Asset Management and Custody Services

Environmental risk score		Social risk score		Governance risk score	
1.14	✓	9.05	–	9.51	–

View: ESG seems to be predominantly focused on investment rather than being applied at a whole-of-group level, though Challenger's ESG ambitions are encouraging.

History/background

Challenger was established in 1985 under the name of Challenger International Ltd and listed on the ASX in 1987. It entered the annuities market in 1997 via an acquisition of Equity Life Ltd.

Challenger operates a funds management business, a life division and a deposit-taking business. Challenger Life is Australia's largest annuity provider. Challenger Bank is an online bank offering savings and lending products, Challenger Investment Management is an institutional fixed-interest manager, and Fidante is an investment management business that works with high-quality investment managers across a range of asset classes.

ESG performance

Its corporate sustainability strategy reflects its most material ESG opportunities and is built on four pillars:

- financially resilient customers and communities
- constructive public policy settings (through advocacy and research)
- doing things right (business activities that consider multiple stakeholders and the environment)
- responsible investment (incorporating ESG).

Challenger's board is ultimately responsible for ESG governance. ESG is discussed and considered at each board group risk committee (GRC) meeting. The board is kept informed by reports from management through the group ESG steering committee.

Challenger produces a raft of reports and policies relating to sustainability, including a sustainability report, a climate change statement, a responsible investment policy, a human rights statement and a modern slavery statement. There is not a lot of readily available detail relating to carbon emissions and no net zero ambitions, however, it is still in the process of identifying and assessing climate-related risks. FY23 saw its sustainability report align to TCFD standards but transparency of data and reporting disclosures should be improved.

In its FY23 sustainability report it identified the following future commitments:

- It will develop a plan to reduce scopes 1 and 2 emissions and aim to become carbon neutral.

- It will improve its ESG data, especially around climate and GHG emissions, across its asset (investment) portfolio. Ideally, this work would be undertaken across the whole group's operations.

- It will improve its ESG reporting and disclosures, and align them with international frameworks such as ISSB, TCFD, SASB and Partnership of Carbon Accounting Financials (PCAF).

- It will undertake a range of climate scenario testing across the investment portfolio and wider business to aid in the proactive management of ESG risk and opportunities.

- ESG will be integrated into strategy and operations.

Every three years the group undertakes an ESG materiality assessment and maps the ESG issues to a materiality matrix. Climate change is one of its nine material topics. Challenger is not a UN Global Compact signatory but has been a UN PRI signatory since 2015.

Overall the company's progress has been a bit disappointing, but its future plans are encouraging. It will be interesting to see how they unfold.

ESG risks	ESG measured	Assessment	Result
ESG exposure	ESG risk rating assessment		✓
	ESG exposure risk classification	Low	✓
	ESG risk exposure score	41.90	X
	ESG excess exposure score	0.90	X
	ESG risk score momentum	(0.58)	✓
ESG sub-industry risk	ESG sub-industry rank	42/397	✓
	ESG risk compared to sub-industry peers	(10.95)	✓
	ESG risk beta	1.02	X
Management of ESG risk	Management of ESG risks score	55.49	—
	Classification of management ESG risks	Strong	✓
	ESG risk management score momentum	0.27	✓
Company controversy	Level of company controversy exposure	None	✓
	Notable ESG issues	Data privacy and security	

Carbon emissions	Measured risks	Assessment	Result
	Carbon overall risk	Low	✓
	Carbon overall risk score	4.61	✓
	Carbon total emissions, scopes 1, 2 and 3	4128.80	✓
	Carbon level of involvement	0	✓
	Level of fossil fuel involvement	0%	✓
	Carbon intensity, scopes 1, 2 and 3	1.86	✓

Concluding remarks

This sector's approaches are a mixed bag. Some groups are far more advanced on ESG data, reporting and ambitions than others, though they were all assessed as having low ESG risks.

On overall ESG risk scores, they were all pretty similar—hence the low risk assessment—but NAB had the highest risk followed by Challenger; WHSP had the lowest.

QBE, Challenger, NAB and NIB were all assessed as being strong in their management of ESG risks, while Magellan and WHSP were assessed as average.

Interestingly, Magellan and WHSP had lower ESG risks than their sub-industry peers, as assessed by ESG risk beta. QBE had the highest and NAB and NIB came in equal second.

On improvements in ESG risk, NAB has been improving its ESG risk year on year and showed the best momentum of its industry sector. NIB and Challenger have improving ESG risks, while QBE, Magellan and WHSP have deteriorated. QBE's deterioration was slight in comparison to that of Magellan and WHSP.

Looking at carbon metrics, QBE had the lowest overall carbon risk score of 2.17. WHSP had the highest at 15.26, which equates to medium risk.

WHSP had by far the largest carbon emissions of the financial sector with scopes 1, 2 and 3 emissions assessed at 676 088.86 metric tonnes of CO_2e, more than seven times higher than those of the second-highest emitting company in the sector, NAB. As WHSP's highest emissions were scope 1, its own operations, it should be able to determine a strategy to better control this. Its emissions level put it in the top third of emitters of all the companies assessed in this book. The next highest in this sector was NAB; the lowest was Magellan. None of the companies in this chapter have any direct fossil fuel involvement.

7. Healthcare

This sector comprises companies that operate within the healthcare industry and encompasses a range of activities such as research and development, manufacture and distribution of pharmaceuticals and medical products, and hospitals and diagnostic laboratories.

Responsible investors often favour this sector since its capacity to improve quality of life means it ticks the social box in ESG, but this is arguably also the sector's biggest risk. This is because while companies operating in this sector can deliver outsize positive social impacts, if they get it wrong they can create a serious negative impact. Typically, therefore, companies in this sector have their highest ESG risks in social or human-centred issues. As a highly regulated sector, healthcare tends to rate well on the management of governance risks. Of the four companies in this chapter, only Ebos delivered a slightly higher governance risk compared to its social risk, although it was at the margin.

Given ongoing research and innovation, healthcare is an ever-changing space that cannot always be anticipated. For example, while the COVID pandemic posed a huge global threat, it provided great business opportunities. Companies involved in developing vaccines, anti-viral medications and testing kits could barely keep up with demand, and their balance sheets enjoyed a huge boost. Manufacturers and suppliers of personal protective equipment (PPE) including gloves and masks also saw demand increase exponentially. Now, semaglutide-based drugs such as Ozempic, originally developed for the treatment of type 2, diabetes became a weight loss phenomenon which was unexpected and pharmaceutical companies couldn't keep up with the off label consumer demand. A side effect has been that shortages persist for the treatment of diabetes.

Every company needs to contribute to progress towards net zero and healthcare has a role to play in climate action and decarbonisation. Australia's healthcare sector is responsible for 7 per cent of the nation's carbon footprint, with approximately half attributable to hospitals, whose emissions are mostly from energy used for heating and cooling facilities, or scope 2. Of the companies reviewed in this sector, Ansell and Sonic Healthcare were assessed as having medium GHG emissions and Ebos and Nanosonics as having low emissions.

Sonic Healthcare Limited

ASX code: SHL www.sonichealthcare.com

Market capitalisation:	$13 733.41 million
Sector:	Healthcare
Morningstar Sustainalytics peer group classification:	Medical Services

Environmental risk score		Social risk score		Governance risk score	
0.05	✓	10.85	–	7.52	✓

View: It's great to see net zero commitments incorporate scope 3, but better still would be to see climate change scenarios analysis and a comprehensive enforcement of the supplier policy.

History/background

Sonic Healthcare, which was founded in 1987, is a globally recognised healthcare provider that operates in the areas of pathology, radiology, laboratory medicine, general practice medicine and corporate medical services. It is the third-largest medical diagnostics company in the world. It claims one of its competitive advantages is its federated management structure, which provides support and resources while keeping local teams in place.

Its business consists of three specialist divisions:

- Laboratory medicine/pathology. There are seven businesses operating in this division across Australia, New Zealand, the USA and Europe. It is the largest pathology provider in Australia, the third-largest laboratory medicine company in the US and the largest provider of laboratory medicine/pathology services in Germany and Switzerland. It also has a presence in Belgium, the UK and New Zealand.

- Sonic Healthcare Australia Radiology. Sonic Healthcare is the second-largest radiology provider in Australia. it consists of eight practice groups with more than 120 radiology centres across the country.

- Sonic Healthcare Australia Clinical Services. This division delivers general practice medicine and corporate medical services, operating in partnership with more than 2000 independent general practitioners across more than 200 medical centres. This division includes IPN medical centres, Sonic HealthPlus and Australian Skin Cancer Clinics.

The company was a beneficiary of the COVID pandemic owing to demand for PCR testing, which was provided by approximately 60 of its labs globally. It saw huge revenue boosts in laboratory business at the time, but significantly reduced demand for COVID-related services saw those revenues stabilise in FY23.

ESG performance

Sonic is on the pathway to sustainability and is transparent in its reporting and use of global standards. Its approach to sustainability has four pillars:

1. Environment — climate change and circular economy and waste

2. People — employee attraction, engagement and development; workforce health, safety and wellbeing

3. Communities — service quality and safety; access and affordability

4. Governance — ethics, integrity, compliance, privacy, information security and human rights.

Sonic's board is responsible for the oversight of the sustainability strategy and approval of the sustainability report. The risk management committee helps the board by identifying and monitoring the material ESG risks. Implementation and management of the sustainability strategy and associated policies are the responsibility of the CEO and the director of sustainability in conjunction with the sustainability steering committee, which is made up of divisional CEOs and global executive team members.

Short-term incentives for executives are linked to the company's progress on governance and sustainability objectives. These include TCFD risk assessment determining opportunities and risks relating to climate, establishing a scope 3 emissions estimation and boundary, inclusion of sustainability clauses in all significant new supplier contracts and submission of the Climate Disclosure Project questionnaire.

On the environment, the company aims to be net zero across all scopes by 2050. It has a defined net zero strategy with interim milestones to achieve this. Sonic is aligned to the Paris Agreement and the Science Based Targets initiative (SBTi) to limit temperature rises to 1.5 degrees Celsius above preindustrial levels by 2050.

Its ambition is to reduce scopes 1 and 2 GHG emissions by 43 per cent from the FY21 baseline by 2030. It will achieve this by transitioning to renewable energy sources and reducing its GHG emissions progressively.

Sonic targets obtaining 80 per cent of energy from renewable sources by 2030. Because of Australia's heavy reliance on fossil fuels 56 per cent of Sonic's scope 2 GHG emissions are attributable to Australia despite its accounting for only about one-third of the global business. To manage this, Sonic has been negotiating contracts to increase renewable energy purchased across its large Australian usage sites. At the time of writing, 30 per cent of all its Australian energy consumption was from certified renewable sources and it is contracted to increase this percentage by 10 per cent per annum, which means that by 2030 it will reach 100 per cent. Since 1 January 2023 100 per cent of its German operation energy consumption has been from certified renewable sources. Sonic's operations in the US, the UK and Europe are in the process of reviewing best renewable energy options in their regions so Sonic can reach its 2030 target of 80 per cent energy coming from certified renewable sources globally.

It achieved a 10 per cent reduction in GHG emissions in FY23 compared to the FY21 baseline through a variety of methods. These include:

- investing in energy efficiency measures

- optimising onsite energy generation and storage (via solar power)

- increasing its use of hybrid/electric vehicles in its fleet over time until it completes the conversion of the global fleet by 2040

- reducing waste to landfill by 10 per cent by FY26.

It is being more careful in separating clinical (contaminated) waste, which constitutes about 15 per cent of waste, from nonclinical waste. Through education it is improving.

FY23 saw Sonic undertake a qualitative TCFD disclosure and complete an estimate of scope 3 emissions. It has mapped out the different categories within scope 3 and assigned a GHG estimation to each. More than 80 per cent of FY23 GHG emissions are scope 3, 50 per cent of which was sourced from purchased goods and services. This work will inform the company's climate risk management priorities and will aid in disclosures for existing and future reporting requirements. In FY22 Sonic undertook a materiality assessment considering a range of stakeholders to determine key risks. These were cross-checked against SASB industry peers to determine alignment and this process will continue in a targeted way.

A key plank of Sonic's sustainable policy is sustainable procurement. It has a supplier policy that outlines expectations, including suppliers setting credible emissions-reduction targets aligned with the Paris Agreement and SBTi. Suppliers must abide by the standards set out in the policy if they want to enter into contracts with Sonic. Compliance is monitored through regular reviews, and work is being done to formalise the onboarding process and assurance program to capture sustainability standards — this is expected to go live in FY25.

Sonic maps its sustainability efforts to relevant SDGs. It has a modern slavery framework and produces an annual modern slavery statement. Its annual sustainability report is comprehensive. The company has a raft of policies to support its sustainability efforts and policies on labour standards and human rights, diversity, modern slavery and suppliers. It reports in alignment with the GRI Standards.

Scenario analysis across a range of possible climate scenarios to capture opportunities and threats to the business. Currently the supplier policy is applied only to new, sizable suppliers; I'd like to see it adopted across all suppliers, new and existing, large and small. Given the supplier policy was put in place only in FY23, perhaps this will happen over time. Sonic is not a signatory to the UN Global Compact.

ESG risks	ESG measured	Assessment		Result
ESG exposure	ESG risk rating assessment			✓
	ESG exposure risk classification	Low		✓
	ESG risk exposure score	32.05		—
	ESG excess exposure score	(1.95)		✓
	ESG risk score momentum	0.39		X
ESG sub-industry risk	ESG sub-industry rank	11/111		✓
	ESG risk compared to sub-industry peers	(4.41)		✓
	ESG risk beta	0.94		✓
Management of ESG risk	Management of ESG risks score	45.34		—
	Classification of management of ESG risks	Average		—
	ESG risk management score momentum	(0.27)		X
Company controversy	Level of company controversy exposure	Low		✓
	Notable ESG issues	Business ethics		

Carbon emissions	Measured risks	Assessment	Result
	Carbon overall risk	Negligible	✓
	Carbon overall risk score	0	✓
	Carbon total emissions, scopes 1, 2 and 3	113,268.00	—
	Carbon level of involvement	0	✓
	Level of fossil fuel involvement	0%	✓
	Carbon intensity, scopes 1, 2 and 3	16.92	✓

Nanosonics Limited

ASX code: NAN   www.nanosonics.com.au

Market capitalisation:	$13 733.41 million
Sector:	Healthcare
Morningstar Sustainalytics peer group classification:	Medical Supplies

Environmental risk score		Social risk score		Governance risk score	
1.82	✓	10.38	–	6.79	✓

View: The company's ESG agenda is still in its early days, with no net zero commitment and no decarbonisation pathway, but in 2023 work began on understanding its GHG emissions.

History/background

Nanosonics is an Australian company that manufactures and distributes innovative cleaning solutions for medical devices. It also conducts research into developing commercial products for infection control and decontamination. Its focus is on preventing the transmission of infections through appropriate disinfection of medical devices, primarily ultrasound probes and related accessories.

Its flagship product is the trophon® device, which disinfects ultrasound probes via an automated closed system. Nanosonics says that at its heart trophon is a sustainable cleaning solution that eliminates reliance on toxic chemicals and large quantities of water in the cleaning phase. trophon® uses hydrogen peroxide disinfectant, and the by-products of the disinfection process are environmentally friendly oxygen and water. At the end of its life approximately 80 per cent of the dismantled device (based on total weight) is recycled.

Nanosonics is in the process of creating a new cleaning technology, Nanosonics CORIS®, for cleaning endoscopes, which is especially challenging due to the small size of the instrument. Nanosonics' solution provides an automated cleaning process that can handle small and large channels, including areas that cannot be effectively brushed manually. The efficacy of manual cleaning depends heavily on the individual technician, and research suggests that despite regular cleaning, endoscopes risk persistent contamination, heightening the risk of patient infection. In essence, then, the new product will help manage infection control through an automated cleaning process.

ESG performance

Nanosonics manages ESG through four pillars:

- Communities — includes product safety and quality

- Governance — includes labour, environmental and social practices in the supply chain, business ethics and ethical marketing

- Environment — labour, environmental and social practices in the supply chain; energy, waste management and climate change; and responsible product stewardship

- People and culture — work, health and safety; talent, recruitment and retention.

It has undertaken a materiality assessment under the guidance of an external consultant in alignment with GRI and SASB standards. The results are mapped under each of the four pillars and are then monitored and periodically refreshed.

The board is responsible for providing strategic guidance and oversight of ESG issues. The sustainability committee is responsible for managing ESG-related issues throughout the company and is supported by the community engagement committee.

The code of conduct and ethics drives ESG initiatives across the workforce. Environmental and other ESG impacts are captured and monitored with the objective of minimising adverse outcomes.

Nanosonics reports that it recognises the importance of strong policies on climate change, including reducing GHG emissions, reducing landfill waste (especially hazardous and chemical waste) and managing water responsibly. It aims to reduce the company's environmental footprint by using recyclable and reusable materials where possible, responsibly sourcing raw materials and minimising waste by prevention and recycling. It has joined APCO and seeks to align with that organisation's 2025 target, which is 100 per cent reusable, recyclable or compostable packaging. To that end it has determined its sustainable packaging strategy and incorporated this into new product development. In FY24 it aims to introduce ESG factors into the new supplier process, optimise materials in packaging and cease using 'chemicals of concern' such as PVC.

Nanosonics has spent time defining its climate change risks, and seeks to establish a set of targets for emissions reduction and develop a strategy for GHG emissions in FY24. It aims to gain an understanding of scopes 1, 2 and 3 emissions and to demonstrate an improvement in all three scopes. Its FY23 sustainability work shows its biggest GHG emissions are in scope 3.

Other projects include developing a supplier code of conduct, diverting 55 per cent of waste to recycling, adhering to APCO 2025, and working on modern slavery and a reconciliation action plan. It is mapping its activities to relevant SDGs.

It has set no targets or benchmarks on GHG emissions yet. It would be good to see it undertake analysis across several climate change scenarios, and set out a pathway to decarbonisation across all three scopes. It is not clear whether Nanosonics endorses the Paris Agreement or seeks alignment with SBTi. It acknowledges that climate change is a threat and that it has a part to play in GHG reduction, but is not clear about its commitment to net zero. It would be good to see more granular information across scopes 1, 2 and 3 to understand where the GHG emissions are being generated and details on plans for reducing them. It is not a signatory to the UN Global Compact.

ESG risks	ESG measured	Assessment	Result
ESG Exposure	ESG risk rating assessment	▮▮▮▮☐	✓
	ESG exposure risk classification	Low	✓
	ESG risk exposure score	30.0	—
	ESG excess exposure score	1.00	X
	ESG risk score momentum	(0.09)	✓
ESG sub-industry risk	ESG sub-industry rank	34/59	—
	ESG risk compared to sub-industry peers	0.95	X
	ESG risk beta	1.03	X
Management of ESG risk	Management of ESG risks score	38.97	—
	Classification of management of ESG risks	Average	—
	ESG risk management score momentum	5.20	✓
Company controversy	Level of company controversy exposure	None	✓
	Notable ESG issues	Product governance	

Carbon emissions	Measured risks	Assessment	Result
	Carbon overall risk	Negligible	✓
	Carbon overall risk score	0	✓
	Carbon total emissions, scopes 1, 2 and 3	2,113,19	✓
	Carbon level of involvement	0	✓
	Level of fossil fuel involvement	0%	✓
	Carbon intensity, scopes 1, 2 and 3	28.30	✓

Ansell Limited

ASX code: ANN   www.ansell.com

Market capitalisation:	$2974.26 million
Sector:	Healthcare
Morningstar Sustainalytics peer group classification:	Medical Supplies

Environmental risk score		Social risk score		Governance risk score	
0.88	✓	8.63	–	5.89	✓

View: Ansell is committed to net zero within its own operation by 2040, but scope 3 remains the final frontier for this company.

History/background

Ansell is a global company with a 130-year history. It has corporate headquarters in Australia, Belgium, the USA and Malaysia and more than 14 000 employees in over 55 countries, but it is legally based in Australia.

It operates across two major business units: Healthcare Global and Industrial Global. Healthcare Global business units specialise in manufacturing a wide variety of health and safety solutions, especially in personal protective equipment (PPE) and medical gloves. The Industrial Global business unit produces and sells chemical protective clothing designed for a range of industrial applications. It is known for its innovative product range, made possible by its commitment to and investment in research and development, including sustainable PPE solutions such as HyFlex® 11-842 gloves, made with recyclable materials, and GAMMEX® Non-Latex Sensitive, a non-latex glove. Each product in this range is accompanied by its own fact sheet, providing information outlining its environmental benefits.

ESG performance

Ansell acknowledges that sustainability has become an important differentiator. Its mission is to ensure that everything it does begins and ends with safety, and that extends to protecting the world we live in. It divides sustainability into two main areas: people and planet.

People covers safe and inclusive workplaces and community support. It aligns this to three SDGs: good health, decent work and economic growth, and reduced inequalities.

Planet encompasses reduction of environmental impact across its operations through innovative solutions, including in energy and emissions, climate and biodiversity risk, water and waste. These are aligned to four SDGs: clean water and sanitation, affordable and clean energy, responsible consumption and production, and climate action.

It has four sustainability work streams that encompass people, planet and product (such as sustainable packaging), and sustainable communications and training.

The company has committed to GHG reduction targets that are science based and in line with the Paris Agreement for its scopes 1 and 2 emissions. Its ambition is to deliver net zero by 2040, and it has outlined in detail both the plan and how it is tracking against the plan. It has set a target of 42 per cent reduction off its FY20 baseline, and it plans to achieve this through a combination of decarbonisation activities, such as progressing its use of renewable energy to 100 per cent in its operations, and using carbon offsets for the residual emissions, which it has set at less than 10 per cent.

Ansell acknowledges that scope 3 emissions-reduction targets are important, as scope 3 make up the bulk of the company's carbon footprint — approximately 80 per cent of GHG emissions on the FY20 baseline. However, its complex supply chain requires it to undertake engagement work with its suppliers to ascertain what those emissions are. It is seeking to formalise its engagement approach with its suppliers to determine decarbonisation expectations. It will be interesting to see how the company approaches a reduction in GHG emissions for scope 3.

Ansell also seeks to introduce in all manufacturing plants certified energy management systems including zero waste to landfill, reduction of fossil fuel material, increasing recycled and bio-based materials, and making all packaging material recyclable, compostable or reusable. It also seeks to reduce water usage by 35 per cent by 2025 off the FY20 baseline.

The company has completed a climate risk assessment and scenario modelling. A detailed report tracks key performance indicators for people and planet. Comprehensive information on Ansell's approach to managing all material topics is provided in a separate sustainability management approach report. Its environmental sustainability policy sets out the company's commitment to sustainability, including the management of physical and transitional risks and opportunities associated with climate change.

The CEO and executive leadership team are accountable for the company's sustainability strategy and provide regular updates and recommendations to the board, which has ultimate responsibility for both. Further support is provided by the sustainability and risk committee, which monitors the effectiveness of Ansell's policies and programs, and the audit and compliance committee, which ensures disclosures are in alignment with TCFD. The executive team's remuneration is linked to ESG metrics. The labour rights committee is responsible for managing modern slavery and labour rights risks in the company's own operations and across the supply chain.

Ansell has made many sustainability-related commitments including membership of the UN Global Compact and full alignment with TCFD recommendations. Its sustainability report conforms with GRI Standards. It has committed to align with climate groups RE100 and EP100. Its approach is transparent, ambitious and comprehensive.

Finally, it has developed Ansell Earth, which delivers product life cycle pillars on PPE, material, manufacturing, packaging, use and end of use, providing information on sustainability at each stage to help in the achievement of its sustainability goals.

ESG risks	ESG measured	Assessment	Result
ESG exposure	ESG risk rating assessment	▮▮▮▮▯	✓
	ESG exposure risk classification	Low	✓
	ESG risk exposure score	30.20	—
	ESG excess exposure score	1.20	X
	ESG risk score momentum	(0.70)	✓
ESG sub-industry risk	ESG sub-industry rank	12/59	✓
	ESG risk compared to sub-industry peers	(2.63)	✓
	ESG risk beta	1.04	X
Management of ESG risk	Management of ESG risks score	52.03	—
	Classification of management of ESG risks	Strong	✓
	ESG risk management score momentum	3.02	✓
Company controversy	Level of company controversy exposure	Moderate	—
	Notable ESG issues	Product governance	

Carbon emissions	Measured risks	Assessment	Result
	Carbon overall risk	Negligible	✓
	Carbon overall risk score	0	✓
	Carbon total emissions, scopes 1, 2 and 3	276 740.18	—
	Carbon level of involvement	0	✓
	Level of fossil fuel involvement	0%	✓
	Carbon intensity, scopes 1, 2 and 3	138.88	—

Ebos Group Limited

ASX code: EBO
www.ebosgroup.com

Market capitalisation:	$6601.64 million
Sector:	Healthcare
Morningstar Sustainalytics peer group classification:	Medical Distribution

Environmental risk score		Social risk score		Governance risk score	
2.93	✓	6.69	✓	6.72	✓

View: GHG emissions data is not comprehensively reported and the company's decarbonisation ambitions are unclear.

History/background

EBOS has a history that dates back to 1922 when, as the Early Brothers Trading Company, based in Christchurch, it sold lamps for horse-drawn carriages. Over the years it branched out to sell a variety of products, including healthcare supplies. In 1954 the company changed its name to Early Brothers Dental and Surgical Supplies and narrowed its focus to healthcare. The company listed on the New Zealand Stock Exchange in 1967 and rebranded as EBOS Group Limited in 1986. It entered the Australian market in 1996 and listed on the ASX in 2013.

EBOS Group, with headquarters in Australia and New Zealand, is a diversified business that distributes wholesale healthcare products to healthcare providers such as hospitals and pharmacies. It distributes consumer healthcare and beauty products such as over-the-counter vitamins and medicines, personal care items and beauty products, and supplies an array of animal care products to veterinary clinics and pet owners, including animal pharmaceuticals and nutritional products. Part of its competitive advantage is the wide variety of products it distributes through a network that allows it to reach a diversified customer base efficiently. Some of its success is attributable to successful strategic acquisitions that have complemented the existing product base and helped strengthen its market position.

ESG performance

On sustainability EBOS is making progress towards integrating ESG into its business strategy but is not as advanced as some of its competitors.

The board has ultimate responsibility for sustainability, overseeing the ESG framework and strategy including climate-related risks and opportunities. The CEO and executive leadership team are responsible for delivering the ESG strategy. Since 2020 the board has been supported by the ESG steering committee, made up of executive leaders who are responsible for delivering the group's ESG strategy, benchmarking and evaluating performance and emerging risks and opportunities. The committee was expanded in FY23 and includes representatives from the healthcare, animal care and medical technology teams. The ESG steering committee reports regularly to the board.

EBOS has undertaken a materiality assessment of its sustainability issues, guided by the AA1000 Stakeholder Engagement Standard, identifying 20 material ESG topics separated into five pillars:

1. health and animal care partners

2. consumers and patients

3. community and environment

4. our people

5. responsible business.

The group plans to make comprehensive climate-related disclosures in 2024 to comply with New Zealand external reporting board requirements. It references the importance of limiting global warming to 1.5 degrees Celsius above preindustrial levels and is on a pathway to becoming an accredited carbon neutral organisation. In FY23 its scope 1 emissions were net zero through the use of carbon credits to offset its GHG emissions. However, it plans to reduce these emissions through the use of renewable energy and has five sites generating energy from solar power.

FY23 saw the launch of its ethical sourcing strategy, which is supported by a supplier code of conduct outlining expectations for suppliers who seek to partner with EBOS. It is committed to reducing plastic waste and has a sustainable packaging strategy that supports the Australian national packaging targets for 2025. EBOS plans for all grocery brands to be packaged using reusable, recyclable or compostable materials.

The company is working on data collection and improved management systems to capture energy, water and carbon data, but it is a long way from a comprehensive data inventory. It reports on GRI, TCFD and SASB standards, but there is no reporting on scope 3 emissions, no net zero commitment across scopes 1, 2 and 3, no baseline, no clarity on whether it is planning to conform to the Paris Agreement and SBTi, and no pathway to net zero. Further, no assessment has been made of the risks and opportunities for the business across a range of climate change scenarios.

EBOS needs much more clarity and ambition on GHG emission commitments. It is starting to build some momentum in ESG by gathering data, setting up policies and committees and providing some reporting, but it still has a way to go to catch up to the leaders in this space. It doesn't seem to be involved in ESG-related memberships and associations such as the UN Global Compact that would demonstrate a commitment and accountability. It may get there but it is not there yet, which is probably why it ranks 21 of 47 in its sub-industry.

ESG risks	ESG measured	Assessment	Result
ESG exposure	ESG risk rating assessment		✓
	ESG exposure risk classification	Low	✓
	ESG risk exposure score	26.20	✓
	ESG excess exposure score	0.20	X
	ESG risk score momentum	0.36	X
ESG sub-industry risk	ESG sub-industry rank	21/47	–
	ESG risk compared to sub-industry peers	(0.30)	✓
	ESG risk beta	1.01	X
Management of ESG risk	Management of ESG risks score	39.50	–
	Classification of management of ESG risks	Average	–
	ESG risk management score momentum	4.17	✓
Company controversy	Level of company controversy exposure	Low	✓
	Notable ESG issues	Product governance	

Carbon emissions	Measured risks	Assessment	Result
	Carbon overall risk	Medium	–
	Carbon overall risk score	11.22	–
	Carbon total emissions, scopes 1, 2 and 3	39 560.88	✓
	Carbon level of involvement	0	✓
	Level of fossil fuel involvement	0%	✓
	Carbon intensity, scopes 1, 2 and 3	5.63	✓

Concluding remarks

The four companies chosen in this sector were all assessed as exhibiting low ESG risks. Each, however, is at a different stage on its ESG journey. Nanosonics and Ansell operate in the same industry subgroup, Medical Supplies, whereas EBOS falls into Medical Distribution and Sonic Healthcare, Medical Services. All have similar risk exposures although EBOS is marginally lower. On management of ESG risks only Ansell was assessed as having a strong management approach, with the other three companies assessed as average. Sonic Healthcare's management score was the next highest in the cohort, with stronger ESG management capabilities than either Nanosonics or EBOS.

All companies report to globally recognised frameworks such as the GRI Standards. Ansell and Sonic declared their alignment to the Paris Agreement target of limiting global warming to 1.5 degrees, but the views and commitment of Nanosonics and EBOS were opaque. They need to provide clarity on this important issue. Only Ansell is a signatory to the UN Global Compact.

Ansell has progressed farthest in providing comprehensive data and clear plans in relation to its decarbonisation activities.

Sonic Healthcare was assessed as having the lowest environmental risk, followed by Ansell, with EBOS having the highest, but really the environmental risks across these companies were exceptionally low. Sonic had the highest social risk closely followed by Nanosonics, and EBOS had the lowest. On governance all did well, demonstrating robust governance processes, but Ansell had the lowest risk followed by EBOS.

Nanosonics, Ansell and Sonic Healthcare were all assessed as having negligible carbon risks; EBOS was slightly higher at medium risk. Only EBOS had estimated data, with the others providing reported data for scopes 1 and 2. Sonic Healthcare was the only company reporting scope 3 data (as of 2021).

Ansell had the highest outright emissions across scopes 1, 2 and 3; Nanosonics had the lowest.

The two companies that have progressed furthest across a range of sustainability metrics are Ansell and Sonic Healthcare. EBOS has progressed least but is building out its capability. Sonic had the highest ranking in the sub-peer group, Ansell had the best sustainability ranking in the healthcare sector based on lowest overall ESG risks followed by EBOS, Sonic Healthcare then Nanosonics.

8. Industrials

This sector comprises companies that operate across a number of broad segments, including capital goods, construction, commercial and professional services, and transportation and logistics. Industrials captures the part of the economy that produces and distributes capital goods. Capital goods are products used to create other goods and services, such as machinery, equipment and vehicles. The industrials sector is often associated with manufacturing, engineering and the construction industries, and with airports, toll roads and marine ports.

The sector is an important driver of economic growth. These companies can be the beneficiaries of infrastructure development, urbanisation and technology. Many are adopting sustainable practices and looking to leverage technology in order to improve efficiency and overall customer experience while reducing their negative environmental and social impacts.

This sector can be sensitive to economic volatility, as it tends to be capital and maintenance intensive; it can also be vulnerable to operational and technical risks. The companies included in the cohort operate across a diverse range of subsectors including highways and railroads, electronic equipment, marine ports, airports and business support services.

Transurban Group Limited

ASX code: TCL

www.transurban.com

Market capitalisation:	$39 929.76 million
Sector:	Industrials
Morningstar Sustainalytics peer group classification:	Highways and Railroads

Environmental risk score		Social risk score		Governance risk score	
1.77	✓	3.15	✓	3.89	✓

View: Transurban has impressive sustainability chops and aims to achieve net zero across all three scopes by 2050.

History/background

Transurban Group Limited (TCL) manages and develops urban toll road networks in Australia, Canada and the United States. It is one of the largest stocks in the industrial sector of the ASX 200.

The company was founded in March 1996 to operate Melbourne's CityLink contract, which connects three of the city's major freeways. It has since expanded its portfolio to include 18 motorways in Australia and four in North America. Some of its major assets are:

- CityLink in Melbourne
- M2, M5, M7, M8, NorthConnex and Cross City Tunnel in Sydney
- Gateway, Logan, AirportlinkM7, Clem7, Go Between Bridge and Legacy Way in Brisbane
- 495, 95 and 395 Express Lanes and 95 Express Lanes Extension in Greater Washington
- A25 motorway in Montreal.

Transurban's business model is based on developing, operating and maintaining toll roads that provide faster, safer and more reliable travel for customers. It collects toll revenue from its roads; influencing factors include traffic volume, toll price, economic conditions and customer behaviour. It also invests in new projects and acquisitions that enhance its existing network or create new opportunities for growth.

Transurban's competitive advantage is its extensive experience and expertise in toll road management, its access to high-quality traffic data and modelling, its strong relationships with governments and communities, and its diversified and resilient revenue streams. It faces competition from other infrastructure investors and operators, as well as alternative modes of transport and emerging technologies. However, Transurban has demonstrated its ability to innovate and adapt to changing customer needs and market conditions, as well as to deliver social and environmental benefits through its toll road projects. For example, it builds bike paths, regenerates land alongside roads to improve wildlife habitat, and provides green spaces and public art to benefit communities affected by their proximity to major transport routes.

ESG performance

Transurban may seem like an unlikely candidate for a sustainability portfolio, given road transport's role as a major source of GHG emissions as well as air and noise pollution. With the increasing take-up of electric vehicles, fossil fuel pollution should diminish, but in the meantime there's no avoiding the fact that Transurban's financial success is bound up with increased road use, which is a fundamental challenge when assessing sustainability. Despite this paradox, the company has developed a comprehensive approach to sustainability.

Transurban has a four-pillar approach:

- People — make life better

- Planet — use resources wisely

- Places — build better transport

- Partnerships — lead and unite.

Its sustainability strategy is aligned with the UN's SDGs. It has identified nine SDGs that are most relevant to its business and reports on how it contributes to these goals.

Transurban provides a climate change framework that outlines its actions and targets on the path to achieving net zero emissions across all scopes by 2050. It is awaiting SBTi validation for its net zero 2050 target.

It aims to reduce its scopes 1 and 2 emissions by 50 per cent from the FY19 baseline by 2030. Its scope 3 emissions are split into purchased goods and services and major projects. For purchased goods and services it seeks to reduce emissions by 22 per cent from the FY19 baseline and for major projects it aims to achieve a 55 per cent reduction in emissions. These targets have been validated by the SBTi, consistent with the Paris Agreement. Transurban was the first top-20 ASX-listed company to have its 2030 emissions-reduction targets validated by the SBTi.

To achieve these goals it has committed to a number of activities across scopes 1, 2 and 3.

On scopes 1 and 2, as of FY23 it is operating with 80 per cent renewable energy, including installing on-site solar panels, optimising tunnel ventilation and upgrading to LED lighting that together have reduced electricity demand by 20 344mWh per annum.

To hit its 2030 milestones, it plans to transition its fleet to zero-emissions vehicles and encourage contractors to do the same.

On scope 3, as of FY23 it has established mandatory infrastructure sustainability ratings for all Australian projects, reducing emissions across nine projects. It has engaged with its major suppliers on decarbonisation and GHG reporting and targets. This has resulted in 32 of its largest 100 suppliers adopting GHG reduction targets and 26 per cent of suppliers sourcing renewable energy. Further, it is collaborating with MECLA on decarbonising the Australian construction industry. To achieve 2030 milestones, it plans to encourage suppliers to transition to renewable energy and set science-based targets for GHG reductions, ideally to net zero. Major projects will specify increased renewable energy, reduced fossil fuel use and increased usage of low-carbon materials. Finally, it is looking to collaborate with major suppliers on decarbonisation of the supply chain.

Transurban tested its resilience to climate change across a range of climate-related scenarios considering physical and transition risks. The approach it took was based on the International Energy Agency's four scenarios, which assess the potential impacts of climate change on assets, operations, financial performance and strategy. It evaluated the possible impacts of each scenario and determined a range of actions it needed to take to mitigate the risks.

Transurban is involved with various partners and associations with direct links to improving sustainability including the UN Global Compact, the SBTi, the Climate Leaders Coalition (as a founding member) and the Infrastructure Sustainability Council of Australia (ISCA). It has achieved Infrastructure Sustainability ratings for several of its projects, including NorthConnex, West Gate Tunnel and 395 Express Lanes.

Transurban partners with various other organisations and initiatives that support its sustainability and decarbonisation goals. These include the Australian Renewable Energy Agency (ARENA), the Electric Vehicle Council, the Clean Energy Finance Corporation (CEFC) and the Global Road Safety Partnership (GRSP), which is a network of government, civil society and private sector organisations that work together to improve road safety and reduce road trauma.

Internally, it also recognises reporting frameworks such as GRI, SASB and TCFD to communicate its sustainability performance and strategy to its stakeholders.

ESG risks	ESG measured	Assessment	Result
ESG exposure	ESG risk rating assessment		✓
	ESG exposure risk classification	Negligible	✓
	ESG risk exposure score	21.05	✓
	ESG excess exposure score	0.05	X
	ESG risk score momentum	(0.22)	✓
ESG sub-industry risk	ESG sub-industry rank	12/53	✓
	ESG risk compared to sub-industry peers	(2.47)	✓
	ESG risk beta	1.00	—
Management of ESG risk	Management of ESG risks score	60.92	—
	Classification of management of ESG risks	Strong	✓
	ESG risk management score momentum	1.08	✓
Company controversy	Level of company controversy exposure	Low	✓
	Notable ESG issues	Product governance	

Carbon emissions	Measured risks	Assessment	Result
	Carbon overall risk	Negligible	✓
	Carbon overall risk score	0	✓
	Carbon total emissions, scopes 1, 2 and 3	631 051.00	X
	Carbon level of involvement	0	✓
	Level of fossil fuel involvement	0%	✓
	Carbon intensity, scopes 1, 2 and 3	298.17	—

Atlas Arteria Limited

ASX code: ALX   www.atlasarteria.com

Market capitalisation:	$8414.84 million
Sector:	Industrials
Morningstar Sustainalytics peer group classification:	Highways and Railroads

Environmental risk score		Social risk score		Governance risk score	
0.79	✓	2.64	✓	3.88	✓

View: Atlas Asteria Limited has a pathway to net zero for scopes 1 and 2, but has yet to set scope 3 targets.

History/background

Atlas Arteria Ltd is a global owner, operator and developer of toll roads, with a portfolio of five toll roads in France, Germany and the United States — namely, ADELAC, APRR, Chicago Skyway, Dulles Greenway and Warnow Tunnel.

It was created out of the reorganisation of Macquarie Infrastructure Group into two separate ASX-listed toll road groups in 2010 — Atlas Arteria and Macquarie Infrastructure Corporation (now Macquarie Infrastructure Holdings, LLC). Atlas Arteria was externally managed by Macquarie Fund Advisors Pty Limited until 31 March 2019, when it transitioned to its current management team.

The company's perceived competitive advantage is its diversified portfolio of high-quality toll roads in attractive markets, its strong operational and financial performance, its disciplined capital allocation and its focus on sustainability.

ESG performance

Like Transurban, its dependence on road transport makes Atlas an odd fit for this book, but again an active sustainability program and transition to environmentally better modes of transport make its inclusion less surprising.

On sustainability the company has four priority areas:

1. Safety — for employees, contractors and customers

2. Customers and community — customer satisfaction and engagement, fair pricing, community engagement

3. People—health and wellbeing, an inclusive and engaged workforce

4. Environment—GHG emissions and climate change, protecting the natural environment.

These priority areas are supported by four business fundamentals: good governance, an ethical culture, an emphasis on sustainable growth, and innovation and technology.

Every two years the company conducts a materiality assessment to identify the most significant environmental, social and governance risks and opportunities for its business and stakeholders. The materiality assessment involves a desktop review of industry trends, peer benchmarking, stakeholder engagement and internal workshops. The results are presented in the company's sustainability framework, which guides its strategy and reporting.

It identifies 16 material topics, the largest risks being climate change, cybersecurity, and the regulatory and political environment.

The company faces physical and transition risks and opportunities from the impacts of climate change on its toll roads, such as extreme weather events, changes in policy, technology and customer behaviour, and potential litigation. It has analysed and assessed the physical and transition risks and opportunities for its toll roads in different climate scenarios, using the TCFD framework and International Energy Agency (IEA) scenarios. The company found its toll roads to be resilient to the physical impacts of climate change but recognises it may face some transition risks from changes in policy, technology and customer behaviour. It is developing mitigation strategies and action plans to address these risks and opportunities.

Atlas Arteria aims to achieve net zero emissions from its operations by 2050. The pathway to achieving this includes a reduction in scopes 1 and 2 emissions of 25 per cent by FY25 against the FY19 baseline and 46 per cent by 2030. However, these ambitions do not take into account the recently acquired 66.7 per cent majority interest stake in Chicago Skyway. A scope 3 baseline upstream emissions assessment has been undertaken for FY19 for wholly owned businesses and corporations, primarily capturing emissions generated by customer use of its roads. As yet there are no targets for scope 3.

Altas Arteria has committed to reducing its emissions as of FY22, the most recent data available since at the time of writing the FY23 sustainability report is yet to be released. It achieved a reduction in scopes 1 and 2 emissions of 9.8 per cent against the FY21 baseline. This was achieved through energy savings from eliminating inefficient air conditioning equipment, an LED replacement program, energy-efficient equipment upgrades, the use of renewable energy, including commissioning a solar farm near the A19, and building a low-carbon culture among employees. It has a 23 per cent conversion to electric vehicles within its light vehicle fleet, compared to 4 per cent in FY21. Its ambition is to reach 75 per cent EVs by FY25. It also has 100 per cent EV charging stations at its 98 service areas, which means there are now 700 charging points for customers across the network, reducing range anxiety. It has completed 12 wildlife crossings and is on track to deliver a further seven by FY23.

On governance, the board is responsible for setting the strategic direction and approving policies and frameworks for sustainability. The board delegates the day-to-day management of sustainability to the CEO and the senior leadership team, which consists of the chief financial officer, the chief operating officer, the general counsel and company secretary and the head of investor relations. The team monitors the performance and progress of sustainability initiatives and reports regularly to the board. The board is further supported by the TCFD working group, which focuses on climate-related issues. The working group includes representatives from key business areas across the company and provides a forum for analysing and evaluating climate-related issues, ensuring their clear communication from the business functions through to management and the board.

To date Atlas Arteria does not use GRI but it does report on sustainability against SASB standards. It is not a signatory to the UN Global Compact.

The company is a member of the ISCA, the Global Road Safety Partnership (GRSP) and the International Road Federation (IRF).

ESG risks	ESG measured	Assessment	Result
ESG exposure	ESG risk rating assessment		✓
	ESG exposure risk classification	Negligible	✓
	ESG risk exposure score	20.60	✓
	ESG excess exposure score	(0.40)	✓
	ESG risk score momentum	(1.32)	✓
ESG sub-industry risk	ESG sub-industry rank	6/53	✓
	ESG risk compared to sub-industry peers	(3.98)	✓
	ESG risk beta	0.98	✓
Management of ESG risk	Management of ESG risks score	67.57	—
	Classification of management of ESG risks	Strong	✓
	ESG risk management score momentum	9.67	✓
Company controversy	Level of company controversy exposure	None	✓
	Notable ESG issues	Community relations	

Carbon emissions	Measured risks	Assessment	Result
	Carbon overall risk	Negligible	✓
	Carbon overall risk score	0	✓
	Carbon total emissions, scopes 1, 2 and 3	2 196 276.00	X
	Carbon level of involvement	0	✓
	Level of fossil fuel involvement	0%	✓
	Carbon intensity, scopes 1, 2 and 3	30 090.01	X

Imdex Limited

ASX code: ANN   www.imdexlimited.com

Market capitalisation:	$924.09 million
Sector:	Industrials
Morningstar Sustainalytics peer group classification:	Electronic Equipment

Environmental risk score		Social risk score		Governance risk score	
3.29	✓	3.90	✓	4.71	✓

View: Imdex is a sustainability laggard, with little evidence of initiatives aimed at reducing emissions or using internationally recognised frameworks, which makes it hard to assess.

History/background

Imdex Limited is an Australian mining technology company that provides integrated solutions to the minerals industry. It develops and delivers drilling optimisation products, cloud-connected rock knowledge sensors, and data and analytics to improve the process of identifying and extracting mineral resources for drilling contractors and resource companies globally. The company's technology enables faster, safer and more efficient drilling operations, and better decision making.

Pilbara Gold NL was founded in 1980 as a drilling fluids company and was listed on the ASX in 1987. Over the years it has expanded its product offering and geographic footprint through acquisitions and organic growth. In 2003 the company acquired AMC, a leading drilling fluids and equipment provider, and in 2007 it acquired REFLEX, a leading downhole instrumentation and data management provider. It also established joint ventures and partnerships with other technology companies such as ioGlobal, Rock Knowledge and Flexidrill. The company rebranded itself as Imdex in 2017 to reflect its integrated mining technology solutions.

Imdex operates through two brands: AMC and REFLEX. AMC provides drilling fluids, drilling equipment, and environmental solutions to optimise drilling performance and reduce costs. REFLEX provides advanced downhole instrumentation, data management solutions, and analytical software for geological modelling to enhance rock knowledge and data quality. The company's products and services cover the entire mining value chain, from exploration to extraction.

Imdex's competitive advantage lies in its innovative and integrated mining technology solutions that deliver real-time data and insights to its customers. The company's solutions are cloud-connected, interoperable and scalable, enabling seamless data transfer and analysis across different platforms and devices. The company's solutions are also driller-operable, user-friendly and reliable, reducing the need for specialised personnel and equipment on site. The company has a global presence and a loyal customer base, with more than 6000 IMDEXHUB-IQ™ users and over 15 000 instruments deployed worldwide. The company invests in research and development and collaborates with industry partners and associations to stay ahead of market trends and customer needs.

ESG performance

This company does not have a comprehensive sustainability report or a clear alignment with any of the widely recognised sustainability standards or frameworks. It is therefore difficult to assess its sustainability performance and progress in a consistent or comparable way.

Imdex has established an ESG committee endorsed by the board, and in FY21 it completed a materiality assessment to determine material ESG topics across the business. The topics identified were:

- People — ensuring a safe and inclusive global workplace
- Innovation — driving the sustainability of the global minerals industry via technology
- Environment — contributing to a low emissions future
- Society — supporting economic developments and local communities
- Governance — upholding ethical and sustainable business practices.

The company has a range of products, services and embedded policies that support the sustainable operations of its mining industry stakeholders. These include biodegradable drilling fluids, operational efficiencies, a conflict-of-interest policy, ethics training, anti-bribery and anti-corruption training, a risk, compliance and legal framework, an employee code of conduct, a speak-up policy and information security management.

While the board of directors has ultimate responsibility for the sustainability policy, it is supported by the ESG committee, which works with other committees and focuses on enhancing disclosure, engaging stakeholders and embedding sustainability throughout the global business. In FY24 it proposes to establish a separate ESG committee reporting directly to the board.

A key objective is preparing a sustainability report in accordance with the GRI Standards within three years. It will also assess its climate risk against the TCFD recommendations.

As it stands today, however, the company falls short on a number of key metrics. For example, the company has not performed scenario analysis to evaluate the potential impacts of climate change on its business and stakeholders. Such analysis is an important and useful organisational tool for assessing the potential business implications of climate-related risks and opportunities under different future states, and to identify physical and transition risks. The findings can then be incorporated into its sustainability strategy.

The company has not explicitly aligned itself with the Paris Agreement and the SBTi. Its 2022 sustainability report contains no GHG emissions data.

Imdex's sustainability reporting appendix did map to GRI and SASB standards but the dearth of data makes it difficult to assess the company's performance and accountability for its net zero ambition.

ESG risks	ESG measured	Assessment	Result
ESG exposure	ESG risk rating assessment		✓
	ESG exposure risk classification	Low	✓
	ESG risk exposure score	21.80	✓
	ESG excess exposure score	(0.20)	✓
	ESG risk score momentum	0	—
ESG sub-industry risk	ESG sub-industry rank	28/138	✓
	ESG risk compared to sub-industry peers	(3.21)	✓
	ESG risk beta	0.99	✓
Management of ESG risk	Management of ESG risks score	46.92	—
	Classification of management of ESG risks	Average	—
	ESG risk management score momentum	0.00	—
Company controversy	Level of company controversy exposure	None	—
	Notable ESG issues	Carbon – own operations	

Carbon emissions	Measured risks	Assessment	Result
	Carbon overall risk	Medium	—
	Carbon overall risk score	10.56	—
	Carbon total emissions, scopes 1, 2 and 3	5920.11	✓
	Carbon level of involvement	0	✓
	Level of fossil fuel involvement	0%	✓
	Carbon intensity, scopes 1, 2 and 3	30.54	✓

Qube Holdings Limited

ASX code: QUB

www.qube.com.au

Market capitalisation:	$5155.30 million
Sector:	Industrials
Morningstar Sustainalytics peer group classification:	Marine Ports

Environmental risk score		Social risk score		Governance risk score	
3.48	✓	7.98	✓	4.92	✓

View: Qube is still in the process of building out ESG data, particularly for scope 3, for which data is yet to be provided.

History/background

Qube Holdings Ltd provides logistics solutions for the import and export supply chain in Australia and internationally. It operates through two core divisions: the Operating Division and a 50 per cent interest in Patrick Terminals.

The Operating Division consists of two business units: Qube Logistics & Infrastructure and Qube Ports & Bulk. Qube Logistics & Infrastructure provides road and rail transport, warehousing and distribution, container parks and related services, and intermodal logistics hubs. Qube Ports & Bulk provides port services, bulk materials handling, and transport solutions for the mining and resources sector. Patrick Terminals is a leading container terminal operator in Australia, with facilities in Brisbane, Sydney, Melbourne and Fremantle.

The company was formed in 2011 from the merger of Qube Logistics and Kaplan Equity, which were both spinoffs from the former Patrick Corporation. The merger created a diversified logistics company with a strong presence in the Australian market. The company has since expanded its operations and portfolio through acquisitions, organic growth and joint ventures.

Qube's competitive advantage lies in its integrated and innovative logistics solutions that deliver value and efficiency to its customers and stakeholders. The company's solutions are supported by its extensive network of assets, infrastructure and technology, which enables seamless and reliable data transfer and analysis across different platforms and devices. The company's solutions are tailored to the specific needs and requirements of each customer and industry, including automotive, agriculture, mining and retail. The company has a strong market position and a loyal customer base, with long-term contracts and partnerships with major importers, exporters and shipping lines. It invests in research and development and collaborates with industry associations and regulators to stay ahead of market trends and customer needs.

ESG performance

Its sustainability priorities are:

- Safety—zero harm
- Wellbeing—nurture people to allow them to reach their full potential
- Planet—net zero scope 1 emissions by 2050
- Opportunity—feed the aspirations of all
- Performance—strive to do better.

Qube completed a materiality assessment in FY22 and risks and opportunities, aligned to SDGs, were grouped into five material issues:

1. Supply chain transparency—including ESG impacts
2. Industry-leading ESG disclosures to set credible targets
3. Servicing Australia's sustainable future—transition to renewable energy, shift towards rail
4. Ensuring a successful transition for Qube's workforce
5. Building resilience in a changing global environment—including extreme weather, economic and geopolitical shocks.

It has committed to reducing scope 1 emissions by 50 per cent by FY30 against the FY18 baseline and to delivering net zero by 2050. On scope 2 emissions, it aims to power its premises with 100 per cent renewable energy by FY30. It has outlined several measures needed to achieve these targets:

- Efficiency—for example, shifting from road to rail and managing fuel via optimisation
- Technology—for example, transitioning heavy fleet to Euro 5 and 6 standards and biofuel adaptable
- Alternative fuels—for example, sourcing biofuels and commercially viable renewable fuels, electrification and hydrogen
- Renewable energy—onsite and offsite
- Carbon offsets—if required, source or generate carbon offsets.

It also provides a course of action across each sector—road, rail and premises. Qube ports and bulk facilities are compliant with ISO14001 environmental standards, and are in the process of achieving the same certification for the remaining ports and bulk and logistics sites.

Qube continues to educate senior management on climate-related issues. It has established decarbonisation KPIs for each managing director's report and has added climate-related risk and opportunities into the risk management process. Further, 90 per cent of heavy vehicles now meet Euro 5/6 standards; Qube's target is 95 per cent by FY27. It plans to convert 50 per cent of its light vehicle fleet to hybrid electric by FY27 and 70 per cent by FY30. Sixty-one of the smaller mobile assets such as forklifts have been converted to battery operation, and it will continue to transition mobile assets in FY24. Other targets include trialling alternative fuels and electrification of the fleet where it is viable. It also seeks to improve productivity by being more efficient, carrying more load by double stacking containers, using trailer combinations and route optimisation. On scope 2 it will continue to roll out rooftop solar and LED upgrades and is evaluating purchasing renewable power.

Qube also plans to improve environmental data collection in FY24, which will form the basis of its management and reporting of environmental risks and opportunities. In FY21/22 it undertook a climate-related risk assessment, explored a number of scenarios and developed a model to understand and evaluate the risks. In FY24 it plans on evolving this analysis by aligning the risk analysis with ISSB standards.

ESG risks	ESG measured	Assessment	Result
ESG exposure	ESG risk rating assessment	▰▰▰▰▱	✓
	ESG exposure risk classification	Low	✓
	ESG risk exposure score	27.00	—
	ESG excess exposure score	0.00	—
	ESG risk score momentum	0.06	X
ESG sub-industry risk	ESG sub-industry rank	20/46	—
	ESG risk compared to sub-industry peers	0.01	X
	ESG risk beta	1.00	—
Management of ESG risk	Management of ESG risks score	40.94	—
	Classification of management of ESG risks	Average	—
	ESG risk management score momentum	(0.22)	X
Company controversy	Level of company controversy exposure	Moderate	—
	Notable ESG issues	Occupational health and safety	

Carbon emissions	Measured risks	Assessment	Result
	Carbon overall risk	Negligible	✓
	Carbon overall risk score	0	✓
	Carbon total emissions, scopes 1, 2 and 3	167 649.01	—
	Carbon level of involvement	0	✓
	Level of fossil fuel involvement	0%	✓
	Carbon intensity, scopes 1, 2 and 3	119.03	—

Auckland International Airport Limited

ASX code: AIA   www.aucklandairport.co.nz

Market capitalisation:	$10 870.12 million
Sector:	Industrials
Morningstar Sustainalytics peer group classification:	Airports

Environmental risk score		Social risk score		Governance risk score	
3.51	✓	10.54	–	5.51	✓

View: Its ambitious scope 1 and 2 net zero targets lead the way, well ahead of scope 3 data collection and understanding.

History/background

Auckland International Airport Limited operates the largest and busiest airport in New Zealand, serving over 21 million passengers and more than 200 000 flights annually. The airport connects Auckland to more than 50 domestic and more than 40 international destinations, and makes a significant contribution to the New Zealand economy. The airport also owns and manages a property portfolio of more than 1500 hectares, comprising commercial, industrial, retail and hotel developments. The airport's vision is to be the hub of choice for travel, trade and tourism in Australasia.

Auckland Airport was established in 1966 as a joint venture between the Auckland City Council and the Auckland Regional Authority, with the New Zealand Government as a minority shareholder. The airport was incorporated in 1988 and listed on the New Zealand and Australian stock exchanges in 1998. It has since expanded its operations and infrastructure through acquisitions, partnerships and investments. Notable milestones include the opening of the international terminal in 1977, the domestic terminal in 1985, the second runway in 2005 and the Novotel hotel in 2011. The airport also acquired a 24.55 per cent stake in North Queensland Airports in 2010, a 24.99 per cent stake in Queenstown Airport in 2010 and a 19.9 per cent stake in Tainui Auckland Airport Hotel in 2012.

Auckland Airport's competitive advantage lies in its strategic location, its diversified revenue streams and its long-term growth potential. The airport is situated in the largest and fastest-growing city in New Zealand and serves as a gateway to the Pacific Islands and a hub for trans-Tasman and long-haul flights. The airport generates revenue from aeronautical, retail, property and hotel activities, which provide a balanced and resilient income base. It also has a clear vision and plan to invest in its infrastructure, technology and customer experience to cater for the expected growth in passenger and cargo demand. The airport has a strong market position and a loyal customer base, with long-term contracts and partnerships with major airlines, retailers and tenants.

ESG performance

Auckland Airport's sustainability framework has four key pillars:

- Purpose — includes a target of 100 per cent sustainable procurement by 2030 based on ISO20400 guidelines

- People — includes safety, gender balance and 20 per cent Maori/Pasifika ethnicity in leadership positions by 2030

- Place — net zero scopes 1 and 2 emissions by 2030; 20 per cent reduction in portable water use by FY30 from FY19 baseline; 20 per cent reduction in waste to landfill from aeronautical operation by FY30 from FY19 baseline

- Community — 40 per cent of employees participating in community volunteer programs by FY30; create a pathway for females and Maori/ Pasifika into trades with 30 per cent of staff sourced from targeted apprentice scheme by FY30.

Every three years it undertakes an ESG materiality assessment to understand the most significant issues for the business. It has identified eight, which are aligned to nine UN SDGs:

1. safety, health, wellbeing and security

2. wider economic contribution

3. customer experience

4. aircraft noise

5. responsible employer

6. climate change mitigation and adaptation

7. minimising environmental footprint

8. community and tangata whenua involvement.

The air travel industry contributes significantly to climate change. Auckland Airport acknowledges this and is taking a proactive approach to managing and reducing its carbon emissions.

On scopes 1 and 2, its goal is to deliver net zero emissions by 2030. This will require a 90 per cent reduction of GHG emissions from the FY19 baseline. This is best practice aligned with the Paris Agreement to keep temperature rises below 1.5 degrees Celsius. To deliver on these ambitious goals will require a significant commitment to change, and Auckland Airport has outlined in its FY23 sustainability report how it means to implement that change, including electrification of the vehicle fleet, replacing natural gas with electric alternatives, acquiring electricity from on- and off-site renewable energy sources, and using refrigerants with the lowest global warming potential.

Despite these measures, Auckland Airport predicts 10 per cent of baseline FY19 emissions will remain by FY30. These residual emissions are expected to be offset by the purchase of carbon removal purchase agreements.

However, scopes 1 and 2 make up only a small component of its GHG emissions. Most occur in scope 3, and here it has yet to set a target. Nevertheless, the airport is working with its airline, ground handling, and air navigation partners to increase operational efficiency and reduce fuel burn, by providing EV chargers, ground power units, pre-conditioned air, and fuel-saving flight paths. The airport is anticipating and preparing for the adoption of future aircraft technologies and fuels, such as sustainable aviation fuel, and electric and hydrogen-powered aircraft, by ensuring the right ground infrastructure is in place. Its 30-year plan makes provision for these future requirements. It acknowledges that reducing the impact of aviation on the environment is an important challenge, and while scopes 1 and 2 have been decreasing over time, scope 3 has been increasing. Water and waste have also increased due to the significant uptick in passengers since COVID restrictions were lifted. It has been working on capturing more comprehensive scope 3 emissions data, which has added to the significant uptick of scope 3 year on year.

Auckland Airport was an early member of the Climate Leaders Coalition to help transition to a low-carbon economy. The airport is certified by CEMARS, a leading carbon measurement and reduction scheme, and has been recognised by the Airport Carbon Accreditation program for its efforts to reduce its carbon footprint.

It has identified and assessed a range of physical and transitional climate-related risks and opportunities, such as extreme weather events, sea level rise, changes in customer preferences, policy and regulatory changes, and reputational impacts. It has also conducted climate scenario analysis across three possible futures, drawing from the tourism sector and property and construction sector-wide scenarios. The airport has experienced extreme weather events that have had a financial impact. In January 2023 it suffered significant flooding due to high rainfall, and shortly thereafter it was impacted by Cyclone Gabrielle, when strong winds made it unsafe for ground crews to operate.

It reports in line with TCFD, and while XRB reporting will become mandatory in FY24 it began reporting in FY23, a year in advance. It has disclosed its carbon emissions and energy consumption data, as well as its progress towards its targets, using internationally recognised frameworks and standards, such as the Greenhouse Gas Protocol, the Airport Carbon Accreditation program and the GRI Standards.

Ten per cent of the short-term incentive program for the CEO and direct reports is linked to climate change risk and opportunities.

ESG risks	ESG measured	Assessment	Result
ESG Exposure	ESG risk rating assessment		✓
	ESG exposure risk classification	Low	✓
	ESG risk exposure score	31.85	−
	ESG excess exposure score	(1.15)	✓
	ESG risk score momentum	0.65	✗
ESG sub-industry risk	ESG sub-industry rank	32/86	✓
	ESG risk compared to sub-industry peers	(0.64)	✓
	ESG risk beta	0.97	✓
Management of ESG risk	Management of ESG risks score	40.85	−
	Classification of management of ESG risks	Average	−
	ESG risk management score momentum	(2.67)	✗
Company controversy	Level of company controversy exposure	None	✓
	Notable ESG issues	Product governance	

Carbon emissions	Measured risks	Assessment	Result
	Carbon overall risk	Negligible	✓
	Carbon overall risk score	0	✓
	Carbon total emissions, scopes 1, 2 and 3	10 617.72	✓
	Carbon level of involvement	0	✓
	Level of fossil fuel involvement	0%	✓
	Carbon intensity, scopes 1, 2 and 3	57.93	−

Brambles Limited

ASX code: BXB

www.brambles.com

Market capitalisation:	$18 533.32 million
Sector:	Industrials
Morningstar Sustainalytics peer group classification:	Business Support Services

Environmental risk score		Social risk score		Governance risk score	
1.03	✓	8.16	✓	4.00	✓

View: Brambles is very advanced in terms of sustainability, with a clear pathway to achieving net zero across scopes 1, 2 and 3 by 2040.

History/background

Brambles Limited provides supply-chain logistics services based on the provision of reusable pallets, crates and containers for shared use by various participants in the supply chain. It sees itself as a pioneer in the sharing economy, and one of the most sustainable. It operates in more than 60 countries, primarily through the CHEP (Commonwealth Handling Equipment Pool) brand, and serves the fast-moving consumer goods, fresh produce, beverage, retail and general manufacturing industries. It also has specialist businesses serving the automotive, aerospace, and oil and gas sectors.

Brambles traces its history back to 1875, when Walter Bramble established a butchery in Newcastle, Australia. The business gradually expanded into transport and logistics. Brambles entered the pallet pooling business in 1958 by buying CHEP from the Australian Government. Brambles has since grown into a global leader in supply-chain equipment and solutions, with operations in the Asia Pacific, Europe, North America, Latin America and Africa. It has also diversified into other businesses, such as records management, waste disposal, railway leasing and shipping, some of which have been divested over the years.

Brambles' competitive advantage lies in its circular business model, network effect and supply-chain expertise. Its circular business model facilitates the 'share and reuse' of the world's largest pool of reusable pallets and containers, which enables Brambles to serve its customers while minimising impact on the environment and improving the efficiency and safety of supply chains around the world. The company's network effect is derived from the scale and density of its service centre network and the strength of its customer relationships in every major market in which it operates. Brambles' supply-chain expertise has been developed over 70 years of managing customers' supply chains around the world and it leverages data analytics and digital technologies to deliver value-added solutions. Brambles is also recognised as one of the world's most sustainable corporations, ranking third in the Corporate Knights' Global 100 in 2023.

ESG performance

Brambles' sustainability pillars have three broad programs: Business Positive, Planet Positive and Communities Positive. Underlying each are the key areas of focus and impact:

Business Positive:

- Supply chain positive — 'share and reuse' model, circularity
- Positive collaboration — impact of customer collaborations
- Workplace positive — inclusion and diversity, with at least 40 per cent women in management.

Planet Positive:

- Forest positive — two trees to grow for every tree used; ensure 100 per cent sustainable sourcing of timber of more forestry markets to chain of custody (CoC) certification
- Climate positive — commit to a 1.5 degrees Celsius climate future, aligning with the 2015 Paris Agreement and a science-based carbon emissions target; achieve 100 per cent of electricity from renewable sources and carbon neutral operations for scopes 1 and 2 emissions
- Waste positive — zero product materials sent to landfills at all Brambles and subcontracted locations; upcycle post-consumer plastic into platforms.

Communities Positive:

- Food positive — collaborate with food banks to serve rescued food to 10 million people
- Circular economy transformation — advocate, educate and inspire one million people to become circular economy changemakers
- Positive impacts for people and our planet — committed to developing natural and social capital accounting approaches.

·

These pillars are also aligned with the UN's SDGs.

Every two years Brambles completes a materiality assessment to identify and prioritise the sustainability issues most relevant for the company and its stakeholders. Engagement with key stakeholders has helped develop a materiality matrix that outlines the top issues ranked for relative importance to Brambles and its stakeholders. The matrix is divided into four quadrants: high, medium-high, medium-low and low. The issues in the high quadrant are considered most material and are the focus of the company's sustainability strategy and reporting.

The company has identified the climate-related risks and opportunities for its business covering its entire value chain across three different scenarios. It has also analysed its GHG emissions and set science-based targets to reduce its carbon footprint and align with the 1.5 degrees Celsius scenario. Brambles has disclosed its climate scenario analysis and its response to the Task Force on Climate-related Financial Disclosures (TCFD) in its sustainability review and its TCFD disclosure document. The company has a clear pathway to decarbonisation and measures itself against science-based targets. It is monitoring its progress across all scopes against its FY20 baseline. Its climate transition plan is based on three main pillars: accelerate, scale up and remove. It will accelerate its emissions reduction by optimising its logistics, increasing its use of zero-emissions vehicles and switching to renewable energy sources. Brambles will scale up its circular business model by expanding its product portfolio, increasing its customer collaborations and enhancing its digital capabilities. The company will mitigate any remaining emissions by investing in nature-based solutions, such as forest restoration and conservation.

It sources timber that is 100 per cent sustainable, 72.6 per cent with a full chain of custody. The circular business model drives a variety of positive environmental impacts that Brambles can account for. Its operations already use 100 per cent renewable energy. It has successfully launched an eight-year €500 million green bond aligned with the International Capital Market Association's Green Bond Principles and the Loan Market Association Green Loan Principles. Brambles' green bond is the first by an Australian company to be fully dedicated to the circular economy, reflecting the company's leading position as a circular business pioneer through its 'share and reuse' pooling model. Brambles will use the proceeds of the green bond to finance and/or refinance sustainable assets and expenditures with positive environmental benefits, such as reusable timber and plastic pallets, crates and containers, equipment used to maintain and repair the share and reuse assets, projects for automated inspection, sorting and repair of pallets, and other assets that support the functioning of the circular economy business model.

Brambles issues sustainability certificates to its customers to help quantify the environmental benefits of using its products and services, such as trees saved by using Brambles' solutions over single-use alternatives. The certificates use a robust peer-reviewed life cycle assessment (LCA) calculation, giving customers confidence regarding results.

Brambles won the Australasian Investor Relations Award 2023 for best ESG and Sustainability Reporting by an Australasian company and provides comprehensive information to investors through its annual report, sustainability review and climate change supplement. It uses various frameworks such as TCFD, GRI and the Value Reporting Foundation to report and disclose its sustainability performance and impacts, and these too communicate how Brambles manages climate-related risks and opportunities, how it follows the global standards and principles for sustainability reporting, and how it integrates its financial and non-financial value creation. Brambles also provides industry-specific sustainability indicators based on SASB standards.

Brambles provides detailed reporting. It has achieved carbon neutral targets for scopes 1 and 2, ahead of FY25 targets, and aims for net zero across scopes 1, 2 and 3 by 2040.

ESG risks	ESG measured	Assessment	Result
ESG exposure	ESG risk rating assessment		✓
	ESG exposure risk classification	Low	✓
	ESG risk exposure score	30.45	—
	ESG excess exposure score	(0.55)	✓
	ESG risk score momentum	(0.93)	✓
ESG sub-industry risk	ESG sub-industry rank	12/174	✓
	ESG risk compared to sub-industry peers	(7.61)	✓
	ESG risk beta	0.98	✓
Management of ESG risk	Management of ESG risks score	59.14	—
	Classification of management of ESG risks	Strong	✓
	ESG risk management score momentum	4.57	✓
Company controversy	Level of company controversy exposure	None	✓
	Notable ESG issues	Product governance	

Carbon emissions	Measured risks	Assessment	Result
	Carbon overall risk	Low	✓
	Carbon overall risk score	1.01	✓
	Carbon total emissions, scopes 1, 2 and 3	1 625 080	X
	Carbon level of involvement	0	✓
	Level of fossil fuel involvement	0%	✓
	Carbon intensity, scopes 1, 2 and 3	317.28	—

Concluding remarks

All companies selected in the industrials sector were assessed as having low or negligible ESG risks. Transurban and Atlas Arteria, both which operate in the highways and railroads sector, secured the best possible rating, and are considered to have negligible ESG risks. The highest ESG risks were attributed to Auckland International Airport followed by Qube Holdings (subsector marine ports). Brambles and Imdex were in the middle of this pack on ESG risks.

On sub-industry ranking Brambles performed best, followed by Atlas Arteria, Imdex, Transurban and Auckland International Airport, with Qube Holdings ranking last.

Brambles, Atlas and Transurban were all assessed as having strong ESG management and were considered to be managing their risk well, with Atlas Arteria coming out marginally higher than Transurban. Imdex, Qube and Auckland International Airport were assessed as having average management of ESG risks. Atlas and Brambles in particular had high scores on positive momentum in the management of their ESG risk.

On overall climate ambition Brambles took the cake with its commitment to deliver net zero across all three scopes by 2040. Transurban seeks to reach net zero across all three scopes by 2050 and has had its interim FY30 targets validated by SBTi; it is awaiting SBTi validation of its 2050 target.

Imdex seems to have made the least progress on its net zero journey, having no targets across any of the scopes. Qube, Atlas Arteria and Auckland International Airport had scopes 1 and 2 targets but none for scope 3.

On carbon data, Atlas Arteria had the highest total emissions followed by Brambles then Transurban Group.

9. Real estate and utilities

The real estate sector is leading the way on sustainability. All seven stocks captured in this chapter have the highest possible sustainability rating with negligible ESG risk. No other sector has as many high-scoring companies. This is likely driven by Australia's National Australian Built Environment Rating System (NABERS). Launched in 1998, NABERS measures the environmental performance of buildings and tenancies and allows for comparability on sustainability across different building types. This has helped Australian real estate manage ESG risks. A NABERS rating is a high priority in this sector.

Sustainable properties have been linked to a range of financial benefits including reduced building operations costs due to a range of initiatives such as energy efficiency resulting from better insulation, use of renewable energy such as solar panels and reduced water waste. These initiatives flow on to create higher market value for these buildings, reduced vacancy rates and the attraction of higher quality tenants who are prepared to pay higher rentals for a NABERS building.

Environmental considerations in this sector include energy efficiency, energy sources, sustainable construction materials, circularity, waste, pollution, water and biodiversity. From a social perspective, workforce conditions across the supply chain, impacts on communities, and a building's accessibility, inclusivity, safety and health impacts are all important. Governance is where all these considerations come together in corporate values, implementation, reporting, risk management, value creation, policy and compliance.

One area for improvement in this sector is scope 3 carbon emissions, which are likely to be captured in the mandatory climate-related disclosure regime of the future.

The utilities sector encompasses companies that supply essential services such as electricity, gas and water to consumers and businesses. Two companies captured in this sector have strong ESG credentials. Both operate in the renewable energy space; both generate 100 per cent renewable energy; both are based in New Zealand and dual listed on the ASX. The utilities sector tends to have more stable and predictable return profiles and lower market correlations, which makes it more defensive in nature although it does have exposure to regulatory risks.

Dexus Limited

ASX code: DXI   www.dexus.com

Market capitalisation:	7571.98 million
Sector:	Real estate
Morningstar Sustainalytics peer group classification:	REITs

Environmental risk score		Social risk score		Governance risk score	
1.90	✓	1.54	✓	3.54	✓

View: Dexus achieved net zero in corporate business and management property portfolio in FY22.

History/background

Dexus is a leading Australian real estate group that invests only in Australia, with a focus on quality CBD office properties and a significant third-party funds management platform and trading business. The company's history traces back to Deutsche Bank, which managed externally several property trusts from 1984 to 2004. In 2004, the trusts that comprise Dexus were stapled to form DB RREEF Trust, with the group also acquiring 50 per cent of the management rights from Deutsche Bank at that time. In 2008, DB RREEF Trust was rebranded as Dexus, and the remaining management rights were acquired from Deutsche Bank, creating an internally managed vehicle.

Dexus has five key business activities: investing, managing, developing, transacting and trading high-quality properties. The company invests in office, industrial, healthcare, retail, and infrastructure assets and investments. It directly owns approximately $17 billion of properties and manages a further $44 billion of investments in its funds management business.

ESG performance

On sustainability, Dexus has identified three areas of priority: customer prosperity, climate action and enhancing communities. Climate action is accelerating the transition to decarbonisation. To that end Dexus has committed to limiting global warming to 1.5 degrees Celsius in line with the Paris Agreement and has set net zero and science-based targets, which are certified by SBTi. Its ambition is to achieve a

70 per cent reduction in scopes 1 and 2 emissions across its property portfolios by FY30 against an FY18 baseline. In addition, it has committed to reducing customer-related emissions by 25 per cent over the same time frame. In fact, it was able to achieve net zero in scopes 1 and 2 across its property portfolio in FY22. It also committed to RE100 in FY20, committing to achieve 100 per cent electricity from renewables by FY30, but this was already achieved in FY22.

Dexus provides a comprehensive and detailed sustainability report and data pack that align with the highest international standards including GRI, SASB and IIRF.

Dexus undertakes regular materiality assessments to identify key issues that inform its strategy. It also maps the impact of its activities to evaluate its performance. It has been undertaking regular materiality assessments since 2011. The most recent assessment was undertaken in FY23 and identified 17 potential issues, with five topics chosen as the most material:

1. Customer engagement and experience

2. Decarbonisation and circularity

3. Economic performance and resilience

4. Asset environmental performance and optimisation

5. Championing a high-performance workplace culture.

It undertakes regular scenario analysis to understand business risks and opportunities as they relate to climate impacts, which also influences the group's strategy. In the last report, published in 2020, three different scenarios were considered, and details of the work undertaken and possible actions can be found in the 'Towards Climate resilience report' on the website.

On governance the board has ultimate accountability but several committees support the board, including a board ESG committee, which has oversight of the implementation and management of sustainability/ESG practices and initiatives throughout Dexus. There is also a group management committee, a corporate executive committee and targeted working groups with expertise in specific areas such as social and community, reconciliation action, climate action and environment.

Dexus publishes a Corporate Governance Statement that presents its governance framework against the ASX Corporate Governance Principles & Recommendations — Fourth Edition (ASX Principles), disclosing how Dexus meets the ASX Principles. It has a robust supply chain management framework to encourage and influence suppliers to address sustainability impacts and create shared value. The framework covers policies, procedures and implementation including procurement and supplier monitoring. In addition, an environmental impacts management framework helps guide the achievement of high environmental performance standards across the group's property portfolio. This framework covers policies and systems as well as environmental delivery.

Looking at materiality through an environmental lens, the company has identified the following issues: energy consumption, water consumption, waste management and biodiversity.

Dexus has a climate change resilience strategy that tackles decarbonisation, adapting to physical and transition risks, influencing the value chain and robust governance. It has assessed climate resilience across a short-, medium- and long-term time frame, and to ensure effective governance it is captured in the climate action management framework.

Dexus is a signatory to the UN Global Compact and RE100. It adheres to TCFD and the Global Real Estate Sustainability Benchmark (GRESB) and is a member of the Green Building Council of Australia (GBCA).

ESG risks	**ESG measured**	**Assessment**	**Result**
ESG exposure	ESG risk rating assessment		√
	ESG exposure risk classification	Negligible	√
	ESG risk exposure score	25.70	√
	ESG excess exposure score	(2.30)	√
	ESG risk score momentum	0.18	X
ESG sub-industry risk	ESG sub-industry rank	7/448	√
	ESG risk compared to sub-industry peers	(8.42)	√
	ESG risk beta	0.92	√
Management of ESG risk	Management of ESG risks score	73.99	√
	Classification of management ESG risks	Strong	√
	ESG risk management score momentum	(0.48)	X
Company controversy	Level of company controversy exposure	0	√
	Notable ESG issues	Product governance	

Carbon emissions	**Measured risks**	**Assessment**	**Result**
	Carbon overall risk	Low	√
	Carbon overall risk score	3.50	√
	Carbon total emissions, scopes 1, 2 and 3	135 296.00	–
	Carbon level of involvement	0	√
	Level of fossil fuel involvement	0%	√
	Carbon intensity, scopes 1, 2 and 3	181.30	–

Mirvac Group

ASX code: MGR www.mirvac.com

Market capitalisation:	$24 377.61 million
Sector:	Real estate
Morningstar Sustainalytics peer group classification:	REITs

Environmental risk score		Social risk score		Governance risk score	
0.82	✓	2.72	✓	5.10	✓

View: Mirvac has already achieved net positive carbon across scopes 1 and 2, and seeks to deliver net positive carbon across all scopes by 2030.

History/background

Mirvac Group is an Australian property group that builds urban communities with sustainable design and architecture through smart business strategy and vision. The company invests in office, industrial, retail and residential properties, and has a significant third-party funds management platform.

Mirvac Group was founded in 1972 by Bob Hamilton and Henry Pollack. Its first project was a block of 12 apartments in Rose Bay, Sydney. In October 2004 Mirvac Group purchased the James Fielding Group.

It has four key business divisions:

- Office and Industrial develops and manages high-quality office and industrial assets in Australia's major cities.

- Retail develops and manages retail assets in Australia's major cities.

- Residential develops and manages residential assets in Australia's major cities.

- Mirvac Funds manages third-party capital across a range of real estate sectors.

ESG performance

The company's sustainability strategy prioritises three areas: customer prosperity, climate action and enhancing communities. Mirvac's sustainability strategy, 'This Changes Everything', sets clear targets to ensure the company continues to have a positive environmental and social impact and to make better choices. The company aimed to achieve net positive emissions across scopes 1 and 2 by 2030 by enhancing energy efficiency and increasing the use of renewable energy across its portfolio, although it has already achieved this goal and now seeks to add scope 3 and achieve net positive across all scopes by FY30.

Mirvac outlines its approach to delivering net positive carbon in its report 'Net Positive Carbon by 2030'. Net positive is better than net zero as it means reducing carbon beyond what the company itself emits, although part of this will be achieved through carbon offsets. In this report it considers three climate scenarios to predict how its carbon emissions might vary depending on future climate outcomes. Its approach to reducing scope 3 is threefold: reducing embodied carbon, collaborating with customers to reduce their emissions and investing in high-quality carbon offsets.

Embodied carbon is GHG within building materials and construction processes that are emitted during the development and construction of the building. It is looking at using recycled materials, dematerialisation (using less), using lower carbon inputs such as low-carbon concrete, steel and aluminium, and exploring whether it can use more timber and retain existing building structures.

Collaborating with customers works best when it retains the assets and has tenants, but key activities include all-electric buildings using 100 per cent renewable energy and maximising energy efficiency by removing air leaks, installing efficient appliances and installing rooftop solar.

Carbon offsets are used to cover emissions it is not yet able to eliminate. It already purchases some carbon offsets for its residual scope 1 emissions, and it expects it will need to incorporate carbon offsets for scope 3 emissions.

Mirvac has signed up to SBTi, which validates its carbon reduction targets and approach. Beyond delivery of positive carbon outcomes, it also seeks to deliver positive waste and water by FY30.

In FY20 Mirvac signed up to RE100 and committed to sourcing 100 per cent renewable energy by 2030. To support its trajectory to net positive emissions, Mirvac has established an interim target of achieving 70 per cent renewable electricity use by 2025.

Periodically it publishes a 'building climate resilience report', which outlines the Mirvac approach to managing climate risks and opportunities. FY23 sees the release of its fifth report as per TCFD requirements.

Mirvac is a signatory to the UN Global Compact. It has partnered with ARENA to develop a new energy-efficient housing model and with the Clean Energy Finance Corporation (CEFC) to develop a new financing model for the construction of energy-efficient buildings. Mirvac also reports in line with GRI Standards.

ESG risks	ESG measured	Assessment	Result
ESG exposure	ESG risk rating assessment	▮▮▮▮▮	✓
	ESG exposure risk classification	Negligible	✓
	ESG risk exposure score	26.65	—
	ESG excess exposure score	(1.35)	✓
	ESG risk score momentum	(0.15)	✓
ESG sub-industry risk	ESG sub-industry rank	14/448	✓
	ESG risk compared to sub-industry peers	(6.75)	✓
	ESG risk beta	0.95	✓
Management of ESG risk	Management of ESG risks score	68.66	✓
	Classification of management ESG risks	Strong	✓
	ESG risk management score momentum	3.10	✓
Company controversy	Level of company controversy exposure	Moderate	—
	Notable ESG issues	Business ethics	

Carbon emissions	Measured risks	Assessment	Result
	Carbon overall risk	Low	✓
	Carbon overall risk score	2.33	✓
	Carbon total emissions, scopes 1, 2 and 3	80 729.00	—
	Carbon level of involvement	0	✓
	Level of fossil fuel involvement	0%	✓
	Carbon intensity, scopes 1, 2 and 3	61.06	—

Stockland Corp Limited

ASX code: SGP   www.stockland.com.au

Market capitalisation:	$9859.02
Sector:	Real estate
Morningstar Sustainalytics peer group classification:	REITs

Environmental risk score		Social risk score		Governance risk score	
2.62	✓	2.51	✓	3.95	✓

View: Stockland has advanced impressively on its sustainability journey.

History/background

Stockland is an Australian property development company that specialises in residential, commercial and industrial property development. The company was founded in 1952 by Albert Scheinberg and Ervin Graf and was listed on the ASX in 1957 through the acquisition of a controlling interest in Simon Hickey Industries Ltd.

It has a diversified portfolio of assets across the retail, residential and logistics sectors. It focuses on delivering a range of master-planned communities and medium-density housing in growth areas across the country.

ESG performance

Stockland's sustainability strategy rests on four pillars:

1. Climate positive — aims to achieve net zero carbon emissions by 2028 and net positive carbon by 2050

2. Circular economy — aims to achieve zero waste to landfill by 2030 and to increase the use of recycled materials in its operations

3. Thriving communities — aims to create thriving communities that are healthy, connected and resilient

4. Responsible investment — aims to invest responsibly and to ensure that these investments align with its sustainability strategy.

It produces a number of sustainability-related reports, approaches and statements including a climate transition action plan and an ESG data pack, covering its environmental management approach, social management approach, governance management approach, a modern slavery statement and a reconciliation action plan.

Stockland's climate transition plan 2023, developed with reference to SBTi and TCFD, provides details on the decarbonisation pathway to net zero. The bulk of the company's emissions come from scope 3 upstream (40 per cent) and downstream (37 per cent) of total carbon emissions against its 2021 baseline. It has set science-based targets on scopes 1, 2 and 3 that align with the 1.5 degree target, and these have been submitted to SBTi for verification. Its ambition is to deliver net zero on scopes 1 and 2 by 2025, to be achieved largely by using 100 per cent renewable energy, with residual emissions covered by carbon offsets. For scope 3 it aims for a 52 per cent reduction from the FY21 baseline by 2030, then to seek to deliver net zero by 2050 across all three scopes. Scope 3 reductions will be achieved by reducing embodied emissions and emissions from tenant energy. To meet the target, it will need to procure low-carbon materials and identify low-carbon product substitutions. It has already started to use low-carbon concrete and is considering moving from steel to timber frames, which would reduce its baseline steel emissions by approximately 45 per cent.

Stockland has undertaken climate risk scenario analysis to understand potential future impacts on the business. Its approach used the IPCC's Representative Concentration Pathway (RCP), which considers physical and transition risks. In relation to its leased assets, decarbonisation could be enhanced by converting assets to all-electric and using 100 per cent renewable energy, as well as considering on-site renewable energy generation such as solar at scale. This analysis impacted its strategic plans related to decarbonisation activities already highlighted.

The group has undertaken a materiality assessment that revealed potential positive and negative double materiality impacts in housing affordability, decarbonisation, climate resilience, Indigenous engagement, social inclusion, health and wellbeing, biodiversity and transition to the circular economy. These are being incorporated into its risk and opportunities matrix.

On governance the board has overall responsibility for sustainability. A sustainability committee supports the board by providing oversight and management of ESG strategy. Each member of the leadership team has ESG, climate risk and sustainability performance objectives, which are a part of their short-term incentive plan. An ESG steering committee assists in the implementation of the strategy. It has undertaken work towards a nature positive transition, seeking to identify the risks and opportunities. It has reviewed biodiversity at its developments and is refining its approach to tracking biodiversity outcomes.

Stockland reports align to TCFD and ISSB guidelines. It is a signatory to the UN Global Compact, a member of the Green Building Council of Australia, the Investor Group on Climate Change and MECLA. It is also a member of the TNFD and SBTN corporate engagement program.

ESG risks	ESG measured	Assessment	Result
ESG exposure	ESG risk rating assessment		✓
	ESG exposure risk classification	Negligible	✓
	ESG risk exposure score	26.40	—
	ESG excess exposure score	0.40	X
	ESG risk score momentum	(0.04)	✓
ESG sub-industry risk	ESG sub-industry rank	26/448	✓
	ESG risk compared to sub-industry peers	(6.33)	✓
	ESG risk beta	1.02	X
Management of ESG risk	Management of ESG risks score	66.52	—
	Classification of management ESG risks	Strong	✓
	ESG risk management score momentum	0.14	✓
Company controversy	Level of company controversy exposure	None	✓
	Notable ESG issues	Product governance	

Carbon emissions	Measured risks	Assessment	Result
	Carbon overall risk	Low	✓
	Carbon overall risk score	5.48	✓
	Carbon total emissions, scopes 1, 2 and 3	85 945.00	—
	Carbon level of involvement	0	✓
	Level of fossil fuel involvement	0%	✓
	Carbon intensity, scopes 1, 2 and 3	42.52	✓

Goodman Group

ASX code: GMG   www.goodman.com

Market capitalisation:	$43 206.39 million
Sector:	Real estate
Morningstar Sustainalytics peer group classification:	REITs

Environmental risk score		Social risk score		Governance risk score	
2.11	✓	3.21	✓	4.36	✓

View: A certified carbon neutral organisation with a broad range of affiliations and partnerships, Goodman is a leader in sustainability.

History/background

The Goodman Group is an Australian integrated commercial and industrial property group that specialises in the development, management and ownership of logistics and business space (such as warehouses, distribution centres and manufacturing facilities). The company was founded in 1989 by Greg Goodman and has grown from one industrial building in South Sydney in the early 1990s to 438 properties in 14 countries across the world today.

The group offers a range of products and services, including:

- development — provides a range of development services, including site acquisition, planning, design, construction and project management

- property management — manages properties on behalf of investors, including leasing, maintenance and asset management

- fund management — manages funds on behalf of institutional investors, including capital raising, investment management and reporting.

ESG performance

Goodman's sustainability strategy is based on three pillars:

- Sustainable properties and places
- People, culture and communities
- Corporate governance and performance.

For each pillar a range of specific ESG targets are monitored and reported on, and are linked to appropriate UN SDGs.

It has identified eight material ESG priorities within those pillars, and these priorities drive its strategy. They are:

1. Actively contributing to the net zero transition

2. Owning strategically located properties close to consumers in key global markets

3. Developing and adapting innovative, efficient and flexible properties with a future focus

4. Demonstrating Goodman's values and promoting diversity, inclusiveness and social equity

5. Investing responsibly, with defined governance and sustainable capital structures

6. Promoting workplace safety and wellbeing

7. Delivering resilient assets that support human health and value natural capital

8. Influencing the sustainability practices of its value chain.

In addition, it has identified a number of emerging issues, including biodiversity, TNFD and First Nations engagement. It also highlights changing reporting requirements, although it believes it is well placed to deliver on these.

Goodman is a certified carbon neutral organisation through validation by Climate Active. Goodman's carbon reduction commitments include a 42 per cent reduction in absolute scopes 1 and 2 GHG emissions by 2030 from a 2021 baseline, and a 50 per cent reduction in square-metre intensity of scope 3 emissions by 2030 from the 2021 baseline covering the use of its buildings by its customers and the use of the buildings it has sold. These emissions-reduction commitments have been validated by SBTi.

On governance, Goodman's board and its sustainability and innovation committee oversee the climate risk management approach. The committee oversees climate disclosures and monitors progress aligned with validated science-based targets. The board and the committee oversee other climate-related targets, including onsite renewable electricity solutions for customers and Goodman's own carbon neutral operations. Its risk management framework, risk register and group investment committee process determine its approach to managing risk.

It has a number of affiliations and partnerships including with TCFD, GRESB, Greenpower, Climate Active, MECLA, the CLC and Reconciliation Australia. It also reports to the GRI standards.

ESG risks	ESG measured	Assessment	Result
ESG exposure	ESG risk rating assessment		✓
	ESG exposure risk classification	Negligible	✓
	ESG risk exposure score	25.20	✓
	ESG excess exposure score	(2.80)	✓
	ESG risk score momentum	0.14	X
ESG sub-industry risk	ESG sub-industry rank	38/448	✓
	ESG risk compared to sub-industry peers	(5.72)	✓
	ESG risk beta	0.90	✓
Management of ESG risk	Management of ESG risks score	62.60	—
	Classification of management ESG risks	Strong	✓
	ESG risk management score momentum	1.06	✓
Company controversy	Level of company controversy exposure	Low	✓
	Notable ESG issues	Product governance	

Carbon emissions	Measured risks	Assessment	Result
	Carbon overall risk	Low	✓
	Carbon overall risk score	4.15	✓
	Carbon total emissions, scopes 1, 2 and 3	52 868.00	✓
	Carbon level of involvement	0	✓
	Level of fossil fuel involvement	0%	✓
	Carbon intensity, scopes 1, 2 and 3	38.63	✓

Scentre Group

ASX code: SCG
www.scentregroup.com

Market capitalisation:	$68 772.51 million
Sector:	Real estate
Morningstar Sustainalytics peer group classification:	REITs

Environmental risk score		Social risk score		Governance risk score	
1.95	✓	2.53	✓	4.37	✓

View: Targeting net zero 2030 for scopes 1 and 2, Scentre needs to do more to capture scope 3, but this work is underway.

History/background

Scentre Group is an Australian property company that owns and operates a platform of 42 Westfield destinations, 37 located in Australia and five in New Zealand. The company was created in June 2014 through the merger of Westfield Retail Trust and Westfield Group's Australian and New Zealand management business.

It offers a range of products and services, including development, property management and fund management. Scentre Group's Westfield destinations are designed as places people choose to come and spend time. Westfield believes its centres provide the most efficient and productive means for businesses to engage and transact with customers. It delivers a mix of retail, fashion, dining, fresh food, and entertainment, each component important in the overall Westfield customer experience.

ESG performance

Scentre's sustainability approach rests on four pillars: community, talent, environmental impact and economic performance. Each of these pillars is mapped to appropriate SDGs. Focusing on environment, its ambition is to achieve net zero in scopes 1 and 2 by FY30 from an FY14 baseline for the wholly owned Westfield destinations. So far it has achieved a 38 per cent reduction, so it believes it is on track to achieve this goal. Emissions-reduction activities it has undertaken include on-site solar generation, renewable energy procurement, LED lighting upgrades and Next Gen Analytics to help optimise energy efficiency. This wide-ranging program covers maintenance activities, reprogramming of air conditioners and improvements to building management systems. It is piloting heat pump technology as a possible solution to replace end-of-life boilers at their sites.

Another goal was to achieve an average 4.5 stars NABERS energy rating across its property portfolio by FY25, but it achieved this goal early, in FY22.

Its recycling and waste management program aims to increase waste recovery by 90 per cent by FY30 (52 per cent of waste was recovered as of FY22). A secondary goal was to maintain waste recovery above 95 per cent for all major developments (it averaged 89 per cent across four major developments in 2022, so it's a bit behind here). Another goal is to reduce water usage (FY22 was actually up 11 per cent from FY21, but it notes that usage is lower than pre-COVID levels).

Scentre is undertaking a materiality assessment to identify the ESG issues that matter most to its business. The high-priority issues identified in FY22 are:

- energy and greenhouse gas emissions
- waste
- water
- health and safety
- physical and online security
- employment and labour practices.

These issues have remained consistent and are incorporated into its risk management framework and influences its business priorities.

Its climate report outlines a range of scenarios aligning with the updated IPCC Special Report on Global Warming, their potential impacts on its business and its approach to mitigating these risks.

The board, supported by committees, is responsible for the governance of the group. The CEO is responsible for the day-to-day management and implementation of strategic objectives. Unlike some of its competitors, no specific committee manages ESG. Mention is made of its enterprise risk management framework capturing material economic, operational, environmental and social sustainability risks. The audit and risk committee reviews processes for assessing material exposure to environmental risk including economic risks associated with climate change. We need to see greater integration of sustainable risk into the governance process.

Reporting is in line with the GRI standards and TCFD. It produces a sustainability report and a climate statement and also provides a responsible business data pack, a modern slavery statement and a corporate governance statement. It is a signatory to the UN Global Compact.

Scentre is on a great pathway to sustainability but there are some areas that invite improvement. It is assessing whether to seek SBTi validation of its GHG emission targets. It would be good to see scope 3 incorporated into its targets, and to that end it is seeking to understand its baseline data and to develop definitions of scope 3. It needs to understand the materiality of embodied carbon and scope 3 emissions and begin measuring these. Also missing is alignment to TNFD, but it is reviewing this too to see if it can be incorporated into the business.

ESG risks	ESG measured	Assessment	Result
ESG exposure	ESG risk rating assessment	▮▮▮▮▮	✓
	ESG exposure risk classification	Negligible	✓
	ESG risk exposure score	29.05	—
	ESG excess exposure score	1.05	X
	ESG risk score momentum	0.54	X
ESG sub-industry risk	ESG sub-industry rank	20/448	✓
	ESG risk compared to sub-industry peers	(6.54)	✓
	ESG risk beta	1.04	X
Management of ESG risk	Management of ESG risks score	70.66	✓
	Classification of management ESG risks	Strong	✓
	ESG risk management score momentum	(0.70)	X
Company controversy	Level of company controversy exposure	Moderate	—
	Notable ESG issues	ESG integration – financials	

Carbon emissions	Measured risks	Assessment	Result
	Carbon overall risk	Low	✓
	Carbon overall risk score	2.77	✓
	Carbon total emissions, scopes 1, 2 and 3	288 126.00	—
	Carbon level of involvement	0	✓
	Level of fossil fuel involvement	0%	✓
	Carbon intensity, scopes 1, 2 and 3	172.26	—

Vicinity Centres

ASX code: VCX

www.vicinity.com.au

Market capitalisation:	$25 879.69 million
Sector:	Real estate
Morningstar Sustainalytics peer group classification:	REITs

Environmental risk score		Social risk score		Governance risk score	
2.84	✓	1.60	✓	4.76	✓

View: With plans to deliver net zero by 2030 for scopes 1 and 2, and comprehensive monitoring and managing of sustainability risk and opportunities, there's lots to like.

History/background

Vicinity Centres is an Australian real estate investment trust that owns and manages 60 shopping centres across Australia. Its flagship properties include Chadstone in Melbourne and the Queen Victoria Building in Sydney. Established in 1985 as Jennings Properties, it was later renamed as Centro Properties Group. It underwent several acquisitions, restructures and spin-offs before becoming Federation Centres. Vicinity Centres was born from the merger between Novion Property Group and Federation Centres in 2015, which brought together a collection of quality retail property assets. It offers retail property ownership and management services, as well as mixed-use development projects that include residential, office and hotel spaces. It uses data science and strategic insights to provide leasing solutions to its retail partners. The business strategy is underpinned by four pillars: enhancing the investment portfolio, delivering property excellence, maintaining strong financial stewardship and enabling good business.

ESG performance

Its sustainability strategy rests on three pillars: people, place and planet. In relation to planet, it aims to deliver net zero by FY30, increase renewable energy usage and strengthen its ability to adapt to climate-related risks. Its focus is to build on its on-site solar generation projects, improve waste diversion from landfill, incorporate circular design principles into new developments and enhance the climate resilience of its centres via climate scenario risk analysis. Vicinity undertakes climate scenario analysis aligned to TCDF standards: FY22 saw it focus on transition risks, and FY23 on physical climate risk. Vicinity used three scenarios supplied by the Network for Greening the Financial System (NGFS). This helps Vicinity determine the possible range of risks and opportunities and prepare to mitigate the risks and leverage the opportunities.

Vicinity conducts a regular materiality assessment to anticipate and adapt to change. An external assessment was completed in FY22 and it plans to undertake another in FY24. Issues are mapped to a materiality matrix to identify the ESG topics of greatest concern. All issues are mapped to SDGs to align all efforts to contributing to global sustainable development. Some of the topics of highest priority were physical and transition risks of climate change, environmental sustainability, which included reducing scopes 1, 2 and 3 emissions, minimising water use, management of waste and recycling, supporting a circular economy, and sustainable design and construction.

Vicinity approaches managing climate change via decarbonisation. It established a net zero target in 2019 that aims to deliver net zero emissions by FY30 across scopes 1 and 2 for its wholly owned centres in the common mall areas. To achieve this it has been delivering large-scale on-site solar programs, across 20 centres already with two more under construction, has scaled up its energy efficiency initiatives and is reducing carbon-intensive energy sources. During FY22 it began reporting on tenant-related emissions as part of scope 3. It needs to do more work to understand its scope 3 emissions ahead of changing reporting requirements. To date it has reduced scopes 1 and 2 emissions by 41 per cent against its FY16 baseline.

On governance, the board is ultimately responsible for the management and performance of the business supported by various committees. A sustainability committee is chaired by the CEO, incorporates senior management and is supported by the sustainability team. Further, sustainability working groups cover the three pillars of the sustainability strategy. The incorporation of monitoring and managing sustainable risk and opportunities is embedded in the company's governance process.

Vicinity issued a green bond after developing a sustainable finance framework. The proceeds of the bond were used to refinance its lower carbon buildings, defined as those with a NABERS energy rating of five stars or above. Given the demand for green bonds from institutional investors, which has been attracting a 'greenium' (investors have been prepared to pay more for green bonds so the company borrows at a more attractive rate), this not only diversifies its funding sources but may slightly improve the cost of funding.

Vicinity currently reports annually against the NGER compliance reporting framework and publishes an annual TCFD statement. It reports in line with the GRI standards and is a signatory to the UN Global Compact.

Possible areas for improvement are use of SBTi for validation of net zero targets and incorporation of scope 3 into the targets. Vicinity is working to better account for scope 3. Once it understands its scope 3 boundaries, it can set a baseline and a target for net zero.

ESG risks	ESG measured	Assessment	Result
ESG exposure	ESG risk rating assessment		✓
	ESG exposure risk classification	Negligible	✓
	ESG risk exposure score	28.10	—
	ESG excess exposure score	0.10	X
	ESG risk score momentum	0.46	X
ESG sub-industry risk	ESG sub-industry rank	28/448	✓
	ESG risk compared to sub-industry peers	(6.20)	✓
	ESG risk beta	1.00	—
Management of ESG risk	Management of ESG risks score	68.35	✓
	Classification of management ESG risks	Strong	✓
	ESG risk management score momentum	(0.41)	X
Company controversy	Level of company controversy exposure	Low	✓
	Notable ESG issues	ESG integration – financials	

Carbon emissions	Measured risks	Assessment	Result
	Carbon overall risk	Low	✓
	Carbon overall risk score	5.20	✓
	Carbon total emissions, scopes 1, 2 and 3	171 344.00	—
	Carbon level of involvement	0	✓
	Level of fossil fuel involvement	0%	✓
	Carbon intensity, scopes 1, 2 and 3	199.83	—

Mercury NZ Limited

ASX code: MCY　　　　　　　　　　　　　　　　www.mercury.co.nz

Market capitalisation:	$8062.32 million
Sector:	Utilities
Morningstar Sustainalytics peer group classification:	Renewable Power Production

Environmental risk score		Social risk score		Governance risk score	
3.21	✓	10.06	–	6.50	✓

View: Mercury's pathway to net zero is set and in line with SBTi targets for utilities of 2040.

History/background

Mercury NZ Limited is an electricity company in New Zealand that invests in, develops and produces electricity from 100 per cent renewable energy sources — hydro, geothermal and wind. It sells energy, broadband, and mobile services and products to retail and wholesale customers. Formerly known as Mighty River Power Limited, it changed its name to Mercury NZ Limited in 2016.

It owns and operates nine hydroelectric power stations and five geothermal power stations, as well as a small gas-fired peaking plant. It also has a 19.99 per cent stake in Tilt Renewables, a wind and solar power company. It is listed on both the Australian and New Zealand stock exchanges. It sees its business as a key enabler in the energy transition. It outlines what it calls the energy trilemma: energy security, environmental stability and energy equity must all be delivered if the energy transition is to be successful.

Mercury's sustainability strategy is built on five pillars:

1. Customer — focus on loyalty by inspiring, rewarding and making it easier for customers

2. People — safety and wellbeing, high performance and development

3. Commercial — operational excellence, development of generation resources and sustainable business growth

4. Partnerships — shared values and a long-term focus

5. Kaitiakitanga — recognising and respecting natural resources and doing its bit to manage climate change.

It seeks to align these pillars to a range of SDGs including affordable and clean energy, decent work and economic growth, and sustainable cities and communities.

ESG performance

Each year Mercury undertakes a materiality assessment, which it has grouped across its five pillars. The material issues are social and relationship, natural manufactured, human intellectual and financial. It outlines its activity in response to these material issues.

Its scenario analysis across three different climate scenarios was completed in FY23. Opportunities identified by this process are increasing demand for electricity due to decarbonisation and increasing investor demand for renewable energy. Risks include variable weather patterns, which could impact energy generation and result in damage to assets, poor government policy, and supply chain constraints due to the rise in demand for renewable energy, which could cause a supply squeeze on renewable electricity generation equipment.

Its climate transition action plan outlines Mercury's ambition to achieve net zero by FY40, which is in line with the Science Based Targets initiative (SBTi) specification for electric utilities. To deliver on this target, Mercury will need to reduce scope 1 emissions by 70 per cent and reduce scopes 2 and 3 absolute emissions by 90 per cent from their baseline year FY22, with any remaining emissions offset through carbon removals. Its interim target is to reduce scopes 2 and 3 emissions by 42 per cent by FY30. These targets are currently undergoing a validation process with SBTi. It will reduce emissions by building renewable generation, trialling reinjecting geothermal emissions back into their geothermal reservoirs and electrification of the motor fleet. It will engage with its customers to switch from gas to electricity and investigate other gas alternatives such as biofuels. It will also engage with its supply chain to encourage decarbonisation.

Mercury is looking to increase its supply of renewable electricity via a pipeline of new projects that includes a wind, geothermal and battery project. It will also look to upgrade its hydro and geothermal power stations. Mercury says most of its scope 1 emissions relate to geothermal generation. New technology has the potential to solve this issue. Early trials of reinjection at one of its geothermal plants has reduced annual emissions by 25 per cent. This new tech will require monitoring of the impacts on the plant to determine if it is commercially viable.

The board has responsibility for the strategic oversight and direction of the company. The risk assurance and audit committee oversees climate-related risk and opportunities. A range of committees support the board, the chief executive and the executive management team. A component of short-term incentive remuneration is aligned to a set of key performance indicators which include climate-related objectives.

Mercury has many partnerships and affiliations. It is a founding member of the Climate Leaders Coalition, which brings together 60 New Zealand businesses that have pledged to take action on climate change and report on their greenhouse gas emissions. It is a signatory to the UN Global Compact, a member of the Sustainable Business Council and the Sustainable Electricity Association of New Zealand, and is accredited by Renewable Energy Assurance Limited. Mercury reports in line with the GRI standards.

ESG risks	ESG measured	Assessment	Result
ESG exposure	ESG risk rating assessment		✓
	ESG exposure risk classification	Low	✓
	ESG risk exposure score	33.00	—
	ESG excess exposure score	(1.00)	✓
	ESG risk score momentum	0.44	X
ESG sub-industry risk	ESG sub-industry rank	30/93	✓
	ESG risk compared to sub-industry peers	(2.43)	✓
	ESG risk beta	0.97	✓
Management of ESG risk	Management of ESG risks score	42.37	—
	Classification of management ESG risks	Average	—
	ESG risk management score momentum	1.36	✓
Company controversy	Level of company controversy exposure	Low	✓
	Notable ESG issues	Community relations	

Carbon emissions	Measured risks	Assessment	Result
	Carbon overall risk	Negligible	✓
	Carbon overall risk score	0	✓
	Carbon total emissions, scopes 1, 2 and 3	294 127.00	—
	Carbon level of involvement	0	✓
	Level of fossil fuel involvement	0%	✓
	Carbon intensity, scopes 1, 2 and 3	204.43	—

Meridian Energy Limited

ASX code: MEZ www.meridianenergy.com.au

Market capitalisation:	$12 548.42 million
Sector:	Utilities
Morningstar Sustainalytics peer group classification:	Independent Power Production and Traders

Environmental risk score		Social risk score		Governance risk score	
3.27	✓	8.88	–	6.13	✓

View: Meridian is a renewable energy producer with strong ambition in carbon reduction validated by SBTi, but scope 3 is yet to be incorporated.

History/background

Meridian Energy is a New Zealand electricity generator and retailer that produces power only from 100 per cent renewable sources such as wind, water and sun. It operates 12 power stations in New Zealand and five in Australia and sells electricity through its Meridian and Powershop brands.

Meridian Energy was formed in 1999 after the breakup of the Electricity Corporation of New Zealand (ECNZ), a state-owned enterprise that controlled most of the country's electricity generation and transmission. Meridian inherited the Waitaki River and Manapouri hydro schemes, which remain its main assets. In 2013 Meridian was partially privatised by the New Zealand Government, which sold 49 per cent of its shares to the public while retaining a 51 per cent stake.

Since its establishment, Meridian has invested in developing new renewable energy projects, such as wind farms and solar arrays, both in New Zealand and Australia. It has also expanded its customer base by acquiring other electricity retailers, such as OnEnergy and Powershop. Meridian is committed to sustainability and has several partnerships and initiatives that support its environmental, social and financial goals.

The company's purpose is clean energy for a fairer and healthier world. Its strategy consists of promoting a more sustainable planet, greater sustainability for customers, more sustainable communities and a more sustainable company.

ESG performance

Meridian Energy bases its climate action plan on science-based targets of limiting global warming to 1.5 degrees Celsius. It aims to achieve net zero for its own operations, with the assistance of carbon offsets, by FY25. Scope 3 is not included, however, and according to its integrated annual report of 2023 this makes up 95 per cent of its GHG emissions. Its next target is to halve its gross operational emissions by FY30 off the FY21 baseline across all scopes, which it calls 'half by 30'. This ambition has been validated by SBTi. Its pathway to achieving this target is through:

- renewable generation, growing its pipeline of renewable energy projects and seeking out new opportunities in renewable energy such as hydrogen

- customer decarbonisation, which includes helping customers replace fossil fuel boilers with electrode boilers and heat pumps and increasing electric vehicle charging networks

- managing emissions, including by reducing carbon emissions to meet net zero goals.

Meridian is a signatory to the UN Global Compact. It adopted the TCFD framework to identify climate-related risks and opportunities and is reporting in line with XRB, a year before it is required to. Its annual report is aligned with the GRI standards.

ESG risks	ESG measured	Assessment	Result
ESG exposure	ESG risk rating assessment		✓
	ESG exposure risk classification	Low	✓
	ESG risk exposure score	36.60	X
	ESG excess exposure score	(0.40)	✓
	ESG risk score momentum	(5.29)	✓
ESG sub-industry risk	ESG sub-industry rank	9/83	✓
	ESG risk compared to sub-industry peers	(16.70)	✓
	ESG risk beta	0.99	✓
Management of ESG risk	Management of ESG risks score	52.95	—
	Classification of management ESG risks	Strong	✓
	ESG risk management score momentum	6.02	✓
Company controversy	Level of company controversy exposure	Low	✓
	Notable ESG issues	Product governance	

Carbon emissions	Measured risks	Assessment	Result
	Carbon overall risk	Negligible	✓
	Carbon overall risk score	0	✓
	Carbon total emissions, scopes 1, 2 and 3	917 127.00	X
	Carbon level of involvement	0	✓
	Level of fossil fuel involvement	0%	✓
	Carbon intensity, scopes 1, 2 and 3	301.57	—

Concluding remarks

The real estate sector is well advanced on its sustainable journey relative to other sectors; in fact, all stocks selected have negligible ESG risk, which is the best possible rating outcome.

In addition, all management teams of the real estate stocks were assessed as strong, which means they are considered to be managing ESG risks extremely competently. Looking at the data, Dexus achieved the highest raw management score followed by Scentre, Mirvac and Vicinity, but all were assessed as strong so the differences between the companies' management teams are at the margin.

On ESG momentum Mirvac had the highest improved momentum followed by Stockland, with the others assessed exhibiting slightly higher ESG risks year on year. Mirvac's momentum was very positive on its management of ESG risks, although Goodman also scored well on this metric.

On carbon metrics all the real estate companies in the chapter were classified as low risk. Goodman had the lowest carbon exposure followed by Mirvac then Vicinity.

On total carbon emissions across scopes 1, 2 and 3, remembering this data is lagged and was current as of 2021, Scentre was the highest, followed by Vicinity and Dexus. Next was Stockland and Mirvac; Goodman was the lowest.

A number of the companies did well on carbon solution metrics, which captured a range of activities including renewable energy production. Vicinty Centres was the best here with the highest level of involvement in carbon solutions, followed by Stockland, Mirvac then Dexus. Scentre and Goodman were assessed at having zero exposure to carbon solutions.

The utility stocks selected also rated very well on overall ESG risk, but not as well as the real estate stocks. On management of ESG risks Meridian was assessed as strong whereas Mercury was assessed as average.

Meridian Energy was the standout on improved ESG capability, with extremely strong positive momentum year on year for its ESG risks; Mercury had increased ESG risk but only marginally. Likewise for management of ESG risks, Meridian exhibited high positive momentum in management of ESG risks. Mercury also exhibited positive momentum in its management of ESG risks, although not to the same magnitude as Meridian. A good result nonetheless.

On carbon risk both companies were deemed to have no carbon risk. Meridian, however, had significantly higher scopes 1, 2 and 3 emissions than Mercury.

Both companies were assessed as having high levels of involvement in carbon solutions, which captured a range of activities including renewable energy production.

10. Technology

This sector includes a diverse collection of companies across data processing, enterprise and infrastructure software, distribution and other tech management solutions. It is often favoured by sustainable investors because it tends to do well across various ESG metrics. These companies are often innovative and able to develop software solutions to contribute to decarbonisation ambitions by delivering efficiency gains for sustainability challenges.

Most companies in this sector have relatively low scopes 1 and 2 emissions, but the elephant in the room is scope 3; many companies are not directly tackling scope 3. A number of these companies are still in the process of building out their scope 3 data capture. Of the seven companies selected for this chapter, only two had made net zero commitments and only one had incorporated scope 3 as part of its decarbonisation commitment. Further, a number of companies were carbon neutral partly through the use of carbon offsets, yet had made no net zero commitments.

Perhaps because this sector does so well on ESG metrics, particularly scopes 1 and 2 carbon emissions, it generally seemed less advanced on decarbonisation efforts than other sectors. Companies operating in this sector typically have not signed the UN Global Compact or joined other organisations that are supporting the advancement of sustainability issues.

IRESS Limited

ASX code: IRE   www.iress.com

Market capitalisation:	1313.13 million
Sector:	Technology
Morningstar Sustainalytics peer group classification:	Data Processing

Environmental risk score		Social risk score		Governance risk score	
1.24	✓	7.76	✓	5.23	✓

View: With no net zero commitments yet it has a lot to do, but it has plans.

History/background

IRESS is a technology company that provides software and information services to the financial services industry in the Asia-Pacific, North America, Africa, the UK and Europe. Some of its products and services are:

- Xplan — a financial advice software platform that helps advisers manage their clients, compliance and business performance

- IRESS Order System — a trade order management software that connects traders, brokers and market participants across multiple asset classes and markets

- Financial Synergy — superannuation administration software that supports the delivery of member outcomes and engagement

- QuantHouse — a global provider of end-to-end systematic trading solutions, including ultra-low latency market data, the algo trading development framework and infrastructure solutions.

IRESS was founded in 1993 as Dunai Financial Systems by Peter Dunai, Neil Detering and Hung Do. Two years later, they launched the equity information software product 'Iress'. In 1997, Bridge Information Systems acquired 80 per cent of the company and formed BridgeDFS. In 2000 the company listed on the Australian Securities Exchange as BIS.ASX and changed its name to Iress Market Technology Limited in 2001. Since then, IRESS has expanded its global presence and diversified its product portfolio through a series of acquisitions. In October 2023 SS&C acquired the managed funds administration business from IRESS. IRESS retains ownership of the rest of its products.

ESG performance

IRESS is committed to internationally recognised sustainability risks, including climate change and modern slavery, and supports science-backed targets. It aligns itself with SDGs and reports in line with TCFD.

It has outlined its environmental and social impact roadmap, which rests on four pillars:

- Healthy environment—emissions management and climate change, e waste

- Prospering community—quality education, decent work, charitable services

- People wellbeing—diversity and inclusion, human rights

- Responsible business—corporate governance, risk management.

Internally, it dubs its short- and medium-term goals as winning steps that have ESG objectives embedded in them. The prioritised winning steps are ESG strategy, emissions reduction, IRESS impact (charitable support) and diversity.

IRESS conducted a materiality assessment that identified 20 material topics across four areas: social and IRESS impact, environmental, customer and product, and governance. The material topics in environment are climate change adaptation and resilience, waste and resource efficiency.

It has undertaken a climate risk and opportunity assessment and created a roadmap to improve future climate disclosures. It has set a near-term emissions-reduction target for 2030 to reduce scopes 1 and 2 emissions by 46.2 per cent from an FY19 baseline and to reduce scope 3 emissions by at least 18.5 per cent by 2030. These targets are aligned to SBTi and IRESS has submitted the plans for validation by SBTi. However, approximately 95 per cent of emissions come from scope 3.

Among the activities IRESS is undertaking to reach its emissions targets are continued transition to cloud-based technology and retiring hundreds of physical servers. The cloud provider is committed to using 100 per cent renewable energy. IRESS is also switching to renewable energy for its offices and reducing its electricity consumption by leasing smaller office space and transitioning to energy-efficient buildings.

It has established a robust procurement assessment process, which is enshrined in the IRESS sustainable procurement policy and the supplier code of ethics policy. These outline expectations of shared values including capturing environmental impacts.

On governance, it has revised its audit and risk committee charter to incorporate environmental and social risk. The chief legal officer was appointed as the climate sponsor. Climate-related risks were also added to its enterprise risk register.

It is reporting in accordance with the GRI standards. It has many affiliations, though few (if any) seem to be sustainability related. It is not a signatory to the UN Global Compact. It is picking up the pace on its sustainability journey and has a plan of attack.

ESG risks	ESG measured	Assessment	Result
ESG exposure	ESG risk rating assessment		✓
	ESG exposure risk classification	Low	✓
	ESG risk exposure score	30.45	—
	ESG excess exposure score	(1.55)	✓
	ESG risk score momentum	(0.57)	✓
ESG sub-industry risk	ESG sub-industry rank	6/101	✓
	ESG risk compared to sub-industry peers	(6.75)	✓
	ESG risk beta	0.95	✓
Management of ESG risk	Management of ESG risks score	57.16	—
	Classification of management ESG risks	Strong	✓
	ESG risk management score momentum	2.00	✓
Company controversy	Level of company controversy exposure	None	✓
	Notable ESG issues	Human capital	

Carbon emissions	Measured risks	Assessment	Result
	Carbon overall risk	Negligible	✓
	Carbon overall risk score	0	✓
	Carbon total emissions, scopes 1, 2 and 3	17 290.00	✓
	Carbon level of involvement	0	✓
	Level of fossil fuel involvement	0%	✓
	Carbon intensity, scopes 1, 2 and 3	39.56	✓

Dicker Data Limited

ASX code: DDR www.dickerdata.com.au

Market capitalisation:	$2093.51
Sector:	Technology
Sustainalytics peer group classification:	Technology Distribution

Environmental risk score		Social risk score		Governance risk score	
3.70	✓	3.89	✓	5.21	✓

View: With no commitments to reduce emissions, and no scopes 1, 2 or 3 data, as mandatory climate reporting comes into effect it will have much to do.

History/background

Dicker Data is an Australian-owned and operated, ASX-listed technology hardware, software and cloud distributor. Its products and services include:

- Cloud solutions. Dicker Data works with leading cloud vendors such as Cisco, Citrix, Microsoft and VMware to deliver cloud computing solutions for digital transformation projects.

- Data centre solutions. Dicker Data is a certified distributor of data centre solutions from vendors such as Dell Technologies, Hewlett Packard Enterprise, Lenovo and Intel.

- Cybersecurity solutions. Dicker Data provides comprehensive cybersecurity solutions from vendors such as Aruba, SonicWall, Trend Micro and Veritas to protect data, devices and networks from cyber threats.

- Business applications. Dicker Data delivers business applications that enhance collaboration and productivity from vendors such as Cisco, Citrix and Microsoft.

- Accessories and peripherals. Dicker Data distributes a wide range of technology accessories and peripherals from vendors such as HP, Logitech, Samsung and Seagate.

Dicker Data was founded by David Dicker in 1978 as a distributor of data storage products. Over time it began to distribute a wide range of IT hardware and software products. In 2001 the company went public, listing on the ASX. A couple of years later the company established a partnership with Hewlett Packard, which was a significant moment in the company's history. In 2014 Dicker Data acquired Express Data Holdings, a leading distributor of IT products in Australia and New Zealand. In 2021 it acquired Exeed Group, a New Zealand–based IT distributor, and relocated to its new headquarters in Kurnell, Sydney. In 2022, Dicker Data acquired the security division from Hills, a provider of integrated security and surveillance solutions, and launched Dicker Data Access and Surveillance.

ESG performance

The company says it recognises the importance of sustainable business practices for long-term success but it is relatively early on its journey. There is no reporting in line with TCFD, no climate scenario assessments, no ESG materiality assessment, no climate data and no net zero commitments. It produces no sustainability report, although a few pages in the annual report are dedicated to sustainability. There is also no commitment to the Paris Agreement or other science-backed targets, and no climate reporting although it is mentioned in the corporate governance statement. It is proud of its new headquarters, which has rooftop solar that generates 56 per cent of the power consumed, and it is increasing its solar capacity, which means it may be able to run off grid across a range of weather conditions. It has made an effort to reduce use of new boxes by 50 per cent for outbound shipments and is a member of APCO. It is committed to delivering packaging that is 100 per cent reusable, recyclable or compostable by FY25. It has also reduced single-use plastics.

Despite this minimal approach to sustainability, Dicker Data does well on a range of ESG metrics, even though it seems not to be a key focus. It is concerning how it is going to manage transitioning to the new climate disclosure standards given it seems to be so far behind its peers on this score.

ESG risks	ESG measured	Assessment	Result
ESG exposure	ESG risk rating assessment		✓
	ESG exposure risk classification	Low	✓
	ESG risk exposure score	17.10	✓
	ESG excess exposure score	0.10	X
	ESG risk score momentum	No data	n/a
ESG sub-industry risk	ESG sub-industry rank	34/61	–
	ESG risk compared to sub-industry peers	0.37	X
	ESG risk beta	1.01	X
Management of ESG risk	ESG risk management score momentum	26.14	X
	Classification of management ESG risks	Average	–
	Momentum of management of ESG risks	No data	n/a
Company controversy	Level of company controversy exposure	None	✓
	Notable ESG issues	Carbon – own operations	

Carbon emissions	Measured risks	Assessment	Result
	Carbon overall risk	Medium	–
	Carbon overall risk score	14.14	–
	Carbon total emissions, scopes 1, 2 and 3	20 162.02	✓
	Carbon level of involvement	0	✓
	Level of fossil fuel involvement	0%	✓
	Carbon intensity, scopes 1, 2 and 3	11.09	✓

Technology One Limited

ASX code: TNE   www.technologyonecorp.com

Market capitalisation:	$5090.90 million
Sector:	Technology
Morningstar Sustainalytics peer group classification:	Enterprise and Infrastructure Software

Environmental risk score		Social risk score		Governance risk score	
4.24	✓	8.08	✓	5.18	✓

View: Certified carbon neutral and targeting reduction in scopes 1 and 2 emissions, but scope 3 is where the bulk of its emissions lie.

History/background

Technology One is an Australian enterprise software company that provides software as a service and enterprise resource planning solutions to a range of industries such as local government, education, health and community services, and more. Some of its key products and services are:

- Financials—a comprehensive financial management system that covers accounting, budgeting, reporting and analytics

- Student management—a student administration system that supports the entire student lifecycle, from enrolment to graduation

- Enterprise asset management—a solution that helps organisations manage their physical assets, such as buildings, equipment and infrastructure

- Corporate performance management—a tool that enables strategic planning, performance monitoring and reporting across the organisation.

Technology One was founded by Adrian Di Marco in 1987, when he saw an opportunity to build a new generation of accounting software using relational database technology. He approached investors John and Dugald Mactaggart, a former customer, for financial backing. The company set up its first R&D centre in a demountable office in the car park at Mactaggart's hide processing plant in Brisbane. Since then Technology One has grown to become one of Australia's top 100 ASX-listed companies, with offices in the UK, New Zealand, the South Pacific and Asia. The company has also invested heavily in cloud technology, artificial intelligence and machine learning to deliver innovative solutions to its customers. In 2017 Di Marco stepped down as CEO and Edward Chung took over the role.

ESG performance

The board and committees are involved in the ESG agenda and reporting, and leaders throughout the business ensure ESG impacts are aligned to the company's sustainability focus areas. An ESG framework sets out the sustainability agenda and informs business priorities. A materiality assessment identifies the key ESG risks and opportunities. The framework has five pillars mapped to E, S and G objectives. They are:

- Our world
- Our people
- Our community
- Our customers
- Responsible business.

Technology One recognises the science of climate change and the imperative of permanent GHG reductions in line with Paris Agreement. Like many others in this sector its own operations are GHG light and do not have a significant negative impact (as captured by scopes 1 and 2 emissions), but tackling scope 3 is where the rubber hits the road. It predicts that customers transitioning from an on-premise solution to a SaaS solution by FY25 could see energy use decrease by as much as 80 per cent. Its carbon reduction initiatives cover employee engagement and awareness to help reduce energy consumption, operational reductions by improved energy efficiency, increased use of renewable energy, a reduction of consumption and waste and recycle-and-reuse e waste.

The company is certified by Climate Active as carbon neutral for its global operations. It has invested in certified carbon offset credits to cover the remaining emissions. It has set emissions-reduction targets for scopes 1 and 2 global emissions. The ambition is to reduce emissions by 80 per cent by FY25 and 100 per cent by FY30 from a FY22 baseline. Missing are scope 3 emissions-reduction targets, however, which is where the bulk of its emissions are captured.

Technology One undertakes regular climate scenario analysis to understand the risk and opportunities. In FY22 three different climate scenarios were analysed across physical and transition risks. The process identified 15 issues, and it has outlined activities it can undertake to mitigate these issues, including GHG emissions reduction, improved climate risk disclosures and transparency, vendor assurance of climate risk–related management, and safeguards around critical infrastructure and connectivity.

It regularly assesses material issues using a methodology that is in line with the GRI standards. The issues are then ranked. Of the 15 issues, 11 were ranked 'very high' and four were ranked 'high'. Interestingly, environmental impact and maintaining carbon neutral operations were rated only 'high', rather than 'very high'.

The board oversees progress against strategic programs and approves disclosures, including against the TCFD. The risk management framework and the audit and risk committee oversee material risks. The nominations and governance committee reviews sustainability agenda and progress against key priorities. The executive team is accountable for the implementation of key objectives and programs under the sustainability agenda. Reporting to the chief financial officer, the group company secretary and head of compliance and risk are accountable for the environmental sustainability agenda. Climate risk is embedded in the risk management framework.

Reporting is aligned with TCFD and the GRI standards and linked to SDGs.

ESG risks	ESG measured	Assessment	Result
ESG exposure	ESG risk rating assessment	▰▰▰▰▱	✓
	ESG exposure risk classification	Low	✓
	ESG risk exposure score	32.10	—
	ESG excess exposure score	(1.90)	✓
	ESG risk score momentum	0.21	X
ESG sub-industry risk	ESG sub-industry rank	53/443	✓
	ESG risk compared to sub-industry peers	(4.91)	✓
	ESG risk beta	0.94	✓
Management of ESG risk	Management of ESG risks score	49.13	—
	Classification of management ESG risks	Average	—
	ESG risk management score momentum	(0.07)	X
Company controversy	Level of company controversy exposure	Low	✓
	Notable ESG issues	Human capital	

Carbon emissions	Measured risks	Assessment	Result
	Carbon overall risk	Low	✓
	Carbon overall risk score	5.15	✓
	Carbon total emissions, scopes 1, 2 and 3	5513.30	✓
	Carbon level of involvement	0	✓
	Level of fossil fuel involvement	0%	✓
	Carbon intensity, scopes 1, 2 and 3	24.15	✓

Altium Limited

ASX code: ALU

www.altium.com

Average market capitalisation:	$5934.07 million
Sector:	Technology
Morningstar Sustainalytics peer group classification:	Enterprise and Infrastructure Software

Environmental risk score		Social risk score		Governance risk score	
1.35	✓	11.08	✓	4.61	✓

View: Early on its decarbonisation journey, with no net zero targets in place, Altium is working with external consultants to understand its emissions.

History/background

Altium Ltd provides electronic design automation software to engineers who design printed circuit boards. Some of its key products and services are:

- Altium Designer — a software package for unified electronics design that covers schematic capture, board layout, routing, testing, analysis and FPGA design

- Altium 365 — a cloud platform that enables agile collaboration and design sharing across the entire PCB design process

- Altium NEXUS — a team-based, cloud-enabled printed circuit board (PCB) design solution that supports workflow management and resource allocation

- CircuitStudio — a professional PCB design tool for hobbyists and makers

- CircuitMaker — a free community-driven PCB design tool for open-source hardware projects

- Octopart — a search engine for electronic components and parts that provides data on availability, pricing and specifications.

Altium Ltd was founded in 1985 as Protel Systems Pty Ltd by Nicholas Martin, an electronics designer from the University of Tasmania. The company launched its first product, a DOS-based PCB layout and design tool, in 1985. In 1991 it released the world's first Windows-based PCB design system. In 1999 it went public on the Australian Securities Exchange and changed its name to Altium. Since then it has acquired various companies and technologies to create a unified electronics design solution. In 2020 it initiated its Netflix Moment reorganisation, separating its CAD software from its cloud business and bifurcating its sales organisation into high-volume digital and high-touch value sales teams. In 2021 it sold its embedded software business unit, TASKING, to FSN Capital. Altium is now a global market leader in PCB design software, with offices in the United States, Australia, China, Europe and Japan.

ESG performance

Its sustainability objectives are to understand its impact on the economy, environment and society, increase accountability for an enhanced transparency of the sustainable development of electronic products and improve sustainability information supplied to stakeholders.

Altium focuses on three ESG themes:

- Facilitating environmental sustainability in electronics, collaborating with industry partners to make PCB design processes more efficient, using less materials and energy and creating less waste

- Facilitating access to education for women and girls via a scholarship program to become PCB design engineers

- Transformational governance for its board and company.

These key themes are integrated into its strategic vision.

To determine its material risks, Altium worked with an external advisory group. The main five material risks are data security and privacy, business continuity and platform availability, compliance and ethics, corporate governance and cybersecurity.

On climate change, it is measuring baseline GHG emissions across scopes 1, 2 and 3 in order to understand its largest sources of GHG emissions. It applied a science-based targets methodology to undertake the work and help decide on its future emissions-reduction roadmap. Again, Altium worked with an external consultant to undertake this work.

Given the company is so early on its climate emissions journey, it has not undertaken climate scenario analysis.

Altium reports in line with GRI, SASB and TCFD standards. As a founding member of the IPC Sustainability for Electronics Leadership Council, it is taking an active role in the development of the IPC sustainability strategy.

ESG risks	ESG measured	Assessment	Result
ESG exposure	ESG risk rating assessment		✓
	ESG exposure risk classification	Low	✓
	ESG risk exposure score	28.10	–
	ESG excess exposure score	(1.90)	X
	ESG risk score momentum	0	–
ESG sub-industry risk	ESG sub-industry rank	44/443	✓
	ESG risk compared to sub-industry peers	(5.37)	✓
	ESG risk beta	0.94	✓
Management of ESG risk	Management of ESG risks score	42.26	–
	Classification of management ESG risks	Average	–
	ESG risk management score momentum	0	–
Company controversy	Level of company controversy exposure	None	✓
	Notable ESG issues	Human capital	

Carbon emissions	Measured risks	Assessment	Result
	Carbon overall risk	Negligible	✓
	Carbon overall risk score	0	✓
	Carbon total emissions, scopes 1, 2 and 3	10 557.66	✓
	Carbon level of involvement	0	✓
	Level of fossil fuel involvement	0%	✓
	Carbon intensity, scopes 1, 2 and 3	59.59	✓

NEXTDC Limited

ASX code: NXT

Market capitalisation:	$6717.87 million
Sector:	Technology
Morningstar Sustainalytics peer group classification:	Real Estate Management

Environmental risk score		Social risk score		Governance risk score	
4.85	✓	5.29	✓	6.10	✓

View: NEXTDC is committed to sustainability and recognises the link between good ESG management and financial performance, but has yet to make net zero commitments.

History/background

NEXTDC is an Australian data centre operator that provides colocation solutions, connectivity services and infrastructure management software to various industries. Some of its key products and services are:

- Data centres. NEXTDC operates 11 data centres around Australia, with facilities in Melbourne, Sydney, Brisbane, Perth, Canberra, Adelaide and Maroochydore. Its data centres are certified by the Uptime Institute for Tier III or Tier IV standards, ensuring high levels of availability, reliability and security.

- AXON. This virtual connectivity platform enables customers to access cloud platforms, service providers and vendors through a single interface. AXON allows customers to create and manage network connections on demand, reducing costs and complexity.

- ONEDC. A data centre infrastructure management software that provides customers with real-time visibility and control over their data centre assets and operations, ONEDC allows customers to monitor power, cooling, security and capacity across multiple data centres

- NEXTneutral. This carbon offset program allows customers to reduce their environmental impact by purchasing carbon credits equivalent to their data centre energy consumption. NEXTneutral supports projects that generate renewable energy, protect biodiversity and improve social outcomes.

NEXTDC was founded by Bevan Slattery in 2010, with the vision of building and operating carrier- and vendor-neutral data centres in Australia and New Zealand. The company listed on the ASX in 2010 and opened its first data centre in Brisbane in 2011. Since then NEXTDC has expanded its network of data centres across the country, as well as investing in cloud technology, artificial intelligence and machine learning to deliver innovative solutions to its customers. NEXTDC has also been recognised by various awards and certifications for its excellence in data centre engineering and design, customer experience and energy efficiency. In 2021 NEXTDC announced its plans to enter the international market, with data centres in development in Malaysia, Japan and New Zealand.

ESG performance

This company has lofty ambitions on sustainability, seeking to lead the way in energy efficiency and sustainability within its data centres. Although currently it has no targeted emissions-reduction plans in place, its ambition is to develop a net zero pathway across all scopes.

As a business, its largest carbon emissions are scope 2, primarily the energy emissions from powering its data centres. This is unusual, as in most companies scope 3 is the highest emission point. Arguably, this favours NEXTDC, as it has direct control over management of scope 2 emissions.

The company has many sustainability ambitions. It is prioritising 100 per cent renewable energy across its facilities, including rooftop solar. It plans to make sustainability gains when upgrading and building new facilities. It will look to take a whole-of-life approach to sustainability reporting, accounting for a data centre's carbon footprint from design to decommission. It will also seek to minimise use of energy wherever possible, and reduce water use and waste. To that end, NEXTDC's S1 Sydney data centre became the first data centre in Australia to achieve TRUE (Total Resource Use and Efficiency) certification, validating its efficient use of resources. It provides good detail around its energy management, power usage effectiveness, water usage and waste management.

Currently it provides scopes 1 and 2 emissions data, but is only selectively monitoring and reporting scope 3 emissions, although it says it is working to improve its scope 3 transparency. One obvious missing component is net zero commitments and a pathway to achieve them, across all scopes.

In its 2023 ESG report it outlines five environmental objectives:

1. Design data centres using the latest technology to reduce energy usage, improving environmental controls and our impact on the environment

2. Operate data centres maximising the designed intent

3. Comply with all applicable legislative and regulatory requirements relating to energy and the environment

4. Increase awareness of how each individual at NEXTDC can contribute towards reducing their impact on energy usage and the environment

5. Maintain communications with employees and external stakeholders on environmental issues and transparently report on our environmental performance to interested parties.

In FY23 it undertook its first scenario analysis to determine the climate-related risk and opportunities in the business. It assessed a range of scenarios, identified potential risks and opportunities, and considered these across current risk controls.

NEXTDC assesses materiality annually to ensure it is managing sustainability risks appropriately. It has identified 10 material risks for FY23; the specific environmental material topics are energy consumption, climate change and environmental sustainability.

On governance the board has ultimate responsibility for assessing risks, including climate-related risks. The audit and risk management committee is responsible for ESG policies and the leadership team is responsible for implementation, aided by the ESG manager and the risk and compliance team. Short-term incentives include climate-related objectives.

In its FY23 ESG report, NEXTDC made the link between ESG and financial performance.

NEXTDC reports in line with TCFD and the GRI standards.

This company shows a lot of positive intention and ambition, but actions matter most. Time to make some net zero commitments!

ESG risks	ESG measured	Assessment	Result
ESG exposure	ESG risk rating assessment	▮▮▮▮▯	✓
	ESG exposure risk classification	Low	✓
	ESG risk exposure score	30.55	—
	ESG excess exposure score	2.55	X
	ESG risk score momentum	(1.35)	✓
ESG sub-industry risk	ESG sub-industry rank	87/164	—
	ESG risk compared to sub-industry peers	0.22	X
	ESG risk beta	1.09	X
Management of ESG Risk	Management of ESG risks score	47.56	—
	Classification of management ESG risks	Average	—
	ESG risk management score momentum	5.90	✓
Company controversy	Level of company controversy exposure	None	✓
	Notable ESG issues	ESG integration – financials	

Carbon emissions	Measured risks	Assessment	Result
	Carbon overall risk	Medium	—
	Carbon overall risk score	12.85	—
	Carbon total emissions, scopes 1, 2 and 3	306 413.01	—
	Carbon level of involvement	0	✓
	Level of fossil fuel involvement	0%	✓
	Carbon intensity, scopes 1, 2 and 3	1698.03	X

Xero Limited

ASX code: XRO www.xero.com.au

Market capitalisation:	$15 606.41 million
Sector:	Technology
Morningstar Sustainalytics peer group classification:	Enterprise and Infrastructure Software

Environmental risk score		Social risk score		Governance risk score	
1.35	✓	9.07	–	5.68	✓

View: With a commitment to net zero by 2050 across all scopes, Xero's interim pathway is consistent with SBTi.

History/background

Xero provides cloud-based accounting software for small businesses. Some of its key products and services are:

- Accounting software—software that connects small business owners with their numbers, their bank and advisors anytime

- Expense management—a tool that helps manage spending and submit or reimburse expense claims

- Bank connections—a feature that allows users to get their bank data into Xero from over 21 000 financial institutions globally

- Accept payments—a function that enables users to accept online payments by credit card, debit card or direct debit straight from their Xero invoice

- Track projects—a solution that tracks time, costs and profitability of project

- GST returns—a service that simplifies the process of filing GST returns in Australia.

- Bank reconciliation—a process that matches transactions in Xero with those in the bank statement

- Manage Xero contacts—a system that stores and organises contact information of customers and suppliers

- Capture data—a capability that allows users to scan and extract data from receipts and bills using Xero's mobile app

- Xero App Store—a marketplace that offers more than 1000 third-party apps and integrations that connect to Xero.

Xero was founded by Rod Drury and Hamish Edwards in 2006 in Wellington, New Zealand, where its headquarters are still located. The company was originally called Accounting 2.01. It went public on the New Zealand Exchange in 2007 and on the ASX in 2012. It transitioned to a sole listing on the ASX in 2018. In 2018 Steve Vamos replaced Rod Drury as CEO, and in 2023, Sukhinder Singh Cassidy took over the role.

ESG performance

Xero's environmental sustainability objectives are to:

- reduce electricity consumption in buildings

- reduce waste and increase recycling

- evaluate its greenhouse gas emissions footprint

- reduce greenhouse gas emissions by encouraging alternative modes of transport for employees

- minimise carbon-intensive travel options such as air travel and encourage video and teleconference meetings

- enhance procurement processes so environmental impacts are a key consideration when engaging with its supply chain—for example, minimising the carbon impact of transportation.

Xero is certified carbon neutral by Climate Active and has been offsetting its carbon emissions since FY19. The company has a decarbonisation program in place, 'Net Zero @ Xero' by 2050. It aims to achieve net zero emissions by 2050. Its interim pathway to net zero is to reduce scopes 1 and 2 emissions by 42 per cent and to reduce scope 3 emissions by 17 per cent by FY30 compared to the FY20 baseline. These emission targets are aligned with science-based target net zero guidance. It will achieve them by increasing its use of renewable energy, more efficient management of energy consumption by light sensors and timer lighting, and providing end-of-trip facilities to alternative modes of transport. For scope 3 it is undertaking work to improve its emissions inventory and to better engage with suppliers and customers.

It is also planning on conducting a supplier assessment and build out a scope 3 reduction roadmap so it can operationalise its emissions-reduction target.

Xero's board is responsible for strategy and performance oversight, which includes ESG issues. The audit and risk management committee provides oversight of the climate strategy, governance and performance. Regular TCFD updates are provided including reporting on progress on emissions reduction. Climate change risk is included on Xero's risk radar. The CFO is the company's climate sponsor and responsible for climate change–related issues, supported by the ESG steering committee and the climate working group. The ESG steering committee is made up of senior leaders within the company. The sustainability team manages implementation of the TCFD roadmap.

Reporting uses global standards such as TCFD. It provides a databook with environmental and social datapoints, a TCFD statement and a supplier code of conduct. It is a signatory to the UN Global Compact. In relation to climate ambition and activities, Xero is the standout company in the technology sector.

ESG risks	ESG measured	Assessment	Result
ESG exposure	ESG risk rating assessment		✓
	ESG exposure risk classification	Low	✓
	ESG risk exposure score	30.70	–
	ESG excess exposure score	0.70	X
	ESG risk score momentum	(0.28)	✓
ESG sub-industry risk	ESG sub-industry rank	29/443	✓
	ESG risk compared to sub-industry peers	(6.32)	✓
	ESG risk beta	1.02	X
Management of ESG risk	Management of ESG risks score	50.94	–
	Classification of management ESG risks	Strong	✓
	ESG risk management score momentum	(1.16)	X
Company controversy	Level of company controversy exposure	None	✓
	Notable ESG issues	Human capital	

Carbon emissions	Measured risks	Assessment	Result
	Carbon overall risk	Negligible	✓
	Carbon overall risk score	0	✓
	Carbon total emissions, scopes 1, 2 and 3	4301.00	✓
	Carbon level of involvement	0	✓
	Level of fossil fuel involvement	0%	✓
	Carbon intensity, scopes 1, 2 and 3	7.40	✓

WiseTech Global Limited

ASX code: WTC

www.wisetechglobal.com

Market capitalisation:	$22 265.46 million
Sector:	Technology
Morningstar Sustainalytics peer group classification:	Enterprise and Infrastructure Software

Environmental risk score		Social risk score		Governance risk score	
4.63	✓	9.36	–	5.37	✓

View: Still collecting data, WiseTech is a long way behind the leaders in this space.

History/background

WiseTech provides software solutions for the supply chain management of various industries and organisations. Some of its key products and services are:

- CargoWise—a cloud-based platform that offers end-to-end logistics solutions for freight forwarders, customs brokers, transport providers, warehouse operators and more

- Borderwise—a border compliance software that simplifies the complex processes of customs clearance and trade compliance

- CustomsWare—an on-demand customs clearance solution that is accredited for all customs regimes in Ireland, the Netherlands, Belgium, the United Kingdom, Switzerland, Sweden and Germany

- DataFreight—a software solution that provides customs, freight forwarding and warehouse management capabilities in the United Kingdom.

WiseTech was founded by Richard White and Maree Isaacs in 1994 in Sydney, Australia. They started by writing code for Australian freight forwarders and gradually expanded their product portfolio and customer base through organic growth and acquisitions. WiseTech went public in 2016 and entered the ASX 50 in 2021. WiseTech's mission is to create breakthrough products that enable and empower the supply chains of the world.

ESG performance

WiseTech's sustainability pillars are community, environment, marketplace and its people. Within that it has three priority impact areas: tech education, people and culture, and net zero carbon.

Every year it undertakes a materiality assessment to identify the most materially important sustainability issues for the company, and these priority issues are mapped to each of the four sustainability pillars. For the environment pillar the issues are climate change and decarbonisation and environmental management.

The board has oversight, implementation and management responsibility for sustainability and ESG practices. It is supported by various committees and is updated on a range of issues. FY23 saw the development of Sustainability and ESG principles that guide ESG integration into the business. The sustainability and ESG team reports to the chief financial officer and the team supports senior leaders on the day-to-day management of ESG risks and opportunities.

WiseTech links its various activities back to the relevant UN SDGs. It has identified five UN SDGs to which it directly contributes: quality education, decent work and economic growth, reduced inequities, responsible consumption and production, and climate action.

It is yet to commit to net zero, but it is building out its emissions inventory and adding scope 3 to the already collected scopes 1 and 2 data. Understanding your emissions is the first step to determine how they might be reduced. Currently scopes 1 and 2 emissions are 100 per cent offset by carbon credits.

It does not produce a separate sustainability report, but sustainability information is integrated into the annual report. Its reporting is in line with GRI and SASB. WiseTech is not leading the way in this sector.

ESG risks	ESG measured	Assessment	Result
ESG exposure	ESG risk rating assessment	▓▓▓▓░	✓
	ESG exposure risk classification	Low	✓
	ESG risk exposure score	31.45	—
	ESG excess exposure score	(2.55)	✓
	ESG risk score momentum	0.67	✗
ESG sub-industry risk	ESG sub-industry rank	105/443	✓
	ESG risk compared to sub-industry peers	(3.05)	✓
	ESG risk beta	0.93	✓
Management of ESG risk	Management of ESG risks score	41.16	—
	Classification of management ESG risks	Average	—
	ESG risk management score momentum	(1.77)	✗
Company controversy	Level of company controversy exposure	None	✓
	Notable ESG issues	Data privacy and security	

Carbon emissions	Measured risks	Assessment	Result
	Carbon overall risk	Low risk	✓
	Carbon overall risk score	7.32	✓
	Carbon total emissions, scopes 1, 2 and 3	9926.28	✓
	Carbon level of involvement	0	✓
	Level of fossil fuel involvement	0%	✓
	Carbon intensity, scopes 1, 2 and 3	26.67	✓

Concluding remarks

The tech sector typically does well on ESG metrics, and perhaps this is why there is a mixed approach to sustainability practices. As the sector it operates in is not as ESG challenged as others, perhaps it hasn't felt compelled to move swiftly into sustainable commitments. Despite all the selected companies being assessed as having low ESG risks, disappointingly only one company, Xero, has net zero reduction targets across all three scopes, and Technology One was the only other company that had net zero commitments, although these did not incorporate scope 3. All other companies had no net zero commitments, despite staring down the barrel of mandatory climate reporting.

IRESS and Xero were assessed as having strong management of ESG risk; the rest of the group were assessed as being average in their management of the risks. Dicker data had the lowest score in its management of ESG risks out of the top stocks in this sector. NEXTDC and IRESS had improving management of ESG risks compared to previous year. Altium was unchanged.

On ESG risk momentum year on year, NEXTDC was assessed as being most improved followed by IRESS and Xero. This metric captures those companies whose risks have improved compared to the previous year.

The companies exhibiting the lowest carbon risks were Xero, Altium and IRESS, all assessed as having negligible risk. Technology One and WiseTech had low risk and Dicker Data and NEXTDC had medium risk.

On scopes 1, 2 and 3 total carbon emissions, Xero had the lowest, followed by Technology One and WiseTech. NEXTDC and Dicker Data had the highest emissions across all scopes, although Dicker Data's were based on estimates as it didn't report its emissions. NEXTDC had the highest scope 2 emissions out of the cohort and Dicker Data had the highest scope 3, followed by IRESS.

Xero is the standout company in this sector. It has net zero commitments across all scopes, its management team is managing ESG risks well and it has positive momentum in its ESG risks. It also had the lowest carbon emissions across all scopes and is a signatory to the UN Global Compact.

PART II
THE TABLES

A. Companies ranked on market capitalisation. Secondary filter: Sustainalytics risk classification, from best (lowest risk) to worst (five-tier rating scale: negligible, low, medium, high, severe)

Company	Sustainalytics ESG risk classification	Market cap ($mil) AUD
BHP Group Ltd	Medium	234 482.13
National Australia Bank Ltd	Low	88 631.32
Fortescue Ltd	Medium	76 943.33
Scentre Group	Negligible	68772.51
Wesfarmers Ltd	Low	59 757.56
Woodside Energy Group Ltd	Medium	58 861.24
Goodman Group	Negligible	43 206.39
Transurban Group	Negligible	39 929.76
Vicinity Centres	Negligible	25 879.69
Mirvac Group	Negligible	24 377.61
QBE Insurance Group Ltd	Low	22 961.48
WiseTech Global Ltd	Low	22 265.46
Amcor PLC	Low	20 707.05
Coles Group Ltd	Low	20 517.54
News Corp DR	Low	19 264.84
Brambles Ltd	Low	18 533.32
Xero Ltd	Low	15 606.41
Origin Energy Ltd	High	14 195.44
South32 Ltd	Medium	13 950.12
Sonic Healthcare Ltd	Low	13 733.41
Meridian Energy Ltd	Low	12 548.42
Washington H. Soul Pattinson & Co Ltd	Low	12 092.42
Mineral Resources Ltd	Medium	11 939.55
Auckland International Airport Ltd	Low	10 870.12
Stockland Corp Ltd	Negligible	9859.02
BlueScope Steel Ltd	Medium	9306.31
Endeavour Group Ltd	Low	8829.53
SEEK Ltd	Low	8459.15
Atlas Arteria Ltd	Negligible	8414.84
Ampol Ltd	High	8157.08
Mercury NZ Ltd	Low	8062.32

(continued)

Company	Sustainalytics ESG risk classification	Market cap ($mil) AUD
Dexus	Negligible	7571.98
NEXTDC Ltd	Low	6717.87
Ebos Group Ltd	Low	6601.64
IDP Education Ltd	Low	6307.10
Lynas Rare Earths Ltd	Medium	6187.68
Altium Ltd	Low	5934.07
Incitec Pivot Ltd	Medium	5671.30
JB Hi-Fi Ltd	Low	5230.54
Qube Holdings Ltd	Low	5155.30
Technology One Ltd	Low	5090.90
Harvey Norman Holdings Ltd	Low	4896.81
Viva Energy Group Ltd	High	4756.03
Challenger Ltd	Low	4103.77
Premier Investments Ltd	Low	3893.98
NIB Holdings Ltd	Low	3664.44
Metcash Ltd	Low	3536.96
Eagers Automotive Ltd	Low	3439.90
Beach Energy Ltd	High	3387.78
Nine Entertainment Co. Holdings Ltd	Low	3149.61
Super Retail Group Ltd	Low	3136.73
Ansell Ltd	Low	2974.26
Deterra Royalties Ltd	Low	2622.10
Sims Ltd	Low	2585.15
De Grey Mining Ltd	Low	2138.80
Dicker Data Ltd	Low	2093.51
Bapcor Ltd	Low	1826.04
InvoCare Ltd	Low	1825.25
EVT Ltd	Low	1761.70
Magellan Financial Group Ltd	Low	1346.90
IRESS Ltd	Low	1313.13
Nanosonics Ltd	Low	1311.05
Imdex Ltd	Low	924.09
Vulcan Energy Resources Ltd	Low	433.62

B. Companies ranked by lowest ESG risk to highest risk by market cap

Company	Sustainalytics ESG Risk Classification
Goodman Group	Negligible
Transurban Group	Negligible
Scentre Group	Negligible
Stockland Corp Ltd	Negligible
Vicinity Centres	Negligible
Atlas Arteria Ltd	Negligible
Mirvac Group	Negligible
Dexus Ltd	Negligible
National Australia Bank Ltd	Low
Wesfarmers Ltd	Low
QBE Insurance Group Ltd	Low
Coles Group Ltd	Low
Amcor PLC	Low
WiseTech Global Ltd	Low
News Corp DR	Low
Brambles Ltd	Low
Xero Ltd	Low
Sonic Healthcare Ltd	Low
Washington H. Soul Pattinson & Co Ltd	Low
Meridian Energy Ltd	Low
Auckland International Airport Ltd	Low
Endeavour Group Ltd	Low
Mercury NZ Ltd	Low
SEEK Ltd	Low
Ebos Group Ltd	Low
NEXTDC Ltd	Low
IDP Education Ltd	Low
Altium Ltd	Low
JB Hi-Fi Ltd	Low
Technology One Ltd	Low
Qube Holdings Ltd	Low
Harvey Norman Holdings Ltd	Low
Challenger Ltd	Low
Premier Investments Ltd	Low
Metcash Ltd	Low

(continued)

Company	Sustainalytics ESG Risk Classification
NIB Holdings Ltd	Low
Eagers Automotive Ltd	Low
Nine Entertainment Co. Holdings Ltd	Low
Super Retail Group Ltd	Low
Ansell Ltd	Low
Deterra Royalties Ltd	Low
Sims Ltd	Low
De Grey Mining Ltd	Low
Dicker Data Ltd	Low
InvoCare Ltd	Low
Bapcor Ltd	Low
EVT Ltd	Low
Magellan Financial Group Ltd	Low
Nanosonics Ltd	Low
IRESS Ltd	Low
Imdex Ltd	Low
Vulcan Energy Resources Ltd	Low
BHP Group Ltd	Medium
Fortescue Metals Group Ltd	Medium
South32 Ltd	Medium
Mineral Resources Ltd	Medium
BlueScope Steel Ltd	Medium
Lynas Rare Earths Ltd	Medium
Incitec Pivot Ltd	Medium
Woodside Energy Group Ltd	High
Origin Energy Ltd	High
Ampol Ltd	High
Viva Energy Group Ltd	High
Beach Energy Ltd	High

C. Absolute ESG risk rank in global universe of 15 708 companies globally, best to worst.

Company	Absolute ESG risk rank – universe
Dexus Ltd	42
Atlas Arteria Ltd	61
Mirvac Group	132
Transurban Group	152
Scentre Group	156
Stockland Corp Ltd	177
Vicinity Centres	194
Goodman Group	249
Super Retail Group Ltd	357
News Corp DR	520
SEEK Ltd	552
Imdex Ltd	618
Deterra Royalties Ltd	630
Bapcor Ltd	755
Dicker Data Ltd	849
Brambles Ltd	972
Washington H. Soul Pattinson & Co Ltd	1293
Eagers Automotive Ltd	1301
IRESS Ltd	1334
IDP Education Ltd	1463
JB Hi-Fi Ltd	1723
De Grey Mining Ltd	1778
Ansell Ltd	1813
Wesfarmers Ltd	1820
Metcash Ltd	1839
InvoCare Ltd	1981
EVT Ltd	2056
Xero Ltd	2141
NEXTDC Ltd	2211
Ebos Group Ltd	2258
Nine Entertainment Co. Holdings Ltd	2269
Qube Holdings Ltd	2282
Vulcan Energy Resources Ltd	2476
Altium Ltd	2608

(continued)

Company	Absolute ESG risk rank – universe
Technology One Ltd	2832
Amcor PLC	2889
Coles Group Ltd	2916
Endeavour Group Ltd	2963
Sims Ltd	3185
Meridian Energy Ltd	3278
Harvey Norman Holdings Ltd	3329
Sonic Healthcare Ltd	3371
Premier Investments Ltd	3422
Nanosonics Ltd	3728
Magellan Financial Group Ltd	3837
NIB Holdings Ltd	3868
QBE Insurance Group Ltd	3913
WiseTech Global Ltd	3985
Auckland International Airport Ltd	4095
Challenger Ltd	4173
National Australia Bank Ltd	4196
Mercury NZ Ltd	4209
Mineral Resources Ltd	5263
Fortescue Metals Group Ltd	5657
Lynas Rare Earths Ltd	6422
South32 Ltd	8085
BHP Group Ltd	9510
Incitec Pivot Ltd	9645
BlueScope Steel Ltd	10 640
Woodside Energy Group Ltd	11 360
Viva Energy Group Ltd	12 636
Ampol Ltd	12 981
Beach Energy Ltd	13 754
Origin Energy Ltd	13 800

D. ESG risk management momentum, from worst to best (deteriorating management of ESG risk)

Name	ESG risk management score momentum
Washington H. Soul Pattinson & Co Ltd	−3.10
Magellan Financial Group Ltd	−3.03
Auckland International Airport Ltd	−2.67
WiseTech Global Ltd	−1.77
Seek Ltd	−1.75
Endeavour Group Ltd	−1.75
BHP Group Ltd	−1.63
Xero Ltd	−1.16
Super Retail Group Ltd	−0.97
News Corp DR	−0.84
Scentre Group	−0.70
Dexus Ltd	−0.48
Vicinity Centres	−0.41
Sonic Healthcare Ltd	−0.27
Qube Holdings Ltd	−0.22
Viva Energy Group Ltd	−0.11
Technology One Ltd	−0.07
Amcor PLC	−0.02
Altium Ltd	0.00
Imdex Ltd	0.00
Stockland Corp Ltd	0.14
Challenger Ltd	0.27
QBE Insurance Group Ltd	0.41
Wesfarmers Ltd	0.55
Incitec Pivot Ltd	0.57
Bapcor Ltd	0.88
Coles Group Ltd	0.94
South32 Ltd	0.95
Goodman Group	1.06
Transurban Group	1.08
Origin Energy Ltd	1.10
Mercury NZ Ltd	1.36
Woodside Energy Group Ltd	1.53
Eagers Automotive Ltd	1.70

(*continued*)

Name	ESG risk management score momentum
IRESS Ltd	2.00
Nine Entertainment Co. Holdings Ltd	2.34
Metcash Ltd	2.36
InvoCare Ltd	2.42
IDP Education Ltd	2.49
Sims Ltd	2.72
Ansell Ltd	3.02
Mirvac Group	3.10
Ampol Ltd	3.10
Beach Energy Ltd	3.10
EVT Ltd	3.11
JB Hi-Fi Ltd	3.38
Harvey Norman Holdings Ltd	3.83
Ebos Group Ltd	4.17
National Australia Bank Ltd	4.23
Brambles Ltd	4.57
Premier Investments Ltd	4.77
Nanosonics Ltd	5.20
NEXTDC Ltd	5.90
Meridian Energy Ltd	6.02
Fortescue Metals Group Ltd	6.49
BlueScope Steel Ltd	6.54
Deterra Royalties Ltd	9.06
NIB Holdings Ltd	9.11
Atlas Arteria Ltd	9.67
Mineral Resources Ltd	15.85
Lynas Rare Earths Ltd	16.06
Vulcan Energy Resources Ltd	25.04
Dicker Data Ltd	no data
De Grey Mining Ltd	no data

E. ESG risk score momentum, from worst to best

Company	ESG risk score momentum
Origin Energy Ltd	3.11
Washington H Soul Pattinson & Co Ltd	2.82
Wesfarmers Ltd	2.04
Amcor PLC	1.73
Ampol Ltd	1.70
South32 Ltd	1.67
Magellan Financial Group Ltd	1.55
BHP Group Ltd	1.40
Harvey Norman Holdings Ltd	0.73
Endeavour Group Ltd	0.73
WiseTech Global Ltd	0.67
Auckland International Airport Ltd	0.65
Viva Energy Group Ltd	0.63
Scentre Group	0.54
Vicinity Centres	0.46
Mercury NZ Ltd	0.44
Sonic Healthcare Ltd	0.39
Ebos Group Ltd	0.36
Premier Investments Ltd	0.30
JB Hi Fi Ltd	0.29
News Corp DR	0.23
Technology One Ltd	0.21
Dexus	0.18
Super Retail Group Ltd	0.17
Goodman Group	0.14
Qube Holdings Ltd	0.06
QBE Insurance Group Ltd	0.02
Seek Ltd	0.00
Altium Ltd	0.00
Imdex Ltd	0.00
Stockland Corp Ltd	−0.04
Nanosonics Ltd	−0.09
Mirvac Group	−0.15
Bapcor Ltd	−0.17
Transurban Group	−0.22

(continued)

Company	ESG risk score momentum
Eagers Automotive Ltd	−0.26
Xero Ltd	−0.28
Coles Group Ltd	−0.36
Nine Entertainment Co. Holdings Ltd	−0.56
IRESS Ltd	−0.57
Challenger Ltd	−0.58
Incitec Pivot Ltd	−0.68
Ansell Ltd	−0.70
Woodside Energy Group Ltd	−0.71
EVT Ltd	−0.71
Metcash Ltd	−0.81
Brambles Ltd	−0.93
InvoCare Ltd	−1.04
Sims Ltd	−1.08
Atlas Arteria Ltd	−1.32
Nextdc Ltd	−1.35
BlueScope Steel Ltd	−1.69
NIB Holdings Ltd	−1.77
Deterra Royalties Ltd	−1.94
National Australia Bank Ltd	−2.27
Fortescue Metals Group Ltd	−2.89
Beach Energy Ltd	−3.52
Meridian Energy Ltd	−5.29
Vulcan Energy Resources Ltd	−8.24
Mineral Resources Ltd	−8.50
De Grey Mining Ltd	No data
Dicker Data Ltd	No data

F. Company controversy level, highest to lowest, with key controversy topic

Name	Company controversy level descriptor	Company highest controversy level	Company highest controversy topic
BHP Group Ltd	High	4	Operations
National Australia Bank Ltd	Significant	3	Business Ethics, Customer
Sims Ltd	Moderate	2	Operations
Incitec Pivot Ltd	Moderate	2	Social Supply Chain
Lynas Rare Earths Ltd	Moderate	2	Operations, Society and Community
BlueScope Steel Ltd	Moderate	2	Operations, Business Ethics, Customer
Mineral Resources Ltd	Moderate	2	Employee
South32 Ltd	Moderate	2	Operations, Business Ethics, Employee
Fortescue Metals Group Ltd	Moderate	2	Employee, Society and Community
Nine Entertainment Co. Holdings Ltd	Moderate	2	Customer
News Corp DR	Moderate	2	Customer
Super Retail Group Ltd	Moderate	2	Employee
Eagers Automotive Ltd	Moderate	2	Business Ethics
Premier Investments Ltd	Moderate	2	Business Ethics, Governance, Employee
Harvey Norman Holdings Ltd	Moderate	2	Business Ethics, Customer
Wesfarmers Ltd	Moderate	2	Employee, Social Supply Chain, Customer
IDP Education Ltd	Moderate	2	Business Ethics
Endeavour Group Ltd Ordinary Shares	Moderate	2	Customer
Coles Group Ltd	Moderate	2	Governance, Employee, Social Supply Chain, Customer
Ampol Ltd	Moderate	2	Business Ethics
Origin Energy Ltd	Moderate	2	Operations, Customer
Woodside Energy Group Ltd	Moderate	2	Operations, Product and Service, Society and Community
QBE Insurance Group Ltd	Moderate	2	Product and Service, Customer

(*continued*)

Name	Company controversy level descriptor	Company highest controversy level	Company highest controversy topic
Ansell Ltd	Moderate	2	Employee, Social Supply Chain
Qube Holdings Ltd	Moderate	2	Business Ethics
Mirvac Group	Moderate	2	Business Ethics
Scentre Group	Moderate	2	Governance
Seek Ltd	Low	1	Business Ethics
InvoCare Ltd	Low	1	Employee
JB Hi-Fi Ltd	Low	1	Customer
Amcor PLC	Low	1	Business Ethics, Employee
Metcash Ltd	Low	1	Customer
Beach Energy Ltd	Low	1	Operations, Society and Community
Viva Energy Group Ltd	Low	1	Operations
NIB Holdings Ltd	Low	1	Business Ethics
Ebos Group Ltd	Low	1	Social Supply Chain, Customer
Sonic Healthcare Ltd	Low	1	Business Ethics, Employee, Customer
Transurban Group	Low	1	Business Ethics, Customer
Vicinity Centres	Low	1	Business Ethics, Governance
Goodman Group	Low	1	Governance
Technology One Ltd	Low	1	Customer
Mercury NZ Ltd	Low	1	Employee
Meridian Energy Ltd	Low	1	Customer
Vulcan Energy Resources Ltd	None	0	No controversy
De Grey Mining Ltd	None	0	No controversy
Deterra Royalties Ltd	None	0	No controversy
EVT Ltd	None	0	No controversy
Bapcor Ltd	None	0	No controversy
Magellan Financial Group Ltd	None	0	No controversy
Challenger Ltd	None	0	No controversy
Washington H. Soul Pattinson & Co Ltd	None	0	No controversy
Nanosonics Ltd	None	0	No controversy

Name	Company controversy level descriptor	Company highest controversy level	Company highest controversy topic
Atlas Arteria Ltd	None	0	No controversy
Imdex Ltd	None	0	No controversy
Auckland International Airport Ltd	None	0	No controversy
Brambles Ltd	None	0	No controversy
Dexus Ltd	None	0	No controversy
Stockland Corp Ltd	None	0	No controversy
IRESS Ltd	None	0	No controversy
Dicker Data Ltd	None	0	No controversy
Altium Ltd	None	0	No controversy
NEXTDC Ltd	None	0	No controversy
Xero Ltd	None	0	No controversy
WiseTech Global Ltd	None	0	No controversy

G. Company environmental risk score, from highest environmental risk to least risk

Name	Sustainalytics environmental risk score
Origin Energy Ltd	22.26
Beach Energy Ltd	21.76
Viva Energy Group Ltd	21.14
Ampol Ltd	19.37
Woodside Energy Group Ltd	17.19
Incitec Pivot Ltd	16.23
BHP Group Ltd	15.28
Amcor PLC	13.55
South32 Ltd	13.21
BlueScope Steel Ltd	12.77
Mineral Resources Ltd	10.68
Fortescue Metals Group Ltd	10.36
Lynas Rare Earths Ltd	9.42
Sims Ltd	8.12
Coles Group Ltd	5.92
Vulcan Energy Resources Ltd	4.86
NEXTDC Ltd	4.85
Wesfarmers Ltd	4.81
WiseTech Global Ltd	4.63
Endeavour Group Ltd	4.46
Bapcor Ltd	4.38
Technology One Ltd	4.24
Harvey Norman Holdings Ltd	4.18
Dicker Data Ltd	3.70
Metcash Ltd	3.69
JB Hi-Fi Ltd	3.60
Auckland International Airport Ltd	3.51
Qube Holdings Ltd	3.48
Imdex Ltd	3.29
Meridian Energy Ltd	3.27
Mercury NZ Ltd	3.21
Ebos Group Ltd	2.93
Vicinity Centres	2.84
Stockland Corp Ltd	2.62

Name	Sustainalytics environmental risk score
Magellan Financial Group Ltd	2.36
Premier Investments Ltd	2.33
Goodman Group	2.11
NIB Holdings Ltd	2.02
Scentre Group	1.95
Dexus Ltd	1.90
Nanosonics Ltd	1.82
Transurban Group	1.77
Altium Ltd	1.35
Xero Ltd	1.35
IRESS Ltd	1.24
Challenger Ltd	1.14
Brambles Ltd	1.03
QBE Insurance Group Ltd	0.91
National Australia Bank Ltd	0.89
Ansell Ltd	0.88
Mirvac Group	0.82
Atlas Arteria Ltd	0.79
De Grey Mining Ltd	0.16
Washington H. Soul Pattinson & Co Ltd	0.14
Deterra Royalties Ltd	0.14
Eagers Automotive Ltd	0.13
SEEK Ltd	0.13
Nine Entertainment Co. Holdings Ltd	0.12
InvoCare Ltd	0.12
EVT Ltd	0.12
Super Retail Group Ltd	0.11
IDP Education Ltd	0.11
Sonic Healthcare Ltd	0.05
News Corp DR	0.02

H. Company social risk score, highest social risk to least risk

Company	Sustainalytics social risk score
BlueScope Steel Ltd	11.50
Altium Ltd	11.08
Sonic Healthcare Ltd	10.85
Auckland International Airport Ltd	10.54
Nanosonics Ltd	10.38
Ampol Ltd	10.27
InvoCare Ltd	10.15
Mercury NZ Ltd	10.06
Premier Investments Ltd	9.83
Eagers Automotive Ltd	9.61
WiseTech Global Ltd	9.36
Origin Energy Ltd	9.30
IDP Education Ltd	9.26
National Australia Bank Ltd	9.07
Xero Ltd	9.07
Challenger Ltd	9.05
Nine Entertainment Co. Holdings Ltd	9.01
Meridian Energy Ltd	8.88
Coles Group Ltd	8.67
Ansell Ltd	8.63
QBE Insurance Group Ltd	8.46
BHP Group Ltd	8.39
South32 Ltd	8.34
Harvey Norman Holdings Ltd	8.31
EVT Ltd	8.17
Brambles Ltd	8.16
SEEK Ltd	8.12
Technology One Ltd	8.08
Qube Holdings Ltd	7.98
Metcash Ltd	7.89
Endeavour Group Ltd	7.81
IRESS Ltd	7.76
Viva Energy Group Ltd	7.74
Beach Energy Ltd	7.68
NIB Holdings Ltd	7.62

Company	Sustainalytics social risk score
Lynas Rare Earths Ltd	7.59
Fortescue Metals Group Ltd	7.56
JB Hi-Fi Ltd	7.55
Woodside Energy Group Ltd	7.51
Magellan Financial Group Ltd	7.45
Vulcan Energy Resources Ltd	7.40
Super Retail Group Ltd	7.28
Wesfarmers Ltd	7.16
Incitec Pivot Ltd	6.93
Ebos Group Ltd	6.69
Mineral Resources Ltd	6.54
Sims Ltd	6.48
NEXTDC Ltd	5.29
De Grey Mining Ltd	5.00
News Corp DR	4.74
Deterra Royalties Ltd	4.67
Bapcor Ltd	4.37
Imdex Ltd	3.90
Dicker Data Ltd	3.89
Goodman Group	3.21
Transurban Group	3.15
Washington H. Soul Pattinson & Co Ltd	3.04
Mirvac Group	2.72
Atlas Arteria Ltd	2.64
Scentre Group	2.53
Stockland Corp Ltd	2.51
Vicinity Centres	1.60
Dexus Ltd	1.54
Amcor PLC	0.88

I. Company governance risk score, highest social risk to least risk

Company	Sustainalytics governance risk score
Washington H. Soul Pattinson & Co Ltd	10.96
De Grey Mining Ltd	10.15
QBE Insurance Group Ltd	9.90
National Australia Bank Ltd	9.79
NIB Holdings Ltd	9.55
Challenger Ltd	9.51
Magellan Financial Group Ltd	9.33
EVT Ltd	7.63
Sonic Healthcare Ltd	7.52
Beach Energy Ltd	7.26
Nine Entertainment Co. Holdings Ltd	7.24
Deterra Royalties Ltd	7.13
Nanosonics Ltd	6.79
News Corp DR	6.72
Ebos Group Ltd	6.72
Mercury NZ Ltd	6.50
Premier Investments Ltd	6.35
Woodside Energy Group Ltd	6.21
Lynas Rare Earths Ltd	6.18
Meridian Energy Ltd	6.13
NEXTDC Ltd	6.10
Ansell Ltd	5.89
Harvey Norman Holdings Ltd	5.86
Xero Ltd	5.68
Auckland International Airport Ltd	5.51
Endeavour Group Ltd	5.46
InvoCare Ltd	5.46
WiseTech Global Ltd	5.37
BlueScope Steel Ltd	5.36
Origin Energy Ltd	5.29
IRESS Ltd	5.23
Dicker Data Ltd	5.21
Technology One Ltd	5.18
IDP Education Ltd	5.17
Mirvac Group	5.10

Company	Sustainalytics governance risk score
Ampol Ltd	4.92
Qube Holdings Ltd	4.92
Incitec Pivot Ltd	4.87
Viva Energy Group Ltd	4.77
Vicinity Centres	4.76
Imdex Ltd	4.71
Altium Ltd	4.61
Vulcan Energy Resources Ltd	4.51
Eagers Automotive Ltd	4.41
Scentre Group	4.37
Goodman Group	4.36
Mineral Resources Ltd	4.24
BHP Group Ltd	4.16
Fortescue Metals Group Ltd	4.12
South32 Ltd	4.06
JB Hi-Fi Ltd	4.04
Brambles Ltd	4.00
Stockland Corp Ltd	3.95
Transurban Group	3.89
Atlas Arteria Ltd	3.88
Metcash Ltd	3.86
Bapcor Ltd	3.70
Dexus Ltd	3.54
Sims Ltd	3.53
Wesfarmers Ltd	3.44
SEEK Ltd	3.35
Super Retail Group Ltd	3.19
Amcor PLC	3.18
Coles Group Ltd	3.06

J. Carbon emissions across scopes 1, 2 and 3 in metric tonnes CO2e as of fiscal year 2021 with reported and estimated data across each scope, ranked worst to best

Company	Carbon total emissions scopes 1, 2 and 3	Carbon scope 1 emissions	Carbon scope 1 emissions source type	Carbon scope 2 emissions	Carbon scope 2 emissions source type	Carbon scope 3 emissions	Carbon Scope 3 Emissions Source Type
BHP Group Ltd	417 500 000.00	10 000 000.00	Reported	5 000 000.00	Reported	402 500 000.00	Reported
Fortescue Metals Group Ltd	249 620 000.00	2 400 000.00	Reported	160 000.00	Reported	247 060 000.00	Reported
South32 Ltd	136 100 000.00	9 700 000.00	Reported	20 400 000.00	Reported	106 000 000.00	Reported
Woodside Energy Group Ltd	81 878 000.00	8 901 000.00	Reported	8 000.00	Reported	72 969 000.00	Reported
Origin Energy Ltd	45 115 087.00	13 397 297.00	Reported	2 099 705.00	Reported	29 618 085.00	Reported
Ampol Ltd	41 894 877.00	692 232.00	Estimated	86 529.00	Estimated	41 116 116.00	Estimated
Viva Energy Group Ltd	36 774 217.00	932 077.00	Reported	269 648.00	Reported	35 572 492.00	Reported
Wesfarmers Ltd	31 760 930.00	869 000.00	Reported	607 000.00	Reported	30 284 930.00	Reported
BlueScope Steel Ltd	23 240 000.00	8 800 000.00	Reported	1 740 000.00	Reported	12 700 000.00	Reported
Amcor PLC	11 787 788.00	529 192.00	Reported	1 432 690.00	Reported	9 825 906.00	Reported
Incitec Pivot Ltd	9 690 020.00	3 112 182.00	Reported	299 838.00	Reported	6 278 000.00	Reported
JB Hi-Fi Ltd	7 405 984.67	360.00	Reported	64 487.00	Reported	7 341 137.67	Estimated
Endeavour Group Ltd	3 520 384.20	279 043.36	Estimated	62 009.64	Estimated	3 179 331.20	Estimated
News Corp DR	2 491 010.00	16 456.00	Reported	106 777.00	Reported	2 367 777.00	Reported
Atlas Arteria Ltd	2 196 276.00	6 974.00	Reported	1 463.00	Reported	2 187 839.00	Reported
Coles Group Ltd	1 845 972.00	287 936.00	Reported	1 291 155.00	Reported	266 881.00	Reported

Company	Carbon total emissions scopes 1, 2 and 3	Carbon scope 1 emissions	Carbon scope 1 emissions source type	Carbon scope 2 emissions	Carbon scope 2 emissions source type	Carbon scope 3 emissions	Carbon Scope 3 Emissions Source Type
Brambles Ltd	1 625 080.00	29 410.00	Reported	30 840.00	Reported	1 564 830.00	Reported
Mineral Resources Ltd	1 149 772.47	296 343.00	Reported	1993.00	Reported	851 436.47	Estimated
Meridian Energy Ltd	917 337.00	1376.00	Reported	3130.00	Reported	912 831.00	Reported
Washington H. Soul Pattinson & Co Ltd	676 088.86	548 355.00	Reported	70 735.00	Reported	56 998.86	Estimated
Transurban Group	631 051.00	4 598.00	Reported	198 086.00	Reported	428 367.00	Reported
Beach Energy Ltd	621 530.52	550 468.00	Reported	21 029.00	Reported	50 033.52	Estimated
Sims Ltd	574 588.95	81 200.00	Reported	74 300.00	Reported	419 088.95	Estimated
Lynas Rare Earths Ltd	517 198.85	59 648.00	Reported	43 917.00	Reported	413 633.85	Estimated
Harvey Norman Holdings Ltd	419 199.12	6383.00	Reported	101 866.00	Reported	310 950.12	Estimated
Eagers Automotive Ltd	366 733.35	33 009.00	Reported	29 561.00	Reported	304 163.35	Estimated
NEXTDC Ltd	306 413.01	665.00	Reported	297 897.00	Reported	7 851.01	Estimated
Mercury NZ Ltd	294 127.00	200 115.00	Reported	1650.00	Reported	92 362.00	Reported
Scentre Group	288 126.00	15 245.00	Reported	206 230.00	Reported	66 651.00	Reported
Ansell Ltd	276 740.18	126 937.00	Reported	101 615.00	Reported	48 188.18	Estimated
Nine Entertainment Co. Holdings Ltd	267 880.87	2141.60	Estimated	6 398.44	Estimated	259 340.83	Estimated
Metcash Ltd	186 754.79	38 059.83	Estimated	34 888.17	Estimated	113 806.79	Estimated
Vicinity Centres	171 344.00	4 205.00	Reported	128 946.00	Reported	38 193.00	Reported
Qube Holdings Ltd	167 649.01	68 630.09	Estimated	51 032.32	Estimated	47 986.60	Estimated

(continued)

Company	Carbon total emissions scopes 1, 2 and 3	Carbon scope 1 emissions	Carbon scope 1 emissions source type	Carbon scope 2 emissions	Carbon scope 2 emissions source type	Carbon scope 3 emissions	Carbon Scope 3 Emissions Source Type
Dexus Ltd	135 296 00	16 561.00	Reported	97 219.00	Reported	21 716.00	Reported
National Australia Bank Ltd	131 586.00	10 821.00	Reported	74 850.00	Reported	45 915.00	Reported
EVT Ltd	128 651.87	15 082.00	Reported	110 377.00	Reported	3 192.87	Estimated
Premier Investments Ltd	127 329.65	31.94	Estimated	265.13	Estimated	127 032.58	Estimated
Sonic Healthcare Ltd	113 268.00	27 716.00	Reported	85 341.00	Reported	211.00	Reported
Stockland Corp Ltd	85 945.00	22 402.00	Reported	46 195.00	Reported	17 348.00	Reported
Deterra Royalties Ltd	81 002.10	2 339.30	Estimated	932.44	Estimated	77 730.36	Estimated
Mirvac Group	80 729.00	6 342.00	Reported	64 018.00	Reported	10 369.00	Reported
Super Retail Group Ltd	62 750.00	945.00	Reported	60 914.00	Reported	891.00	Reported
Goodman Group	52 868.00	2 141.00	Reported	38 419.00	Reported	12 308.00	Reported
Ebos Group Ltd	39 560.88	4 611.89	Estimated	12 600.00	Reported	22 348.99	Estimated
QBE Insurance Group Ltd	26 690.00	5 733.00	Reported	12 807.00	Reported	8 150.00	Reported
IDP Education Ltd	23 890.38	50.00	Reported	4 952.00	Reported	18 888.38	Estimated
Dicker Data Ltd	20 162.02	276.98	Estimated	1 465.60	Estimated	18 419.44	Estimated
IRESS Ltd	17 290.00	180.00	Reported	1 373.00	Reported	15 737.00	Reported
Bapcor Ltd	14 391.41	5 796.71	Estimated	6 255.07	Estimated	2 339.63	Estimated
SEEK Ltd	13 482.00	0.00	Reported	687.00	Reported	12 795.00	Reported

Company	Carbon total emissions scopes 1, 2 and 3	Carbon scope 1 emissions	Carbon scope 1 emissions source type	Carbon scope 2 emissions	Carbon scope 2 emissions source type	Carbon scope 3 emissions	Carbon Scope 3 Emissions Source Type
Auckland International Airport Ltd	10 617.72	1674.00	Reported	3 031.00	Reported	5 912.72	Estimated
Altium Ltd	10 557.66	3.31	Reported	1782.57	Reported	8 771.78	Reported
WiseTech Global Ltd	9 926.28	119.24	Reported	8 417.80	Reported	1389.24	Estimated
InvoCare Ltd	7 800.19	948.35	Estimated	4 719.30	Estimated	2132.54	Estimated
NIB Holdings Ltd	6 917.30	23.80	Reported	419.40	Reported	6 474.10	Reported
Imdex Ltd	5 920.11	315.48	Estimated	1683.42	Estimated	3 921.21	Estimated
Technology One Ltd	5 513.30	0.00	Reported	676.10	Reported	4 837.20	Reported
Xero Ltd	4 301.00	7.00	Reported	470.00	Reported	3 824.00	Reported
Challenger Ltd	4128.80	1.00	Reported	690.20	Reported	3 437.60	Reported
Vulcan Energy Resources Ltd	2 246.97	2.33	Reported	71.77	Reported	2172.87	Reported
Nanosonics Ltd	2113.19	0.00	Reported	1282.00	Reported	831.19	Estimated
Magellan Financial Group Ltd	1958.60	0.00	Reported	113.00	Reported	1845.60	Estimated
De Grey Mining Ltd	177.45	157.50	Estimated	16.26	Estimated	3.69	Estimated

K. Carbon intensity across scopes 1, 2 and 3, from most intense to least intense. Total emissions/revenue in metric tonnes CO_2e per US$ million in revenue

Company	Carbon intensity scopes 1, 2 and 3
Atlas Arteria Ltd	30 090.01
South32 Ltd	25 280.78
Woodside Energy Group Ltd	11 530.49
Fortescue Metals Group Ltd	11 394.15
BHP Group Ltd	6982.76
De Grey Mining Ltd	6772.90
Origin Energy Ltd	5085.50
Viva Energy Group Ltd	3153.81
Incitec Pivot Ltd	3038.61
Ampol Ltd	2666.93
BlueScope Steel Ltd	2461.78
NEXTDC Ltd	1698.03
Lynas Rare Earths Ltd	1442.17
Wesfarmers Ltd	1281.46
JB Hi-Fi Ltd	1132.65
Amcor PLC	916.55
Deterra Royalties Ltd	760.66
Washington H. Soul Pattinson & Co Ltd	646.35
Beach Energy Ltd	542.59
Mineral Resources Ltd	419.93
Endeavour Group Ltd	414.01
Brambles Ltd	317.28
EVT Ltd	306.61
Meridian Energy Ltd	301.57
Transurban Group	298.17
News Corp DR	266.19
Mercury NZ Ltd	204.43
Vicinity Centres	199.83
Dexus Ltd	181.30
Scentre Group	172.26
Nine Entertainment Co. Holdings Ltd	156.67
Ansell Ltd	138.88
Harvey Norman Holdings Ltd	137.82

Company	Carbon intensity scopes 1, 2 and 3
Sims Ltd	132.43
Premier Investments Ltd	120.25
Qube Holdings Ltd	119.03
Coles Group Ltd	64.66
IDP Education Ltd	61.99
Mirvac Group	61.06
Altium Ltd	59.59
Auckland International Airport Ltd	57.93
Eagers Automotive Ltd	57.72
Stockland Corp Ltd	42.52
IRESS Ltd	39.56
Goodman Group	38.63
Imdex Ltd	30.54
Nanosonics Ltd	28.30
WiseTech Global Ltd	26.67
Super Retail Group Ltd	24.78
SEEK Ltd	24.18
Technology One Ltd	24.15
InvoCare Ltd	20.09
Metcash Ltd	17.79
Sonic Healthcare Ltd	16.92
Bapcor Ltd	11.14
Dicker Data Ltd	11.09
National Australia Bank Ltd	8.56
Xero Ltd	7.40
Ebos Group Ltd	5.63
Magellan Financial Group Ltd	3.82
NIB Holdings Ltd	3.63
Challenger Ltd	1.86
QBE Insurance Group Ltd	1.55
Vulcan Energy Resources Ltd	No data

L. Level of fossil fuel involvement, from highest to lowest

Company	Carbon fossil fuel level of involvement range (%)
Woodside Energy Group Ltd	50-100
Origin Energy Ltd	50-100
Ampol Ltd	50-100
Beach Energy Ltd	50-100
Viva Energy Group Ltd	25-49.9
Wesfarmers Ltd	5-9.9
South32 Ltd	0-4.9
BHP Group Ltd	0-4.9
Mineral Resources Ltd	0-4.9
Atlas Arteria Ltd	None
Fortescue Metals Group Ltd	None
De Grey Mining Ltd	None
Incitec Pivot Ltd	None
BlueScope Steel Ltd	None
NEXTDC Ltd	None
Lynas Rare Earths Ltd	None
JB Hi-Fi Ltd	None
Amcor PLC	None
Deterra Royalties Ltd	None
Washington H Soul Pattinson & Co Ltd	None
Endeavour Group Ltd	None
Brambles Ltd	None
EVT Ltd	None
Meridian Energy Ltd	None
Transurban Group	None
News Corp DR	None
Mercury NZ Ltd	None
Vicinity Centres	None
Dexus Ltd	None
Scentre Group	None
Nine Entertainment Co. Holdings Ltd	None
Ansell Ltd	None
Harvey Norman Holdings Ltd	None
Sims Ltd	None
Premier Investments Ltd	None

Company	Carbon fossil fuel level of involvement range (%)
Qube Holdings Ltd	None
Coles Group Ltd	None
IDP Education Ltd	None
Mirvac Group	None
Altium Ltd	None
Auckland International Airport Ltd	None
Eagers Automotive Ltd	None
Stockland Corp Ltd	None
IRESS Ltd	None
Goodman Group	None
Imdex Ltd	None
Nanosonics Ltd	None
WiseTech Global Ltd	None
Super Retail Group Ltd	None
SEEK Ltd	None
Technology One Ltd	None
InvoCare Ltd	None
Metcash Ltd	None
Sonic Healthcare Ltd	None
Bapcor Ltd	None
Dicker Data Ltd	None
National Australia Bank Ltd	None
Xero Ltd	None
Ebos Group Ltd	None
Magellan Financial Group Ltd	None
NIB Holdings Ltd	None
Challenger Ltd	None
QBE Insurance Group Ltd	None
Vulcan Energy Resources Ltd	None

M. Companies sorted by overall carbon risk scores, highest to lowest

Company	Carbon overall risk score	Carbon overall risk category
Beach Energy Ltd	43.50	High risk
Viva Energy Group Ltd	40.16	High risk
Woodside Energy Group Ltd	39.38	High risk
Ampol Ltd	39.07	High risk
Origin Energy Ltd	29.21	Medium risk
South32 Ltd	24.30	Medium risk
Incitec Pivot Ltd	21.09	Medium risk
BHP Group Ltd	18.94	Medium risk
BlueScope Steel Ltd	18.83	Medium risk
Washington H. Soul Pattinson & Co Ltd	15.26	Medium risk
Lynas Rare Earths Ltd	14.64	Medium risk
Dicker Data Ltd	14.14	Medium risk
Bapcor Ltd	13.24	Medium risk
NEXTDC Ltd	12.85	Medium risk
Amcor PLC	12.56	Medium risk
Mineral Resources Ltd	11.92	Medium risk
Endeavour Group Ltd	11.37	Medium risk
Ebos Group Ltd	11.22	Medium risk
Fortescue Metals Group Ltd	10.60	Medium risk
Imdex Ltd	10.56	Medium risk
Harvey Norman Holdings Ltd	9.75	Low risk
Metcash Ltd	8.73	Low risk
Sims Ltd	8.22	Low risk
Coles Group Ltd	8.14	Low risk
WiseTech Global Ltd	7.32	Low risk
JB Hi-Fi Ltd	7.10	Low risk
Magellan Financial Group Ltd	6.66	Low risk
NIB Holdings Ltd	6.56	Low risk
Wesfarmers Ltd	6.45	Low risk
Stockland Corp Ltd	5.58	Low risk
National Australia Bank Ltd	5.24	Low risk
Vicinity Centres	5.20	Low risk
Scentre Group	5.17	Low risk
Technology One Ltd	5.15	Low risk

Company	Carbon overall risk score	Carbon overall risk category
Challenger Ltd	4.61	Low risk
Vulcan Energy Resources Ltd	4.46	Low risk
Goodman Group	4.15	Low risk
Dexus Ltd	3.50	Low risk
Mirvac Group	2.33	Low risk
QBE Insurance Group Ltd	2.17	Low risk
Brambles Ltd	1.01	Low risk
Mercury NZ Ltd	0.00	Negligible risk
Auckland International Airport Ltd	0.00	Negligible risk
Nanosonics Ltd	0.00	Negligible risk
Premier Investments Ltd	0.00	Negligible risk
Sonic Healthcare Ltd	0.00	Negligible risk
Meridian Energy Ltd	0.00	Negligible risk
Altium Ltd	0.00	Negligible risk
Qube Holdings Ltd	0.00	Negligible risk
Nine Entertainment Co. Holdings Ltd	0.00	Negligible risk
Xero Ltd	0.00	Negligible risk
EVT Ltd	0.00	Negligible risk
InvoCare Ltd	0.00	Negligible risk
Ansell Ltd	0.00	Negligible risk
De Grey Mining Ltd	0.00	Negligible risk
IDP Education Ltd	0.00	Negligible risk
IRESS Ltd	0.00	Negligible risk
Eagers Automotive Ltd	0.00	Negligible risk
Deterra Royalties Ltd	0.00	Negligible risk
SEEK Ltd	0.00	Negligible risk
News Corp DR	0.00	Negligible risk
Super Retail Group Ltd	0.00	Negligible risk
Transurban Group	0.00	Negligible risk
Atlas Arteria Ltd	0.00	Negligible risk

N. ESG risk rank per sub-industry in global universe (ranked via best in subsector)

Company	Sector	Sustainalytics sub-industry	ESG risk percentile – sub-industry	ESG risk rank – sub-industry
Meridian Energy Ltd	Utilities	Independent Power Production and Traders	10.66	9/83
Mercury NZ Ltd	Utilities	Renewable Power Production	32.21	30/93
IRESS Ltd	Technology	Data Processing	5.95	6/101
Xero Ltd	Technology	Enterprise and Infrastructure Software	7.27	29/443
Altium Ltd	Technology	Enterprise and Infrastructure Software	10.63	44/443
Technology One Ltd	Technology	Enterprise and Infrastructure Software	12.65	53/443
WiseTech Global Ltd	Technology	Enterprise and Infrastructure Software	24.29	105/443
NEXTDC Ltd	Technology	Real Estate Management	53.23	87/164
Dicker Data Ltd	Technology	Technology Distribution	55.45	34/61
Dexus Ltd	Real estate	REITs	2.33	7/448
Mirvac Group	Real estate	REITs	3.88	14/448
Scentre Group	Real estate	REITs	5.21	20/448
Stockland Corp Ltd	Real estate	REITs	6.54	26/448
Vicinity Centres	Real estate	REITs	6.98	28/448
Goodman Group	Real estate	REITs	9.19	38/448
Brambles Ltd	Industrials	Business Support Services	7.29	12/174
Atlas Arteria Ltd	Industrials	Highways and Railroads	10.52	6/53
Imdex Ltd	Industrials	Electronics Equipment	20.51	28/138
Transurban Group	Industrials	Highways and Railroads	21.94	12/53

Company	Sector	Sustainalytics sub-industry	ESG risk percentile – sub-industry	ESG risk rank – sub-industry
Auckland International Airport Ltd	Industrials	Airports	37.11	32/86
Qube Holdings Ltd	Industrials	Marine Ports	42.80	20/46
Sonic Healthcare Ltd	Healthcare	Medical Services	10.00	11/111
Ansell Ltd	Healthcare	Medical Supplies	19.78	12/59
Ebos Group Ltd	Healthcare	Medical Distribution	44.04	21/47
Nanosonics Ltd	Healthcare	Medical Supplies	57.33	34/59
QBE Insurance Group Ltd	Financial services	Property and Casualty Insurance	3.30	3/87
Magellan Financial Group Ltd	Financial services	Asset Management and Custody Services	10.50	39/397
Challenger Ltd	Financial services	Asset Management and Custody Services	11.25	42/397
National Australia Bank Ltd	Financial services	Diversified Banks	18.57	64/356
NIB Holdings Ltd	Financial services	Life and Health Insurance	30.81	29/94
Washington H. Soul Pattinson & Co Ltd	Financial services	Multi-Sector Holdings	46.81	32/68
Woodside Energy Group Ltd	Energy	Oil and Gas Exploration and Production	11.02	18/169
Beach Energy Ltd	Energy	Oil and Gas Exploration and Production	28.70	48/169
Viva Energy Group Ltd	Energy	Oil and Gas Refining and Marketing	34.73	32/92
Ampol Ltd	Energy	Oil and Gas Refining and Marketing	37.99	35/92
Origin Energy Ltd	Energy	Multi-Utilities	80.78	84/104
Coles Group Ltd	Consumer defensive	Food Retail	7.66	9/120
Metcash Ltd	Consumer defensive	Food Distribution	17.50	8/43

(continued)

Company	Sector	Sustainalytics sub-industry	ESG risk percentile – sub-industry	ESG risk rank – sub-industry
IDP Education Ltd	Consumer defensive	Consumer Services	32.89	49/150
Endeavour Group Ltd Ordinary Shares	Consumer defensive	Specialty Retail	36.60	33/90
Super Retail Group Ltd	Consumer cyclical	Automotive Retail	1.00	1/49
JB Hi-Fi Ltd	Consumer cyclical	Electronics Retail	19.00	7/34
Wesfarmers Ltd	Consumer cyclical	Home Improvement Retail	34.75	16/45
Amcor PLC	Consumer cyclical	Metal and Glass Packaging	37.00	25/67
Bapcor Ltd	Consumer cyclical	Distribution	38.13	13/33
InvoCare Ltd	Consumer cyclical	Consumer Services	52.16	78/150
Harvey Norman Holdings Ltd	Consumer cyclical	Electronics Retail	55.00	19/34
Eagers Automotive Ltd	Consumer cyclical	Automotive Retail	56.69	28/49
Premier Investments Ltd	Consumer cyclical	Retail Apparel	64.56	53/82
News Corp DR	Communication services	Publishing	16.36	10/59
EVT Ltd	Communication services	Movies and Entertainment	24.22	20/82
Seek Ltd	Communication services	HR Services	37.30	23/61
Nine Entertainment Co. Holdings Ltd	Communication services	Broadcasting	52.10	33/63
Deterra Royalties Ltd	Basic materials	Steel	1.00	1/157
Mineral Resources Ltd	Basic materials	Diversified Metals Mining	2.08	3/184
Fortescue Metals Group Ltd	Basic materials	Steel	2.90	4/157

Company	Sector	Sustainalytics sub-industry	ESG risk percentile – sub-industry	ESG risk rank – sub-industry
Vulcan Energy Resources Ltd	Basic materials	Specialty Chemicals	3.11	4/142
Lynas Rare Earths Ltd	Basic materials	Diversified Metals Mining	3.70	6/184
De Grey Mining Ltd	Basic materials	Gold	5.60	5/87
South32 Ltd	Basic materials	Diversified Metals Mining	5.87	10/184
BHP Group Ltd	Basic materials	Diversified Metals Mining	9.66	17/184
Sims Ltd	Basic materials	Facilities Maintenance	10.12	8/77
BlueScope Steel Ltd	Basic materials	Steel	11.15	17/157
Incitec Pivot Ltd	Basic materials	Diversified Chemicals	27.71	18/64